Other Books by the Authors

Barbara Kellerman

Professionalizing Leadership (2018)

Hard Times: Leadership in America (2015)

The End of Leadership (2012)

Leadership: Essential Selections on Power, Authority, and Influence (Editor, 2010).

Followership: How Followers are Creating Change and Changing Leaders (2008)

Women and Leadership: State of Play and Strategies for Change (Coeditor with Deborah Rhode, 2007)

Bad Leadership: What It Is, Why It Happens, How It Matters (2004)

Reinventing Leadership: Making the Connection Between Politics and Business (1999)

The President as World Leader (Coauthor with Ryan Barrilleaux, 1991)

Leadership and Negotiation in the Middle East (Coeditor with Jeffrey Rubin, 1988)

Political Leadership: A Source Book (Editor, 1986)

Women Leaders in American Politics (Coeditor with James David Barber, 1986)

The Political Presidency: Practice of Leadership (1984)

Leadership: Multidisciplinary Perspectives (Editor, 1984)

All the President's Kin: Their Political Roles (1981)

Making Decisions (Coeditor with Percy Hill et al., 1979).

Todd L. Pittinsky

The Caregiving Ambition (Coauthor with Julia B. Bear, forthcoming)

Science, Technology, and Society: New Perspectives and Directions (Editor, 2019)

Us Plus Them: Tapping the Positive Power of Difference (2012)

Restoring Trust: Enduring Challenges and Emerging Answers (Coeditor with Roderick M. Kramer, 2012)

Crossing the Divide: Intergroup Leadership in a World of Difference (Editor, 2009)

Working Fathers (Coauthor with James Levine, 1997)

Leaders Who Lust

Among our most extra-ordinary leaders are those driven
impulse they cannot completely stop – by lust. Lust i
however, an abstraction, it has definition. Definition that,
the impact of leaders who lust, is essential to extract. This
identifies six types of lust with which leaders are linked:

1) Power: the ceaseless craving to control.
2) Money: the limitless desire to accrue great wealth
3) Sex: the constant hunt for sexual gratification.
4) Success: the unstoppable need to achieve.
5) Legitimacy: the tireless claim to identity and equit
6) Legacy: the endless quest to leave a permanent im

Each of the core chapters focuses on different lusts and featu
cast of characters who bring lust to life. In the real world le
who lust can and often do have an enduring impact. This bo
therefore, counterintuitive – it focuses not on moderation, b
immoderation.

Barbara Kellerman is James MacGregor Burns Lecturer in P
Leadership at the Harvard Kennedy School, USA, and Four
Executive Director of the school's Center for Public Leader
She is the winner of the International Leadership Associ
Lifetime Achievement Award and has authored or edited r
books and articles on leadership and followership.

Todd L. Pittinsky is Professor at Stony Brook University (SU
USA, and former Faculty Director of its College of Leadership
Service. He is also Associate Faculty Fellow of the Hannah Ar
Center at Bard College, USA. Previously, he served on the facu
of the Harvard Kennedy School and Harvard Graduate Scho
Education.

Leaders Who Lust

Power, Money, Sex,
Success, Legitimacy, Legacy

BARBARA KELLERMAN
Harvard University

TODD L. PITTINSKY
Stony Brook University

CAMBRIDGE
UNIVERSITY PRESS

CAMBRIDGE
UNIVERSITY PRESS

University Printing House, Cambridge CB2 8BS, United Kingdom

One Liberty Plaza, 20th Floor, New York, NY 10006, USA

477 Williamstown Road, Port Melbourne, VIC 3207, Australia

314–321, 3rd Floor, Plot 3, Splendor Forum, Jasola District Centre,
New Delhi – 110025, India

79 Anson Road, #06–04/06, Singapore 079906

Cambridge University Press is part of the University of Cambridge.

It furthers the University's mission by disseminating knowledge in the pursuit of
education, learning, and research at the highest international levels of excellence.

www.cambridge.org
Information on this title: www.cambridge.org/9781108491167
DOI: 10.1017/9781108867764

First published 2020

Printed in the United Kingdom by TJ International Ltd, Padstow Cornwall

A catalogue record for this publication is available from the British Library.

Library of Congress Cataloging-in-Publication Data
Names: Kellerman, Barbara, author. | Pittinsky, Todd L., author.
Title: Leaders who lust : power, money, sex, success, legitimacy, legacy / Barbara
Kellerman, Harvard University, Todd L. Pittinsky, Stony Brook University.
Description: Cambridge, United Kingdom ; New York, NY : Cambridge University Press,
2020.
Identifiers: LCCN 2020024143 (print) | LCCN 2020024144 (ebook) | ISBN
9781108491167 (hardback) | ISBN 9781108867764 (ebook)
Subjects: LCSH: Leadership – Psychological aspects – Case studies. | Leadership –
Moral and ethical aspects – Case studies. | Desire – Case studies. | Lust – Case studies.
Classification: LCC BF637.L4 K45 2020 (print) | LCC BF637.L4 (ebook) | DDC 158/.4–dc23
LC record available at https://lccn.loc.gov/2020024143
LC ebook record available at https://lccn.loc.gov/2020024144

ISBN 978-1-108-49116-7 Hardback

To Kenneth Dana Greenwald, and to Thomas Dana
Greenwald, again. — BK

* * *

To Harris, Marc, and Lauren; Marin, Luke, and Drew; and,
especially, Alexandru - with hopes that you'll read this
book someday and that by then the world will be a saner
and even more wonderful place. — TLP

When the dominating characteristics of gentleness and rationality slumber ... the wild and brutish part ... becomes restless and goes on the prowl in search of anything that will satisfy its instincts.   Plato

Lust of power is the most flagrant of all passions.   Tacitus

The more [money] a man has the more he wants. Instead of filling a vacuum, it makes one.   Benjamin Franklin

Because women do feel themselves aggrieved and oppressed, and fraudulently deprived of their most sacred rights, we insist that they have immediate admission to all the rights and privileges which belong to them as citizens of these United States.   Elizabeth Cady Stanton

His appetite may grow with eating.
Winston Churchill (speaking of Adolf Hitler, in 1938)

CONTENTS

ACKNOWLEDGMENTS

Thanking Todd Pittinsky for his excellent friendship. Thanking Will Imbrie-Moore for his invariably smart, efficient, and good-tempered research assistance. Thanking Ashley Davis for her presence and presence of mind. Thanking David Repetto and Emily Watton for reasons given below. Thanking Joe Greenwald for his initial support. And thanking close family and friends for being close family and friends. — BK

* * *

First and foremost, I thank my coauthor, Barbara Kellerman, for making this journey interesting and fast-paced. Barbara has a singular lust for life which – if not infectious – is intriguing and has prompted me to be more ambitious in work and life.

Alexandru and Vladi are always wholehearted and ardent supporters. Equal parts cheering squad and distractions, pulling me away from too much work and back to the "real" world.

David Repetto, our commissioning editor, was enthusiastic, professional, and timely – all of which tremendously benefited the project. Grace Morris and Emily Watton were helpful, efficient, and positive.

Narcisa Vladulescu was very generous with her time in helping me make sense of the confusing and often disputed social, political, and historical events in Eastern Europe during and after the fall of the Soviet bloc, the setting within which George Soros largely sought to leave his legacy.

Finally, I owe a debt always to my parents, Janet and Bernard, who put their own desires largely (though not entirely) on hold for so many years, prioritizing instead their family and community. It is a gift that I can never repay, though I will honor and pay it forward as best as I can. And finally, I thank my brothers, who, as a diverse collective, I have known intimately and are always an inspiration – sometimes directly, often indirectly. — TLP

PROLOGUE
Lust as Stimulus

Leadership is an obsession – a national obsession, arguably even a global one. But while in response to this obsession has been the burgeoning, now half-century old, multibillion-dollar leadership industry, it has not been especially effective. The leadership industry has failed to live up to its original, high-minded intention, and it continues to resist changing in ways that are other than cosmetic.

A perennial problem is the industry's relentless emphasis on what leadership should be, rather than on what leadership *is*. For reasons that relate to how it makes money, big money, the industry prefers prescription to description. It prefers imagining and idealizing what we want, rather than examining and analyzing what we have. However, in reality, some leaders are good, some are bad, and some are somewhere in between. Leaders are, like the rest of us, mere mortals. They are an amalgam of mixed motives and miscellaneous ambitions.

This book is a deliberate departure from the prevailing trend. It deals with leaders not as figments of our imaginations, as incarnations of our idealizations, but as they are in the real world. Specifically, this book is an examination and evaluation of leaders driven beyond apparent reason, and who therefore, in some cases for better and in others for worse, stand out.

Leaders are supposed to have a range of admirable attributes. One of these is moderation. Moderation in everything, as opposed to excess in anything. Leadership expert Bill George wrote, for example, "Balanced leaders develop healthier organizations ... Balanced leaders are able to make more thoughtful decisions and lead more effectively."[1] But leadership and balance, leadership and moderation, go hand in hand only some of the time. Other times they do not. In fact, sometimes leadership, including exceedingly effective leadership – think Steve Jobs, who was famously, or infamously, furiously focused and obsessively single-tracked – is quite the opposite. Sometimes leadership is excessive, exemplified by precisely the unbridled behaviors that we are instructed to shun. One could even argue – and we do – that followers can be and frequently are attracted to leaders who are extreme. To leaders who are immoderate, who blatantly and even brazenly behave in ways that obviously are at the end of a spectrum.

In general, leaders want to lead. If they did not want to lead, they would not be leading, either formally (from a position of authority) or informally. But some leaders have, in addition to wanting to lead, another want, a different one that is related, but far fiercer. This other want – or need, or drive, or hunger, or determination, or ambition, or passion – is what we call *lust*.

Our definition of lust is simple, even prosaic. *We define lust as a psychological drive that produces intense wanting, even desperately needing to obtain an object, or to secure a circumstance. When the object has been obtained, or the circumstance secured, there is relief, but only briefly, temporarily.* Lust implies a fervor to acquire, achieve, or consume that is out of the ordinary – that is so extreme it is extraordinary. As Edmund Morris put it, writing about Thomas Edison, "His need to invent was as compulsive as lust."[2] "Lust" though, as we use the word here, demands greater specificity. It demands that the definition be broken into two parts. The first pertains to the craving itself which is, as the words "briefly" and "temporarily" suggest, insatiable. Lust is constant and it is chronic. Enough is never enough. No matter how much is gained or consumed, no matter how much is added or acquired, no matter how much satisfaction or gratification, leaders who lust are never at rest. They remain a bottomless pit. Lust is not, in sum, an impulse that is transient. It is an impulse that persists and is relentless. As Churchill put it, perfectly, when he as much as predicted, in 1938, that Hitler's appetite would "grow with eating," lust regenerates itself. Thus, the lust that we address in this book not only does *not* stop, it continues to grow. Moreover, it never ends of own volition. Leaders who lust never say, "I'm done, I've had enough, I'm satisfied" – unless they are obliged, by someone or for some reason, to do so. To the contrary – leaders who lust continue to lust until the end of their days.

The second part of our definition of "lust" addresses the question, "lust for what?" Leaders who lust can and, as we will see, sometimes do, lust for more than one thing at the same time. But, in general, lust as we conceive of it is trained on a single object (or type of object) or circumstance (or type of circumstance) in particular. The desire is for one thing above all, and this desire is so strong, so overwhelming and overpowering that, if push comes to shove, the rest be damned. So, while the word lust is most closely associated with having a strong desire for sexual satisfaction, lust can equally mean having a strong desire for another type of satisfaction altogether. "Lust for power," for example, is a phrase with which most of us are already familiar.

Our interest, then, is in leaders who are typical in that they want to lead, but who are *atypical* in that they want something else – they *desperately* want something else – in addition. This second want is as relentless as it is fierce – and it is focused. It is focused on objects of desire that we have whittled down to an all-important six – six different types of lust that are the most indicative and important to leadership particularly: (1) lust for power; (2) lust for money; (3) lust for sex; (4) lust for success; (5) lust for legitimacy; and (6) lust for legacy.

Leaders who lust for *power* have a ceaseless craving to control. Leaders who lust for *money* have a limitless desire to accrue greater, and then still greater wealth. Leaders who lust for *sex* go on constant, countless, hunts for sexual gratification. Leaders who lust for *success* have an unstoppable need to achieve. Leaders who lust for *legitimacy* tirelessly claim identity and demand equity. And leaders who lust for *legacy* long, effectively lifelong, to leave an imprint that is permanent.

These lusts are not pure types. As indicated, it is perfectly possible, for example, for a leader to lust for power *and* to lust for money simultaneously. We have found, however, that one type of lust demonstrably dominates. It comes first – it takes priority. Therefore, in each of our cases, our exemplars, we focus on it to the exclusion of the others. Similarly, we do not suggest that there are no types of lust other than these. Rather it is that these six are the most indicative and important – they stand out. Among other reasons, as indicated they stand out because they especially, demonstrably, relate to leadership. Each of our six types of lust feeds into – and is fed by – leadership. Which is another way of saying that it can be difficult to determine which is the chicken and which the egg. Do leaders want to lead because leading enables them more easily to satisfy or to try to satisfy their lust? Or is it instead that their lust is in consequence of their being leaders? Did they, that is, experience their lust and permit it to emerge, to play out, only after they had power and authority? To be clear: our interest is not in which came first. Our interest is in pointing out that, as we will see in the pages that follow, leadership and lust are mutually reinforcing. Their relationship can be and sometimes is symbiotic.

Notwithstanding the question of cause and effect, what is clear is that being in a leadership role can, and usually does, make it easier to satisfy, or to try to, whatever the hunger. This explains at least in part why some men and, yes, some women, are driven to become leaders in the first place. It similarly explains at least in part why some men and, yes, some women, are driven to cling to their positions of leadership no matter how hard the row to hoe, no matter how high the cost. Leading enables them more easily to feed their need – for power, money, sex, success, legitimacy, or legacy. Leaders who lust have a *fire in their belly* that is impossible to douse. Leaders who lust have a *life force* that is impossible to slow not to speak of stop. Leaders who lust have an *appetite so enormous and relentless* it is impossible ever fully to satisfy.

As this book makes apparent, while in some cases lust can derail a leader, or at least threaten to, in other cases it does just the opposite. In these cases, lust, a hunger that is exceptional and out-sized, explains, effects, an impact that is equally exceptional and outsized. We refer to leaders who do not merely *want* to lead. To satisfy their hunger, they *must* lead. This sense of urgency, even of destiny, prompts them to be as audacious as ambitious. In cases such as these, leadership is a vehicle for personal gratification. But because it is *leadership*, which is, by definition, a relationship, it can and sometimes does have an inordinate impact on others. When people with considerable power, authority, or influence lust for a long time, over a period of years, leadership and lust tend to become twinned, at which point it becomes difficult if not impossible to separate the one from the other. For example, leaders who are hell bent on leaving a legacy, such as Mahatma Gandhi, are driven to use every resource they can access to get what *they* need, to get what *they* want, to get what *they* crave to the end of their days.

However, if they are extraordinary, as was obviously Gandhi, they simultaneously leave a legacy that imprints, permanently, the lives of others.

Notwithstanding the obvious importance of lust – it provides an explanation, a motivation, for some of the most important leaders who ever lived – it is entirely absent from the voluminous contemporaneous literature on leadership. To be sure, there is a literature on traits of leadership, or attributes or characteristics of leadership. Moreover, this literature does reference, for example, the drive to "achieve" and to "excel" and "for responsibility."[3] However, it does not even mention the trait, or attribute, or characteristic that we consider of significant if not of paramount importance: *the life force that we call lust*. The intense want or desperate need to obtain an object, or to secure a circumstance, a want or need that can be satisfied, but only temporarily, never permanently. How has this happened? How can it be that the importance of lust, the impact of lust on leadership, has been missed? While Plato referenced lust more than two thousand years ago – some men, he wrote in *The Republic*, some *leaders*, go "on the prowl in search of anything that will satisfy their instincts" – the contemporary leadership industry has seemed almost willfully to ignore it. Here we offer three explanations for why this is so.

First, *lust is ignored by the leadership industry because it cannot be learned, which means it cannot be taught*. The leadership industry is a profit-making enterprise. A big profit-making enterprise that as already mentioned generates significant incomes for many different individuals and many different institutions. These incomes, these profits, are based on the proposition that leadership is a strategy or a skill, or an art or a science, or a talent or a gift, a phenomenon that can, in any case, be enhanced in, or extracted from, the leadership learner by the leadership teacher. Ergo, the industry excludes from its curriculum everything that cannot be taught or learned – at least not as these are conventionally defined.

Second, *lust is ignored by the leadership industry because it is not pretty*. Sometimes, in fact, lust is ugly, seamy, to be shunned rather than embraced. Though as we make clear in this book lust can be a force for good – it can drive people to accomplish good, sometimes great things – lust can also be a force for bad. Sometimes lust is even downright dangerous, all of which explains why, in an industry dedicated to *what should be* rather than to *what is*, lust has been sidelined.

Third, *lust is ignored by the leadership industry because it cannot be measured or even assessed*. Up to now, lust has not been identified, not to speak of quantified. There is no lust-index, or anything remotely like it, so we are left to speculate on what precisely lust is, whether it matters, and, if yes, how much and in which ways. When Angela Duckworth wrote her best-selling book, *Grit: The Power of Passion and Perseverance*, she was faced with the same issue. "How do you measure something so intangible" as grit, she asked. "Something that decades of ... psychologists [haven't] been able to quantify?" It was a curious conundrum, for as Duckworth observed, while grit was recognizable "on sight," no one had developed a way "directly" to "test" for it.[4] In other words, grit, like lust, was obvious, but it was elusive. Grit was recognizable – but it was not quantifiable. Until Duckworth came along, grit was ignored – which did not mean that it did not matter. It did.

Lust is not just beyond the parameters of the leadership industry, it is beyond the parameters of the academy more generally. Scholars, researchers – from whom the industry takes some of its cues – have paid some attention to lust, but not much. Were things different, if experts, academics with credentials, had looked at lust seriously and serially, they would have legitimized it as a subject of intellectual inquiry. Instead, lust is nowhere especially in evidence, not even in the scholarly literature that ostensibly addresses the human condition. It seems that it is seen as somehow unseemly, maybe even as threatening, as an impulse that in any case is difficult if not impossible to control. Therefore, lust has been deemed, tacitly at least, as unimportant if not irrelevant to the contemporaneous leadership literature which, distinct from its earlier counterparts – see, for instance, Freud's *Civilization and Its Discontents*, written in 1929 – is all about being rational. In fact, notwithstanding the now considerable evidence of, for example, our various biases and impulses, in the main the leadership industry remains anchored in the supposition that people generally are rational creatures who act in their own, rational, self-interest.

We can, however, extract from the meager research on lust that does exist a few overarching observations. First, most of the relevant research is in the fields of psychiatry, psychoanalytic psychology, and clinical psychology. The other sciences, including the social sciences, have tended to steer clear. Second, most of the research on lust that does exist is about the lust for sex. Lust – or drive, or appetite, or passion – in realms other than that of sexual attraction is not, apparently, of much interest or concern. Third, most of the research on lust yields results that seem somehow muted, even disembodied. Findings on lust, discussions of lust, even as they pertain to passion, seem tame, tamer in any case than the extremes of the human condition would seem to suggest.[5] Finally, most of the research on lust centers on individuals. Lust as a phenomenon that could have, that does have, larger implications – for groups and organizations (including workplaces), for states and nations – is widely ignored.

Here are some of the "overarching observations," each of which is drawn from the scholarly literature.

1. *Lust has a biological component.* It is primal. It goes all the way back to the earliest stages of human development. This means that to an extent lust is biologically determined. As Robert Sapolsky wrote in his book *Behave: The Biology of Humans at Our Best and Worst*, "certain biological traits are inherited by genetic means."[6]

2. *Lust has a cultural component.* As Sapolsky further wrote, "culture matters. We carry it with us wherever we go."[7] This means that lust is, in addition to being biologically determined, culturally determined. Culture is additive. It, together with our genes, has an impact on what we think and on how we behave.

3. *Lust has an experiential component.* Just as biology and culture leave an imprint on who we are – on what we think and on how we behave – so does individual experience. This means that lust has, in addition to biological and cultural determinants, an experiential one. Our own personal histories, as children, as adolescents, and as adults, are formative.

4. *Lust is biologically different from other impulses, specifically those that are more rational.* Lust stimulates those parts of the brain that are the most responsive to emotions and pleasure.[8]

5. *Lust can overwhelm common sense in otherwise sensible people.*[9] Lust is not, however, linear. It fluctuates. This explains why lustful leaders can be and usually are high functioning, if not all the time then most of the time.

6. *Lust can and sometimes does propel people to pursue short-term satisfactions at the expense of long-term goals.* This contrasts

to other wants, needs, and wishes driven less by present needs, and more by future rewards.[10]

7. *Lust undermines self-control; it promotes self-indulgence.* One of the few experiments on lust investigated its impact on self-control. Subjects who were primed to be lustful displayed a greater tendency to indulge in "unhealthy options" than those who were not so primed.[11]

8. *Lust is not inimical to being careful.* Quite the opposite. The research suggests that lustfulness can focus the mind – can strengthen rather than weaken analytical thinking. This contradicts the popular view that lustfulness leads, necessarily, to recklessness.[12]

9. *Lust varies greatly from one individual to another.* The assertion seems obvious. It is. However, research on greed confirms it has a dispositional component. Put simply, different people display different levels of acquisitiveness.[13] This explains why some of us are constantly on the prowl for, say, material gratification, while others of us don't care much, if at all.

10. *Lust can elicit unethical behavior.* Specifically, researchers found that the greedier the person, the more likely they were to engage in wrongdoing. For example, greedy people are more disposed to take bribes – and more disposed to offer bribes. Why? Because greedy people get greater satisfaction than do their less acquisitive counterparts from the positive outcomes associated with wrongdoing.[14]

11. *Lust is related to but ultimately different from other human motivations such as grit and drive.* We focus on "grit" and "drive" because, as already mentioned in the case of grit, both these words are the titles of recent books that, like this one, address the question of what exactly motivates people to behave in certain ways. More specifically, each of the two books was intended to teach people how to succeed. In the case of grit, Duckworth concluded that talent was not irrelevant or unimportant to achievement, but it was far less relevant and important than was effort. In fact, she found that "as much as talent counts, effort counts twice."[15] Duckworth's conclusion then was that what leads to achievement and, ultimately, to success is not sheer smarts or some other preternatural gift. Rather

it is the sheer passion to persevere. Along similar lines, Daniel Pink's book, *Drive: The Surprising Truth About What Motivates Us*, seeks to uncover "the secret to performance and satisfaction."[16] Here the key to the kingdom is "drive." Unlike other hungers that Pink maintains can be satisfied by external rewards (and punishments), drive can be satisfied only by internal rewards, specifically by having autonomy, gaining mastery, and developing a sense of purpose. Though both these books resemble this one in that they address the question of motivation, there are two critical differences. The first is that grit and drive are presumed not only to be inherently good – but to result in good outcomes. They are presumed attributes that we should strive to acquire. Lust, in contrast, is value neutral: it is not, by definition, either bad or good; nor are the consequences thereof, necessarily, either bad or good. The second difference relates to the first: both Duckworth and Pink are prescriptive. They indicate, or try to, how grit and drive might be learned or developed. We, on the other hand, are not prescriptive. As already indicated, we are descriptive. Lust just is. By the time we reach adulthood, lust cannot only not be learned, is unlikely to be developed, or acquired, or adopted. Lust is, perhaps, more primal. It is in any case more involuntary than voluntary, a hunger closer to uncontrollable than to controllable. We are not insisting that lust is innate. But nor do we claim that reading this book will make you, can make you, or should make you, more (or less) lustful.

12. *Lust can result in good outcomes – or in bad ones.* Perhaps the most direct connection between lust and leadership comes from a study of adolescents and greed. Researchers found that individual differences in dispositional greed are associated with greater income, greater spending, less savings, and more frequent debt. Thus, greed had effects that were positive, such as higher income, *and* effects that were negative, such as higher debt.[17] Lust does not, clearly, readily lend itself to reductionism.

This last point – that lust can yield radically different outcomes – cannot be overemphasized. On the one hand, sometimes leaders who lust harness their enormous energies for the common good. The longest of Gandhi's fasts – primarily to secure India's independence from Great Britain – lasted twenty-one days. But leaders who lust can as readily harness their prodigious energies to foster murder and mayhem. To take a single example of Adolf Hitler's lust for power: "Operation Barbarossa." Operation Barbarossa was the code name for the Nazi invasion of the Soviet Union in June 1941, notwithstanding the German–Soviet non-aggression pact signed less than two years earlier. The operation involved no fewer than three million German soldiers and led to, among countless catastrophes, the Battle of Stalingrad, among the largest and bloodiest actions of the Second World War. To repeat, then, lust is not, as we define it, either good or bad. We recognize it is an excess, and we recognize excess generally is seen as unseemly, unsuitable, undesirable, especially in leaders. But leaders who lust can be good – they can be ethical and effective. In fact, as we will see in the pages that follow, lust can drive leaders to be inordinately, exceptionally, ethical and effective.

We in any case render no judgments. Leaders who commit lust-driven transgression are not exactly rare – but our purpose is simply to surface. To surface leaders who lust. To surface leaders who lust because no one else has. To surface leaders who lust because it seems improbable that anyone else will. To surface leaders who lust because when leadership and lust are in tandem, they can and usually do connote outcomes of consequence. To surface leaders who lust because some leaders who lust are as striking as they are singular – they make history. In fact, in the so-called "hero in history" debate, leaders who lust tend to play an outsized role. That is, there are situations in which leaders are so obviously exceptional and, also, so obviously exceptionally lustful, that they make history, not the other way around.

Plato understood that lust is endemic to the human condition. Dante the same; in his epic poem, *Divine Comedy*, he looked at lust through the lens of love. Love as lust, love as excess, as in when we love another too much, we love God too little. Dante's legendarily impassioned, but equally legendarily illicit lovers, Francesca and Paolo, were punished for their lust, confined forever to one of the circles of hell. As to the relationship between lust and leadership, there is no one better to turn to, arguably, than Shakespeare, who in the late sixteenth and early seventeenth centuries dramatized the tie between the two as has no other wordsmith before or since. See *Julius Caesar*, or *Macbeth*, or *Antony and Cleopatra*, for examples of how in Shakespeare this symbiosis is everywhere in evidence.

This book though focuses not on the past but on the present. We assembled our cases with the following four criteria in mind: contemporaneousness, contextual diversity, demographic diversity, and, first and foremost, vividness and vibrancy. We look at leaders who lust and at the consequences thereof not only for them, and for their followers, but for the rest of us as well. For those of us who have been or remain to be advantaged or disadvantaged by the consequences of leaders who lust. Each of our chapters focuses on one of the different types of lust – power, money, sex, success, legitimacy, and legacy. And, each draws on two people to bring lust to life. We focus on individuals – on individual leaders. Leadership is, however, in all cases, even in exceptional cases, such as those of leaders who lust, a *system*. A system that has three parts – leaders, followers, and contexts – each of which is of critical consequence. We focus therefore not just on leaders, but also on their followers, and on the contexts within which each of these leaders and their followers were located.

Two final points about which we wish to be clear. First, we recognize that our quest for diversity fell short of satisfactory. This applies across the board, for example, obviously though not exclusively to gender diversity. Of our twelve cases, only two are women, which raises several questions. Is this because of our own prejudices, our own implicit biases toward lustful leaders who are men as opposed to women? Or is it perhaps because since the beginning of recorded history most people in positions of power and authority were men not women – which has meant that, until recently, history has been seen almost entirely through the lens of men? Or is it, maybe, a possibility not unrelated, because women are inherently less lustful than men? Because they lust less for leadership and, or, they lust less for power, and money, and sex (or promiscuous sex), and success, and legitimacy, and legacy? Or is the explanation that women's innate tendencies to lustfulness are more socially constrained?

The fact is that while we want to have answers to questions such as these, we do not, at least not yet. We do though presume that sometime in the future we will know more, much more, about gender differences than we do now. We further presume that ultimately the truth will lie somewhere in between – somewhere in between simplistic biological determinism on the one hand (nature) and simplistic assertions about socialization on the other (nurture). We, in any case, have found that while the issue of women and leadership is not directly in our sights, the link between leadership and lust is far more in evidence in men than in women. What exactly this means or why this should be so remains unclear.

Our second point is that the cases, the stories, are intended simply to be illustrative of lust, indicative of lust. Their purpose is not to be definitive or all-inclusive.

As we close the Prologue to this book about leaders who lust, we want to single out a woman who in 2019 and 2020 campaigned inordinately hard, and with considerable success, to become the Democratic nominee for president of the United States. We want to single her out because her lust for success has been in obvious evidence from an early age. She is Elizabeth Warren. In high school in Oklahoma she discovered that debate was a domain where she could compete as an equal if not even as a superior. She took to carrying around a large metal box "with hundreds of index cards with quotes and facts written on them," hoping to learn about some of the big topics of the day, such as health care and nuclear disarmament. Even then, she was seen as a singular striver, highly competitive, with "extraordinary focus and self-discipline." After school was over, Liz Herring, as she was then named, would spend hours each day seeking to hone her skills, to the point where she was described by a former debate teammate, Joe Pryor, as "ruthless in preparation." Decades later he still recalls Warren as unusual, atypical, as being driven to succeed well beyond what those less lustful than she would consider reasonable limits. "She wanted to be the best," Pryor remembered decades later. "She wanted it more than I did. She wanted it more than anybody did." Nor was Warren even as a child exactly shy or retiring. She apparently also badly wanted, maybe strongly needed, always, to be in the lead. A friend from early childhood asked a reporter covering Warren's formative years, "Have you ever been around someone who has to be in charge, who has to be the one that everybody looks up to? That was Betsy Herring."[18]

Whether or not Elizabeth Warren someday occupies the White House is not the point. The point is that what drove her to where she plausibly could be the first American president who is a woman is *lust* – her lust for success. Her early life even in brief is an indicator. An indicator of our first claim: that while leaders who lust are extreme, it is their being extreme that explains their paramount importance and singular significance. An indicator also of our second claim: that leadership absent lust is leadership in part not in full.

1   LUST FOR POWER

Prelude

"Leaders who lust for *power* have a ceaseless craving to control."

Among the most pointed of political aphorisms is Lord Acton's, "Power tends to corrupt and absolute power corrupts absolutely." The line lingers because it's wonderfully well-phrased – and because it rings totally true. Even if absolute power is not something that we've personally experienced, we know from the most rudimentary reading of history that some people are power-hungry in the extreme. To the point where nothing less than absolute power, which corrupts as indefinitely as absolutely, will suffice.

It's easy enough to grasp that having some measure of power is a thing to be desired. Most of us prefer not to be completely powerless, if only because it implies that we are other than free agents, that we are in some way at the mercy of others. Which raises the question of how, exactly, power is being defined. Recent research suggests that it's useful to think of power in two ways: the first is power as autonomy; the second is power as influence. The former is conceived of as generally benign. Power as autonomy means no more than, though no less than, being able to ignore, or, if necessary, able to resist the demands of others. Power as influence, in contrast, suggests control not only over one's self, but over others.

Power as autonomy enhances our feelings of authenticity and self-fulfillment, which is precisely why those who report *having* power tend to report being satisfied, while those who report they are *striving* for power tend to report being *un*satisfied. Power as autonomy also has the virtue of being finite. When the quest for power as autonomy is satisfied, so typically is the appetite for power. Power as autonomy is, in other words, a "quenchable thirst." But the quest for power as influence "paints a completely different picture." Among other things it is unending – appetite for power over another does seem to grow with eating. Though most of the research on power is not conclusive, it is nevertheless suggestive. It suggests that people who tend to be autocratic tend also to be narcissistic. So, one way such leaders enhance themselves is by regularly enlisting new recruits, new followers, over whom they can exert power, This is what is meant by "an insatiable hunger for power."[1] This is what *we* mean by a *lust* for power.

Decades ago, social psychologists David McClelland and David Winter popularized the idea that people are characterized by three different needs: for affiliation, for achievement, and for power. Their use of the word "power" was relational – as in one person's power over another. McClelland and Winter viewed the need for power as value free. Sometimes, they concluded, people wanted power for their own self-aggrandizement; other times people wanted power for the benefit of others. But notwithstanding findings like these, which remind us that power can have effects that are benign as well as malignant, in the United States the need for power has historically been viewed with suspicion.[2] Americans have always been hostile to power – certainly when it is exercised nakedly. Despite seeking a powerful role abroad, at home phrases such as "power-hungry" and "power-mad" testify to a national culture that has, since the inception of the Republic, been suspicious of those who seem too ready to dominate, too quick to control. Though there are of course exceptions to the general rule, by and large leaders in America are expected to balance their need for power with behaviors that are socially acceptable, that convey their willingness to be somewhat cooperative and collaborative as opposed to only demanding and domineering.[3]

While the cultures of many other countries are not hostile to the exercise of power – in fact, numberless cultures and countries have long histories of leaders who were all-powerful – there is a certain trajectory of power that nearly everywhere is familiar.

It looks like this. Initially leaders are circumspect – they incline to conceal their zeal to accrue power and then still more power. But after a while, not so much. After a while, leaders display their pursuit of power, sometimes proudly, even to the point of flaunting it. Again, this trajectory from careful to boastful is typical as opposed to unusual. In fact, it is key. It is key to understanding how it happens that leaders with a lust for power are permitted and ultimately enabled by their followers to accumulate more power, sometimes much, much more power, than is optimum. Accumulate power sometimes to the point of systemic dysfunction. Accumulate power sometimes to the point of making many if not most of their followers miserable. Accumulate power sometimes to the point of doing harm to institutions as well as individuals.

An interesting recent example is Rwanda's president, Paul Kagame. For years Kagame was given great credit for steering his country to political stability and economic recovery from the 1994 genocidal civil war. But during the last decade – Kagame become president in 2000 – he has shown a growing proclivity toward, and preference for, autocratic rule. Gradually, and then not so gradually, rival parties have been "squeezed out of the political system and dozens of regime opponents" have been "detained or died in suspicious circumstances."[4] Notwithstanding, in 2017 Kagame was reelected. Soon thereafter the constitution was changed, enabling him potentially to hold on to the presidency until 2034 – for fully thirty-four years.

Of course, the trajectory we describe works both ways – it pertains to leaders *and* to followers. What happens to leaders has been tagged, "the paradox of power." Specifically, the "very traits that helped leaders accumulate control in the first place all but disappear once they rise to power." For example, instead of being decent and honest, as they were early on, over time they become reckless and rude – and too often corrupt. Something, in other words, can and often does happen to people as they go through the process first of acquiring power and then of exercising it. They can and often do change. Social psychologist Dacher Keltner described the impact of having power as being "incredibly consistent." People with power tend to "start acting like fools." For instance, they are more inclined to flirt inappropriately, to tease or diminish others; and, generally, to behave in ways that earlier in their lives as leaders would have been uncharacteristic.[5]

Exactly why this change takes place is not completely clear. But the evidence is persuasive: one of the problems associated with being a leader (either formal or informal) is that holding power tends, especially over time, to make us less sensitive and sympathetic to the well-being of others. Simultaneously, there is a growing sense of entitlement, which expands as power itself expands. Researchers have found that people with power think that they can break the rules "not only because they can get away with it, but also because they feel at some intuitive level that they are entitled to take what they want." As we will see in the case of Roger Ailes, for example, his "sense of entitlement is crucial" to understanding why he "misbehaved in high office."[6]

What happens to followers who have leaders that change over time into something different? Morph from leaders who generally were well liked and respected into leaders gripped by their own power? How and why followers put up with such leaders – with leaders whose acceptable interest in power has evolved into an insatiable *and* indefensible lust for power – is hard to understand. But there is a small literature on followership that provides some clues about why individuals and institutions, groups and organizations, states and nations, tolerate leaders whose lust for power would seem to be intolerable – a literature that we will draw on.[7] Suffice to say at this point that even the worst leaders can and usually, though not always, do provide their followers with benefits. These can include safety and security, as well as the stability and certainty that hierarchies generally are equipped to provide. These can also include the promise of rewards for going along – as well as the threat of punishments for not going along.

It's important to understand as well that we tend to do what social psychologists refer to as, "escalate our commitment." That is, we tend to continue to follow the path we've been on, even when there is growing and finally convincing evidence that the path we've been on is wrong. We should not be surprised, then, when followers continue to support leaders who initially were good, even if over time they turned bad. But, of course, once leaders turn bad, it's late in the game. Once leaders turn bad, followers usually discover they're stuck with a bad leader who refuses to get out. And they're stuck in a situation in which their own getting out is difficult or even impossible.

Roger Ailes

Long before he became known as the architect of a corporate culture that had an outsized level of tolerance for sexual harassment, Roger Ailes had a reputation as a man to be feared. Ailes *created* Fox News, he *was* Fox News, he *used* Fox News as a cudgel to get people to cower. He was so dominating a figure at the network and beyond that he intimidated even the enormously powerful man to whom he supposedly reported, Australian media mogul Rupert Murdoch. As Murdoch's biographer put it, "People are afraid of Roger. Murdoch is, himself, afraid of Roger."[8]

Ailes relished his reputation as a man to be feared; he thought, like Machiavelli, that it was better to be feared than loved; and used fear as a foundation for the power he lusted for all his life. One former deputy said of him, "What's fun for Roger is the destruction. When the light bulb goes on and he's got the trick to outmaneuver the enemy – that's his passion." Said Ailes about a News Corp board member, "I'm not going to have some fucking liberal tell me how to program my network."[9] Said Ailes about himself, "I only understand friendship or scorched earth."[10] To be dominant was his determinant.

Context

Roger Ailes was born in Warren, Ohio in 1940; he died in Palm Beach, Florida in 2017. His background was working class and his early life not exactly warm and fuzzy. But what probably most affected Ailes's childhood and adolescence was his hemophilia, from which it was discovered he suffered at age two. As a boy Ailes veered between being overly protected by his parents and taking risks that landed him in the hospital. His early difficulties were further compounded during his time in college, when his parents' marriage ended and the house in which he grew up was sold. No surprise then that he married the first of his three wives when he was twenty-one. He quickly moved north with her to Cleveland, where he took an entry level position at a television station. Ailes was assigned to work on a pioneering TV talk show, *The Mike Douglas Show.*

Within five years he was executive producer of the show, which had grown from being a local hit to a national one, with an audience of some six million mostly housewives in some 171 cities.[11] It was during these early years of his career that Ailes developed the "unassailable, blustering confidence that became his hallmark."[12] Especially given he was still young and inexperienced, his self-assurance was remarkable and accounted in part at least for his early success. From the outset he was impressive: smart, quick, self-possessed, and, initially, popular with his colleagues.

But once he vaulted over his competitors to become Mike Douglas's executive producer, Ailes wasted no time trying to take control. Put directly, his lust for power was in evidence early in his career, along with his fierce ambition. One year after becoming executive producer of *The Mike Douglas Show* he started to look for new shows to pitch, and began, in the words of his indispensable biographer, Gabriel Sherman, to "develop his ideas about politics as entertainment."[13] It was Ailes's fusion of the two – politics with entertainment – for which he soon became well known, at least within the industry. Moreover, it, politics as entertainment, was the hybrid that enabled him ultimately to get to the top of the media heap.

It was the political prominence of Richard Nixon that gave Ailes an all-important helping hand at a key moment in his career. And it was the media savvy of Roger Ailes that gave Nixon an all-important helping hand at a key moment in *his* career. Given Nixon's miserable experience in 1960 – he was beaten in a debate on the fledgling medium of television by the young, handsome, and charismatic Democratic candidate for president, John F. Kennedy – he should have known better. But eight years later Ailes still recognized before Nixon did that the media landscape had changed. That during the 1968 presidential campaign television was going to be more important to electoral success than it ever was before. It was this campaign that constituted Ailes's baptism into national politics, and that decided where he would stake his claim to fame. Though he was always prone to exaggerate his role in whatever the drama that unfolded, including in the 1968 campaign, it was from then on that Ailes regularly told of having played the part of Nixon's indispensable media consultant.

Ailes never became a member of the president's inner circle. But throughout Nixon's time in the White House, Ailes remained in one or another way connected to the White House, continuing to straddle the line between the ostensible gravity of politics and the obvious frivolity of entertainment. Ailes was especially determined to habituate his several audiences to the idea that the line between politics and entertainment had blurred to the point of nearly disappearing. Similarly, he tried to sell the idea that consultants (such as he) were not sleazy media manipulators out to make a buck by hawking their wares – their candidates. Rather they were new types of political players who had to be reckoned with. "Like many technological advances," Ailes wrote at the time, "the impact of political television has preceded the understanding of its meaning or its uses. The natural human reaction to this lack of understanding is fear, and this single emotion – fear – overrides much of American life today and has brought about a national negativism which has wrapped around us like a shroud."[14]

During the 1980s and into the early 1990s Ailes remained tied to several Republican stalwarts specifically, and to the Republican Party generally. During these years he was not on center stage, but nor was he far off. Cable news, meantime, was gathering steam. CNN was first launched in 1980. However, it was only in the 1990s – after the network had devoted continuing coverage to major events such as the O. J. Simpson trial and the first Gulf War, both of which attracted large audiences and made hefty profits – that cable news's bright future became clear. By 1993 Ailes had signed on to become chief executive of CNBC, where once again he wasted no time taking over the domain that now was his. In fact, as Sherman tells it, it was during his approximately two years at CNBC that Ailes came into his own – as a leader. "His bold impulsiveness, his paranoia and aggression, his conservative instincts, his megalomania, and his huge gift for television programming, reached their maturity." Pointedly, Sherman adds that Ailes's ambition had never been to fit in. It had always been "to dominate."[15]

Whatever the deficits of Ailes's personal comportment, his professional acumen was without question. In his first year at CNBC, the network's revenues climbed 50 percent and its profits tripled. Meantime media mogul Murdoch had correctly concluded that America's appetite for news was expanding exponentially and that he, Murdoch, was the man to feed it. He met his match in Roger Ailes. Murdoch thought Ailes captivating, "powerful, politically connected [and] funny as hell," and hired him in 1996 to launch the Fox News Channel, intended as an outlet for news targeted specifically at conservative audiences.[16] Murdoch's ambition for Ailes's operation was outsized. The goal was to have Fox News become a global platform, which meant that in a single stroke he gave Ailes the gift he most wanted: a complete media outlet over which he had complete control. Fox would enable Ailes to abet

Republican politics, to trumpet increasingly conservative Republican values, and to pick Republican winners – while providing Americans with a type of entertainment unlike any with which previously they were familiar.

In less than a decade Ailes went on to change the face of television. Among its many outsized achievements, Fox News had the single most successful primetime cable news show, *The O'Reilly Factor*. Like everyone else at the network, Bill O'Reilly straddled the line between journalism and vaudeville in a way that traditionalists found offensive. Though Fox continued to insist, famously, that its coverage of the news was "fair and balanced," it nevertheless rejected many if not most well-established journalistic conventions as being "outmoded in the modern era." Fox's critics howled, of course, charging then as now that Fox's on-air talent was characterized by "hyperbole, intolerance, arrogance, and dismissal of alternative voices."[17]

Running Fox News made Roger Ailes an extremely rich man. It also made him an extremely powerful man. Murdoch gave Ailes what he had never previously given any of his lieutenants: complete control over a corporate and cultural behemoth. Though Murdoch's own sons, James and Lachlan, were competing with Ailes, Murdoch remained determined and undeterred. He left Ailes alone. Ailes could not be overruled by anyone "about what goes on air."[18] Nor for that matter could he be overruled by anyone about anything else.

Evidence

On July 21, 2016, Roger Ailes, amid credible allegations of sexual harassment, resigned as Chairman and CEO of Fox News and Fox Television Stations. It was an ignominious fall from towering heights, for during his twenty-year reign at Fox his power within the organization and, to a remarkable degree, without, was essentially unchallenged.

Inside Fox Ailes ruled with an iron fist. Outside Fox his clout was, if anything, more remarkable – specifically his immense influence in the Republican Party. In addition to Nixon, he was advisor to Republican luminaries including presidents Ronald Reagan and George H. W. Bush, and he remained throughout the last several decades of his life a stalwart of party conservatives. Ailes's genius was to use Fox as a platform from which to exercise political control over the right wing of the Republican Party. Ultimately his power was so widely recognized that he was feared personally and politically by everyone along the full spectrum of the Republican Party, whether establishment or renegade.

Again, it was that hybrid of politics and entertainment that was Ailes's trademark – and weapon of choice. Under Ailes, Fox News embraced the idea that a news network could not only overtly identify with, but also brazenly project a clear political ideology. It was this idea that Ailes turned into ratings gold – and which, in turn, enabled him to become Republican kingpin. As one former News Corporation (Murdoch's company) executive put it, "Everything Roger wanted to do when he started out in politics, he's now doing 24/7 with his network." Added mainstream Republican David Frum, "Republicans originally thought that Fox worked for us. Now we're discovering that we work for Fox."[19] It was remarkable really, the degree to which Fox became Ailes's political platform and personal megaphone. This though was no ordinary platform, or megaphone. Through the magic of the medium, television, it was Roger Ailes, more than any other single individual, who was positioned to project his political perspectives to more conservatives more consistently than anyone else in the Republican Party. Of course, he had a supporting cast, public faces in addition to his, such as O'Reilly, Sean Hannity, and Glenn Beck. But during Ailes's tenure at the top no one doubted even for a moment that it was he who held the reins of power. Ailes created a constant climate of fear and loathing. Everyone was "afraid of Roger Ailes."[20]

Ailes was positioned to satisfy his lust for power for so many years for several reasons. As we have seen, the first was the context within which he operated. Being on the cusp of the explosion of cable television was conducive to a man with his special talent for fusing politics with entertainment. The second was the people with whom he surrounded himself, his followers. Some were genuinely like-minded; others were beholden; still others were weak, scared. The third was Ailes's persona, which, more than a few concurred, was driven by paranoia.[21] He was in any case a force of nature, with a drive, an ambition, a fierce and unrelenting determination that is impossible to teach or to assign. That is in part innate, and in part acquired along the line, and that cannot in any case be stopped or ever fully satisfied. The fourth was Ailes's talent, his gift or even genius for, among other things, television programming, which he deployed to create the juggernaut that became Fox News. And, finally, there was his special relationship with his boss, with Rupert Murdoch, which was so strong it enabled Ailes for years to elbow aside Murdoch's own sons and presumed heirs apparent, the previously mentioned Lachlan and James. As biographer Sherman pointed out shortly before Ailes finally fell, it had been a "long-held goal" of Murdoch's sons to "remove Ailes from Fox News." But until the very end they were frustrated in their attempts because "their father consistently sided" with Ailes and against them.[22] In sum, Ailes had covered every one of his bases, squelched every one of his competitors, even those that were part of the royal – Murdoch – family.

Not only was Fox News broadly credited with turning post-9/11 America into a stalwart of Republicanism, the remarkable success of the network was objectively measurable. "The passion of Roger Ailes's audience was something that never before existed in TV news, a consequence of Fox's hybrid of politics and entertainment. Fox did not have viewers. It had fans." In primetime, Fox's fans watched on average fully 30 percent longer than did CNN viewers. Additionally, while early in the twenty-first century Fox News was earning a relative pittance, some ten years later Wall Street valued the network at more than $12.4 billion. (Ailes meantime was earning some $23 million a year.) By 2012 Fox was on track to turn a profit of $1 billion.[23]

But to most of those who worked for Roger Ailes, who worked under Roger Ailes, the cost was high. As a boss he was unrelenting: his need to dominate, to be dominant, was insatiable. From his early days as a manager, Ailes was often described as brutal in his behaviors even to his peers, and, predictably, especially to subordinates. Andy Friendly described him in 1995 as being erratic, duplicitous, and mean, as well as physically intimidating. "I along with several of my most talented colleagues have and continue to feel emotional and even physical fear dealing with this man every day. From in my face spitting and screaming to verbal threats of 'blowing [my] brains out' to psychological mind games - ..."[24] Routinely Ailes seemed to thrive on, perhaps even psychologically depend on, power trips. In the period after 9/11 Ailes was intent on using Fox to build George W. Bush's image as a war president. To this end Ailes scheduled meetings with his senior leadership team twice a day. The way he ran these meetings was, however, nearly invariably, inordinately difficult to tolerate. "His authoritarian management style could terrorize his inner circle into silence. Executives sat around the room hoping he would not call on them." One later recalled that it was hard even to be in the same room with him. "He looks around and points at people. If you talked, you're fucking dead. You're supposed to take it until your face turns bright red, and you're thinking, *if you move, will the T. rex see you?*"[25]

As an executive Ailes displayed other traits characteristic of leaders who need to feel, need to *be*, all-powerful. Though the term "totalitarian" is virtually never applied to corporate leaders – it is reserved for political leaders – it is not too much to say that Ailes's need to control everything and everyone was reminiscent of no one so much as a dictator. He was intensely secretive, preferring to keep his operations "shrouded in mystery." He developed a system that allowed him to police leaks – in fact, Ailes and his aides had a file "on pretty much everyone." He even talked about "putting hits" in the media on anyone who "got out of line."[26] And, as is typical of such strongmen, Ailes had a cadre of trusted tough guys who reported to him directly. Their main job was of course to carry out the boss's orders. (Bill Shine was one such tough guy – though to Ailes he was so subservient that some people at Fox called him "Bill the Butler."[27] Years later Shine went to work, briefly it turned out, at the White House as Deputy Chief of Staff for Communications under one President Donald J. Trump.)

Ailes liked to give the impression that he was everywhere, rather like Big Brother watching. He told one producer, "Look, I know everything I need to know about you. I talk to the people above you. I talk to the people below you. And I talk to the people on either side of you."[28] His own habits seemed deliberately irregular. Sometimes he would show up for meetings, sometimes not. But if he was not in the room, he might be, or he might not be, listening in on a speakerphone, usually without announcing himself. Ailes's most powerful means of control was Media Relations – a department within Fox that regularly made Fox employees feel like they were working in "a surveillance state." They constantly feared not only being watched but being heard; they worried that their conversations were secretly being recorded.

The reign of Roger Ailes effectively ended on July 6, 2016 when a high-profile former Fox News host by the name of Gretchen Carlson filed a sexual harassment suit against him, alleging that she was fired from her program for refusing Ailes's sexual advances. Carlson's case soon settled – she reportedly walked away with a cool $20 million – but for Ailes it was over. Soon after Carlson went public six more women came forward and spoke to Gabriel Sherman, each similarly alleging that Ailes had sexually harassed them, and that he had spoken "openly of expecting women to perform sexual favors in exchange for job opportunities."[29] Just a few weeks later Rupert Murdoch stood in front of Fox News employees and announced that Ailes was out, that his tenure as both chairman and chief executive was over.

Ailes went on to serve, briefly, as media advisor to Trump when he was a presidential candidate, thereby "further erasing the line between Fox and conservative politicians."[30] But once he was forced out of Fox it was never the same. His base of power was no longer – less than a year later he was dead.

Followers

In 2004 one of us, Kellerman, published a book titled *Bad Leadership: What It Is, Why It Matters, How It Happens*. One of the questions the book addressed was why do followers follow bad leaders? In some cases, the answers are evident. For example, if you live in China and are a Chinese citizen, to escape the dictatorial rule of Xi Jinping you would have to emigrate, a move of which generally only the exceedingly rich can even conceive. However, in other cases, such as those in which you are an employee and your employer, or your manager, is abusive, but you are free nevertheless to leave, the answers are not so evident. To be sure, it's never easy to leave one job and secure another, one that is just as good or even better. But in the United States we are, generally, at liberty to quit our place of employ, an option seriously to consider in the event our boss is the type that in *Bad Leadership* was labeled "Callous." Callous leaders are "uncaring and unkind." They ignore or discount "the needs, wants, and wishes of most members of the group or organization, especially subordinates."[31]

So, again, the question: why do people stay in a workplace in which they're being badly treated, if getting out of such places is an option relatively easy to exercise? *Bad Leadership* examined the case of erstwhile Sunbeam CEO, Al Dunlap, who was, like Roger Ailes, callous and controlling in the extreme. In Dunlap's case, as in most cases of callous leadership, the answer to the question of "why stay?" was complicated, in part because not all followers are alike. They are different, one from the other, which means they have different reasons, different motivations, for staying in situations that make them in some way uncomfortable or unhappy.

To be clear, some followers, even of CEOs as callous as Dunlap and Ailes, are not in the least unsatisfied. Quite the contrary – they are satisfied, or even *very* satisfied. Board members, for instance, are often content to leave callous leaders in place, so long as the operation is running smoothly, especially if it is turning a tidy, not to speak of very tidy, profit. Similarly for shareholders, most of whom think little or even not at all about the welfare of workers, especially when the stock price is climbing. Even upper-, middle-, and low-level employees have reasons to remain passively in place, particularly if they perceive that whatever the disadvantages of the jobs they have, the advantages outweigh them. But, then, there are those, among them many of those who remained at Fox News during the tyrannical reign of Roger Ailes, who baffle those on the outside. Why did they tolerate this man for so long?

Of course, not everyone was submissive all the time. At one point, Bill O'Reilly's power base, specifically his fan base, was so large and so dedicated to him personally and professionally that he became difficult for Ailes to manage. Ailes had lost some of or maybe even most of his power over O'Reilly, who felt, correctly, that he didn't need him and could therefore afford to ignore him. Interestingly, and no doubt tellingly, O'Reilly's bad behavior mirrored Ailes's. Like Ailes he was sequentially angry and out of control. Like Ailes he was sequentially abusive to staffers. Like Ailes he was sequentially charged with sexual harassment. And like Ailes he was finally forced by Fox to get out.[32]

Obviously, the main reason why most of those at Fox put up with Ailes for so long was his astonishing, enduring success. Riding along with him was riding on the gravy train. It was being part of an organization that was crushing the competition. It was being part of an organization in whose mission you frequently deeply believed. And it was being part of an organization that was in the business of both politics and entertainment – equally enticing and exciting. Roger Ailes was not, in other words, in the business of producing plumbing supplies. He was in the business of producing televisions shows with distinct political perspectives that were gaining huge ratings and enviable earnings. He was selling a way of thinking that was changing the face of America. And ... he was a kingmaker. Heady stuff.

At the same time, Ailes was no fool. From the get-go at Fox he made as sure as he could that anyone and everyone who worked for him would be, above all, loyal. Loyal not especially to the company, but loyal directly to him and to his political agenda. Above all he was determined not to let the professional ethics of journalism – which he regarded as rigid and outdated – get in the way of his political mission. To this end, his first order of business was to hire people who were pliable. When Ailes first joined Fox News, he led what he called a "jailbreak" from NBC, bringing along with him "dozens of top staffers." He also recruited some well-known faces such as business anchor Neil Cavuto and morning host Steve Doocy, both loyalists who owed their careers to Ailes. To his senior news team, he further added trusted Republicans, on whom he knew he could reliably depend.[33]

Simultaneously, he "embarked on a purge of existing staffers" at Fox News. Recalled one man who was canned, "There was a litmus test. He [Ailes] was going to figure out who was liberal or conservative when he came in and try to get rid of the liberals." Again, this was all about loyalty, in this case as reflected in ideology. As one former anchor put it, "All outward appearances were that it was just like any other newsroom. But you knew that the way to get ahead was to show your color – and that your color was red."[34] Red as in Republican.

The story of Ailes and his followers cannot though be told without referencing at least briefly what once was the elephant in the room: Fox's two-decades-long culture of sexual harassment. It was a culture that was tolerated by Ailes, arguably cultivated by Ailes, and for which he in any case set the tone. But, to be clear, it was a culture that was made possible not only by the offenders, by the perpetrators, but also by their victims. Victims, followers, so cowed that most did not, dared not, speak up or speak out for nearly two decades.

To keep it simple, we place the offenders into two separate silos. In the first was just one man, in effect the king, Roger Ailes. Since Gretchen Carlson came forward, additional women have been emboldened to do the same – to accuse Ailes of having sexually harassed them. They included, for example, Laurie Luhn, who told internal investigators that Ailes had harassed her for twenty years. They included Julie Roginsky, who claimed that her promotion was "contingent upon having a sexual relationship with Ailes."[35] They included Andrea Tantaros, who alleged that not only was she harassed by Ailes, but that Fox News generally "masqueraded as a defender of traditional family values, but behind the scenes it operated like a sex-fueled, Playboy Mansion-like cult, steeped in intimidation, indecency and misogyny."[36] And they included one of Fox's biggest on-air stars, Megyn Kelly.

Kelly, who ultimately left Fox for a short, failed, but highly lucrative stint at NBC, wrote a book about her life in which she went into detail about her experiences with Ailes. His inappropriate behavior began early on, in 2005, when Kelly had been with the company for just under a year. But, according to her, after escalating in 2006 – when Ailes made highly offensive comments, grabbed her, tried repeatedly to kiss her, and "ominously" seemed to threaten her career – his harassment of her slowed and then finally stopped. Apparently, his lust for power was greater than his lust for sex, which explains why, after a few years of giving Kelly a hard time, Ailes backed off. Her on-air talent was so apparent that he did not want to lose her. She, in turn, hung in with him and with Fox and, several years later, was handsomely rewarded for her patience as well as prowess. Kelly's reason for staying rather than leaving was unambiguous – she was ambitious, very ambitious. "I loved my job," is how she put it. "And didn't want to lose it." She knew, of course, that Ailes could ruin her career. At one point he told her, "I don't like to fight, but when I do, I fight to kill."[37] And so, until Carlson paved the way, Kelly, like the others, stayed silent. Their fear of retribution was a powerful pacifier.

In the second silo were all the other offenders. Ailes was – as implied – by no means the only culprit, by no means the only man at Fox who was a sexual harasser. Not only was O'Reilly a repeat offender, so were other supervisors whose wrongdoings ranged from making inappropriate remarks to engaging, or trying to, in inappropriate behaviors. At one point (in 2016) the *New York Times* spoke with about a dozen women who said they had "experienced some form of sexual harassment at Fox News or the Fox Business Network, and a half dozen more who said they had witnessed it."[38] Several supervisors were implicated, among them the previously mentioned onetime Trump aide, Bill Shine. While Shine never was himself accused of harassing, he was named in multiple lawsuits by women who charged specifically that he had covered up the bad behavior of other men, and generally that he had turned a blind eye to the wrongdoing around him.[39]

Sorting out the relationship between Ailes's unbridled and unending lust for power and his concomitant though less consistent demand for sex is not easy. A 2017 article in *Psychology Today* framed the overarching question this way: "What is the Link Between Sex and Power in Sexual Harassment?"[40] The piece raised several issues that, especially since the advent of the MeToo movement, have been front and center. It turns out that while the evidence about the relationship between the lust for power and the demand for sex remains less than completely clear, three assertions can confidently be made: (1) men who once felt powerless but later on in their lives feel powerful are the most likely to harass sexually; (2) sexual harassment complaints tend not to be against peers, they tend instead to be against men higher in the organizational hierarchy; (3) sexual harassment is much less about desire and much more about domination. This last point is key: "To understand sexual harassment primarily in terms of misplaced sexual desire is wrong for many of the same reasons that it is a mistake to understand rape primarily as a crime of passion or lust."[41] In Ailes's case the bottom line is this. While he was a sexual harasser, the evidence nevertheless is clear. Power was always more important to Roger Ailes, far more important, than was sex.

Hindsight

Roger Ailes left behind four separate and distinct legacies, each of which was significant. First was his imprint on Fox News specifically, where he created a context that reflected his persona. Specifically, Fox reflected his lust for power which, ultimately, was normalized in the organization that he led for so long. Second was his imprint on television news generally, which was transformed by Ailes's genius for mass media. To be sure, he was not the only mogul first to promote and then to profit from innovations in communications. In recent years other somewhat similar alpha males have used new technologies first to consolidate their extraordinary power, and then to wield it. Still, Ailes's impact on mass media was so great he stands almost in a class by himself. Third was Ailes's imprint on the Republican Party, which continues even now to propagate his political agenda. Using Fox News as an extension of the Republican Party – or is it the other way around? – has in fact never been more strikingly in evidence than during the Trump presidency. Finally, there was Ailes's fourth imprint, unmistakably on the MeToo movement, which was fueled before it exploded by Gretchen Carlson's readiness publicly to identify Ailes as a sexual harasser. (The charges against Harvey Weinstein did not surface until a year later.)

Each of these different imprints was left by Roger Ailes as he stood on a single stage – Fox News – which he dominated wholly and completely for twenty years.[42] It is testimony to his extraordinary effectiveness, effectiveness as a leader, that even since his departure, Fox has continued to perform exceptionally well. It remains the gold standard in cable news, in 2019 celebrating thirty-one consecutive months as the most-watched basic cable network.[43] Additionally, Ailes's impact on politics has remained as deep as enduring. He helped Trump win the White House – while Trump, in turn, drew on Ailes to dominate America's political landscape as has no other president since Franklin Delano Roosevelt. Finally, there is the dark side to Ailes's legacy, one with which he will, however, forever be associated: sexual harassment in the workplace – overwhelmingly abuse by much more powerful men of much less powerful women. At an earlier moment in time, Ailes's secret would have been kept. But at this moment in this time a few women found the fortitude to come out and step up. Standards of acceptable behavior are changing, which is why, less than a year after Murdoch sundered him from Fox, Roger Ailes died in a semblance of disgrace.

But, even years after his death, there has been no escaping the shadow of a man widely perceived within Fox News as "a tyrant."[44] Similarly, while "Ailes's aggression became a legend in Republican circles," his reputation as among the most formidable of party stars, as well as party stalwarts, remains intact. As his biographer put it, Republicans put up with him and "his volcanic eruptions because Ailes won."[45]

At the end Ailes could claim a few people who seemed genuinely to like or, at least, to appreciate him. So, when the king finally was kicked out of his castle, some said they lamented the loss. After it was announced that Ailes was leaving, Fox News anchor Brett Baier was quoted, "I think it's very sad, to be honest … Roger was always great to me, and my family." Another Fox anchor, Chris Wallace, was more heartfelt. "Roger Ailes is the best boss I've had in almost a half century of journalism. I admired him tremendously professionally and loved him personally."[46] Even Megyn Kelly wrote in her memoir that once Ailes's harassment of her stopped, they had a "professional relationship in which he was, for the most part, a supportive boss, who mentored and looked out for me." It was Roger, she wrote, "who gave me the chance to prove myself."[47] Just as it was Roger who had earlier sought to intimidate her, to dominate her, and to bed her.

Xi Jinping

In 2019 former Secretary of the Treasury Hank Paulson said about China, which has become one of the two most powerful countries in the world: "I never thought China would aspire to be a Jeffersonian democracy or espouse the liberal world order. I always thought the Communist party would be paramount, but I didn't see the clock being turned back."[48] There are three reasons why Paulson was obliged change his mind: (1) an increasingly assertive military, especially though by no means exclusively in the South China Sea; (2) the revision of China's constitution that removed the two-term limit on China's president; and (3) the expanded role of the Chinese Communist Party which now dominates every aspect of Chinese life – political, economic, and technological, private life as well as public life.

Paulson is not an ordinary citizen. But even a casual observer of what's been happening in China in the last few years would have concluded one Big Thing: President Xi Jinping has gone from having an appetite for power typical of authoritarians, to having an appetite for power typical of totalitarians. In other words, Xi's appetite for power has grown with eating – his lust for power is now everywhere in evidence nationally and, increasingly, everywhere in evidence internationally.

Context

For over two thousand years – some sources put the figure at four thousand – China's far-flung regions were held together by imperial rule. Only in 1912 did this era end, with the establishment of the Republic of China. The Republic was, however, short lived, for reasons that included continuing dynastic divisions, warring warlords, grinding poverty, a central government that was feeble from the start, and war abroad as well as at home. Enter, in 1949, the People's Republic of China, led by a cadre that came to be known as "old generation revolutionaries," of whom Mao Zedong was much the most consequential. For our purposes Mao is best thought of as a revolutionist and tyrant somewhat akin to the Soviet Union's Joseph Stalin; Stalin, to whom Mao's political fortunes were tied for thirty years, and whose brutality especially toward his own people has rarely been equaled.

Long abjectly dependent on Stalin, Mao also learned from Stalin. He learned from the master of survival how to gain power at all costs – and how, at all costs, to hold on to power. In other words, Mao had long had a model and mentor, which explains in part why, after many years of revolutionary struggle, from day one the People's Republic of China was completely controlled by the Chinese Communist Party. But only after Stalin's death, four years later, did Mao emerge fully independent of the Soviet Union, becoming at least in his own mind the leading light of communism worldwide.

Though Russia and China were in many ways dissimilar, they were similar in at least three important ways. The first relates to leadership; the second to followership; and the third to the context within which leadership and followership were exercised.

Leaders in both countries had virtually always been either authoritarians or totalitarians. It is not, in other words, as if either Stalin or Mao or, later, Xi Jinping, painted on a blank slate. To the contrary: both countries had traditions of strongman (and, once in a great while, strongwoman) rule. Accordingly, both countries had followers who, by and large, had no experience of being other than politically submissive. Neither Russia nor China had any history of democracy; nor as a result did their citizens have any meaningful tradition of political participation. The inordinate power of leaders and the inordinate powerlessness of followers – who, when the communists took over, were in both Russia and China largely agrarian and mostly impoverished – were further solidified by the contexts within which they were situated, contexts entirely devoid of the ideas and institutions that undergird democratic governance. Ideas such as freedom and democracy; institutions such as independent legislatures and systems of jurisprudence committed to upholding the law.

Mao's regime – his leadership – was at least as brutal as Stalin's, if not even more so. Frank Dikotter, a professor of modern Chinese history who has dug deep into China's archives, concluded that on account of Mao's catastrophically misguided policies, some 45 million people were worked, starved, or beaten to a premature death.[49] Ironically, though to experts on totalitarianism not surprisingly, Mao also left a legacy of leadership as idolatry. Under his regime it was expected that he be venerated in the extreme: his face was everywhere visible; his words were tantamount to gospel; his cult was personal as well as political. Notwithstanding, when Mao finally died, in 1976, he left China in ruin. Given the poverty that was as abject as it was widespread, the Chinese people had no obvious way forward. And given the lack of a viable ideology – communism had failed in China as dismally as it had in the Soviet Union – the leadership class had no obvious template for national recovery, either political or economic.

Between Mao Zedong and Xi Jinping, China's most important leader by far – the leader who led China out of the muck and mire – was Deng Xiaoping. Through what seems on the surface an aberration, Deng, who came to power in 1978, never held titles commensurate with his impact or importance. He was never head of state or government, or titular head of the Communist Party. Moreover, in keeping with ancient Chinese tradition, especially the teachings of Lao Tsu, Deng believed it best to appear modest. "Hide our capacities and bide our time," was his credo, "be good at maintaining a low profile, and never claim leadership."[50] Notwithstanding his being self-effacing, it is Deng who is credited with leading the Chinese people out of their mid-twentieth-century misery into their late twentieth-century viability. It was he who combined some of the traditional trappings of Communist Party ideology with the kinds of market reforms that ultimately enabled China to transition into the modern era. In time China's late twentieth- and early twenty-first-century trajectory was widely regarded as remarkable – ultimately accounting for more than three quarters of all global poverty reduction between 1990 and 2005. Specifically, according to the World Bank, since the 1980s at least 500 million Chinese escaped what the Bank called "extreme poverty."[51]

Deng was in most of the important ways a striking contrast to Mao. Above all, unlike Mao whose leadership style was arrogant and self-aggrandizing, pompous and grandiose, narrow and rigid, dictatorial and tyrannical, Deng was unassuming and understated, calm and collected. Here is Deng again, carefully but clearly differentiating himself from his formidable but terrifying predecessor: "Observe calmly, handle without panic, hide your strength, build your capabilities, never pursue leadership, and seek accomplishments when opportunities arise."[52] As importantly, between Deng, who retired in 1989, and Xi, who came to power in 2013, were several other Chinese leaders, all of whom were more in the mold of Deng than Mao. They were not rigidly committed either to communism or to the Chinese Communist Party. They were not compelled personally or politically to stand out, above and apart from other members of the Chinese hierarchy. They did not develop a cult of personality. They did not squelch the opposition. And they were not driven to stay in power indefinitely.

This is not to say that China evolved between the death of Mao and the rise of Xi into something altogether different, into a nation notably looser and more liberal. Still, as Paulson's quote attests, there was hope. There were many in the West who thought that China's political system would come in time to be somewhat less autocratic and somewhat more democratic. But, as it turned out, while in the last several years China did change, it was not in the ways that Paulson and many other experts envisioned. As it turned out, Xi Jinping, who came to power in 2012, is driven by a lust for power most strikingly reminiscent not of his more recent predecessors, but of his more distant one, the totalitarian Mao Zedong.

The size and importance of Xi's domain are impossible to exaggerate. Since 1978 China has been the world's fastest growing economy; as swiftly as certainly it became an economic and industrial powerhouse. China's economy now rivals that of the United States; the International Monetary Fund predicts that by 2030 China's gross domestic product will supersede that of every one of its competitors. China ranks first in the world in population – it has some 1.4 billion people – and it ranks fourth in the world in size. In short, Xi's lust for power is located in a context of singular consequence.

Evidence

Xi Jinping, born in 1953, was elected to the all-important post of General Secretary of the Communist Party of China in November 2012. One year later he was elected president of the country – the People's Republic of China. And in 2018 the National People's Congress removed the two five-year term limits on presidents including the incumbent, which means obviously that Xi can legally continue to serve as president indefinitely.

His childhood and adolescence were emblematic of the chaos that characterized Mao's rule. When Xi was born, his father was close to Mao. In fact, his father was not only an esteemed revolutionary hero, he served under Mao as vice premier. However, Xi's privileged early life ended abruptly, in 1962, when in the throes first of the Great Leap Forward and then of the Cultural Revolution, both brutal political campaigns driven mercilessly by Chairman Mao, Xi's father was purged from his leadership post and charged with being an anti-party rightist.

Notwithstanding the turbulence of his early years, Xi became an avid reader of Chinese history. And when years later his father was "rehabilitated," Xi was able, which was unusual at the time, to graduate from a good university. He was 26 when he began his steady climb through the ranks of the government and of the Chinese Communist Party. In 2007 Xi was elevated to the post of Party Chief of Shanghai, a promotion that foreshadowed his appointment to high office at the national level. It was no surprise, then, that less than a year later Xi was elevated to the Standing Committee of the Politburo – which in a single stroke made him one of the nine most powerful men in China. Five years later he was named both General Secretary and Head of the Communist Party Central Military Commission – which made him the country's most important and powerful single political leader.[53] It was from this point on that Xi's lust for power – his continuing and unbridled desire to accumulate more than he already had, and more than any other Chinese leader since Mao – became crystal clear.

Xi's strategy for accumulating power, and then more power, was carefully crafted and impeccably executed. First, he instituted institutional changes, which according to several experts were nothing less than "radical adjustments." These radical adjustments, all calculated to strengthen Xi's hand, included (but were not limited to) downsizing the number of Politburo members from nine to seven; assuming the formal powers associated with chairing each of the most important political committees; downgrading the other political committees, in other words, the competition; establishing new economic committees, such as the one charged with leading market reforms, all of which named Xi chair; and establishing new foreign policy and national security committees, all of which also put Xi at the helm. Institutional changes like these were, of themselves, transformative. They were designed to, and succeeded in, "uplifting Xi's position from being first-among-equals … to being an all-powerful leader with absolute authority in handling domestic and external affairs." These moves, in other words, granted Xi a level of authority that had eluded his immediate predecessors, and they reversed the "trend toward collective leadership since Deng Xiaoping."[54]

Another perspective on Xi's extraordinary accumulation of power over the last seven years is by Oxford sociologist Stein Ringen, who described what he called China's "pillars of power."

These include the party, the military, the executive, the legislature, the police, and the judiciary. For example, since the Communist Party of China dominates China, the leader of the party is China's dominant leader. Ringen writes of the party that it is "present in every government agency, central and local, in every unit of the military, in every town and village and neighborhood, in every school, in every university and university department, and every student residence, in every business, and in every officially registered social organization."[55]

Similarly, Xi also came to have total control over the military, the People's Liberation Army (PLA). The PLA is the ultimate guarantor of the party, which means it is the ultimate guarantor of the state, which means it is prepared to intervene anywhere at home and abroad, whenever and wherever party leaders determine the need arises. The fact that Xi was credited with singlehandedly "achieving a milestone victory" in restructuring the army – early in his tenure at the top he secured an "unprecedentedly large-scale and multifaceted transformation" of the military – contributed significantly to what, also relatively early in his tenure at the top, was widely perceived even at the time as a shift away from collective leadership, back toward one-man rule.[56]

But perhaps nowhere is the shift under Xi Jinping from authoritarian to totalitarian leadership as clear as in his increasingly complete control of the Chinese people. Beginning around 2013 it became more dangerous to be a political activist. Beginning around 2016 it became more dangerous to be a member of the Muslim minority, hundreds of thousands of whom were forcibly held in detention centers known as re-education camps. And beginning around 2017 it became more dangerous to be an ordinary Chinese citizen – as the latest technologies were increasingly used to monitor the masses.

In 2014 China watchers noted that suppression had "increased markedly not only against human rights activists but also against dissidents, underground churches, Falun Gong adherents, petitioners, activist netizens, and liberal scholars." At the same time there was a "tightening of information dissemination and ideological control."[57] Since then this trend – toward greater monitoring of the everyday lives of ordinary people – has expanded and accelerated. Rules and regulations governing citizens are as endless as they are onerous. New technologies are constantly being employed to make monitoring more extensive and efficient.

Access to information has become strictly limited, with internet censorship in China now more widespread and advanced than anywhere else in the world. Offenses against the state include signing online petitions, communicating with groups abroad, and calling for reform and an end to corruption. Committing such offenses is risky to the point of being dangerous: Amnesty International notes that China has "the largest number of imprisoned journalists and cyber-dissidents in the world."[58]

Looking ahead we can anticipate that Xi Jinping's government will take Big-Brotherism to whole new levels. The authorities have already launched what one writer called a "dystopian program" *quantitatively* to monitor its citizens (followers) for the benefit of its leaders.[59] The purpose of the program is essentially to reward citizens for what the government decides is good behavior, such as donating blood, and to punish citizens for what the government decides is bad behavior, such as violating laws, including routine traffic laws. Predictably, the government claims the program is in the people's best interest: "It will guide the citizens to be honest and promote the socialist core values." But the way the program works – it uses tracking technologies linked to cell phones and social apps; it is also installing some 200 million cameras to employ facial recognition technologies – would appear onerous to most Westerners. It obviously does to Stephen Colbert, who cracked, "If you thought the way Facebook tracks you is scary, it's got nothing on the Chinese government."[60]

Followers

Leadership is, by definition, a relationship. Leaders cannot, do not, lead unless they have at least one follower. Even the most potent person on the planet depends on others not only to attain power, but also to maintain power. Moreover, even the most potent person on the planet cannot ascend to power, cannot accrue power in the first place, without getting others in some way to acquiesce at every point in the process.

But how small numbers of leaders become all-powerful remains ultimately a mystery. In the twentieth century three of the most ruthless totalitarians ever were approximately coterminous – Hitler, Stalin, and Mao – which explains why some of the great minds of the twentieth century, Hannah Arendt, for example, asked, in effect, "How this could have happened?" How was it possible for three such evil leaders to gain so much power? And how was it possible for three such evil leaders to maintain so much power – even as they obviously pursued policies with malignant, malevolent intentions?

Without making facile comparisons between Xi on the one hand, and Hitler, Stalin, and Mao on the other, all political leaders who lust for power, whose appetite for power is insatiable, have certain things in common. For example, they seek to control the many not just a few, the masses not just a handful. To this end they use propaganda to propagate their ideology. Xi has grounded his public policies in traditional Chinese thought, especially in Confucianism. During his all-important anti-corruption campaign, for instance – which some saw as a way for him to eliminate enemies, but which did coincide with the widespread opinion that corruption was a problem – Xi quoted Confucius: "The rule of Virtue may be compared to the Pole Star, which stays in its place while the myriad stars pay it homage."[61]

Another tactic that Xi employed to keep his followers in line was to reward them for their fealty. As we have seen, over the last four decades China has gone from economic backwater to global economic powerhouse. While in 2018 China's economic growth started to slow – a trend that if it continued would present Xi with not just an economic problem, but a political one – in 2017 it posted a remarkable 6.9 percent gain. (This figure accounted for fully one third of total global growth.[62]) In other words, for most of Xi's tenure at the top, China's economic accomplishments have been remarkable. Moreover, they have done more than provide hundreds of millions of Chinese with material benefits. China's booming economy has provided them as well with a strong sense of safety and security and, increasingly, a growing feeling of great national pride. In recent years Xi has in fact increasingly encouraged strong feelings of nationalism, even of patriotic fervor, in matters of both domestic and foreign policy. Of course, if the Chinese economy slows, Xi will turn not only to nationalism but to militarism to ensure continuing support for his regime. The same can be said of the threat posed by the populace of Hong Kong. Given the scope of their protests, essentially against the authorities in China, Xi might have felt obliged at some point militarily to intervene – to protect his power and prestige. However, after the advent of the pandemic, public health became paramount.

Which brings us to the necessary counterpart to Xi's promise of reward: his threat of punishment. In other words, rewarding followers for their loyalty is one option; punishing them for failing to fall into line is another. Totalitarian movements are sustained by the unadulterated and unconditional loyalty of their members. Once this façade starts to crack, it's over. Moreover, the success of the system – success as defined by the leader's continuing capacity completely to control – depends on sustaining the leader at the center. Here's how Arendt described the phenomenon: "At the center of the movement as the motor that swings it into motion, sits the Leader. He is separated from the elite formation by an inner circle of the initiated who spread around him an aura of impenetrable mystery ... His position within this intimate circle depends on his ability to spin intrigues among its members ... He owes his rise to leadership to an extreme ability to handle inner-party struggles for power."[63]

We want to be clear here. Xi has not been without authentic allies or even acolytes, any more than were other totalitarian leaders. To take just a single example, Xi's four-decade friendship with Wang Qishan was "arguably the most important factor in the consolidation of Xi's power and the implementation of his ... policy initiatives." Wang has been described as tough, courageous, and highly knowledgeable, especially in finance. One scholar writes that he was absolutely "instrumental" to all of Xi's key policy initiatives, especially at the start of his tenure, when he most needed the support of a few who were supremely competent and totally loyal.[64] It was Wang, moreover, who Xi put in charge of his all-important anti-corruption campaign. The scale of the resulting purge has been described as "almost incomprehensible." Since 2012, the authorities "investigated more than 2.7 million officials and punished more than 1.5 million of them." Among those punished were seven members of the Politburo and the cabinet and about two dozen high-ranking generals; two senior officials were sentenced to death.[65]

Additionally, according to "relatively reliable polling," Xi has been popular with the Chinese people.[66] Of course this putative popularity has been nurtured if not force-fed by an escalating propaganda campaign that places Xi at the center of the universe. In keeping with Chinese history and tradition – though not in keeping with China's more recent attempts to collectivize leadership – Xi and his minions have capitalized on the adulation of ancient emperors, once known as "sons of heaven." In 2017 reporter Cindy Yu wrote, "For the first time since the death of Chairman Mao four decades ago, a leadership personality cult is emerging in

China. You can see it in Beijing's streets, where President Xi Jinping's face appears on posters on bus stops, next to those of revolutionary war heroes. Scarlet banners fly with bold white letters saying, 'Continue Achieving the Success of Socialism ... with Comrade Xi Jinping at the core.'" The city felt, Yu added, as if it were participating in a "coronation."[67]

Nevertheless, in Xi's never-ending quest to continue to control the Chinese people, and to control his followers, the power to punish remains an all-important arrow in his quiver. This is a power which Xi needs – even paranoids have real enemies. First, dictatorships cannot depend on a relatively small number of loyal servants, or even on mass support that might be genuine enough but is not reliably either strong or enduring. Second, Xi's real enemies include many among at least three different groups who have come to despise him: wealthy Chinese who had their lives of luxury destroyed by Xi's anti-corruption campaign; technocratic elites who feel betrayed by, among other treacheries, the squelching of legal and market reforms; and liberals and activists who in recent years were – and are still being – oppressed and suppressed, sometimes brutally. Finally, things happen. A striking example is the wholly unanticipated public health crisis that Xi was forced to face as a result of the coronavirus. It presented his regime with what by early 2020 had become its most significant challenge.

In addition to these is a more general principle: totalitarian regimes must prompt people to become loyal and to remain loyal.[68] Under Xi, prompts intended first to elicit and then to ensure faithful followers include: (1) party and state organs under instructions to collect every piece of information that could possibly be considered politically relevant; (2) security services everywhere with the authority to strike down anyone engaging in activities deemed politically threatening; (3) courts under political and party control; (4) entire hierarchies of public and party officials assessed for performances based not only on merit but also on obedience to authority; (5) registration of some 1.4 billion people in a national data bank; (6) the requirement that every adult carry a photo identity; (7) the maintenance of personal files on all Chinese citizens including information that Westerners would regard as deeply private; (8) censorship, including self-censorship, internet censorship, media censorship, and academic censorship; and (9) controlling discourse in universities by rewarding students, for example with higher grades and scholarships, for reporting to the authorities any professor who strays from the strict party line – from the line of the now all-controlling Communist Party of China.[69]

Hindsight

In the last few years, it has become increasingly obvious that Xi Jinping's lust for power is as we could have predicted – insatiable. In fact, since taking power, in 2012, he gradually but inexorably set about "extinguishing all challenges to his authority."[70] His appetite grew with eating – which means that on the cusp of the third decade of the twenty-first century he is intent on playing a, if not *the*, dominant role on the international stage as well as on the national one.

China has become America's most prominent competitor – ideologically, economically, and militarily. America's foreign policy establishment and its business community have looked increasingly askance at China's retrenchment of economic reforms; China's digital authoritarianism; China's mass incarceration and relentless repression of ethnic minorities (especially Muslims); China's Belt and Road Initiative intended to expand its influence around the world, especially on routes that connect Eurasia and the Indian Ocean; and China's intermittent military adventurism, especially but not exclusively in the area of the South China Sea. In 2019 Chinese and Russian air forces staged their first ever joint aerial patrol; a Chinese oil exploration vessel entered waters claimed by Vietnam; Beijing announced that it was developing a military base in Cambodia, its first in Southeast Asia; and Taiwan, which for decades has been self-governing, has looked with alarm at China's increasing encroachment on Hong Kong.[71]

It's obviously impossible to measure how much of China's expansionism is in direct consequence of Xi's leadership. But this much is clear: the attempt to exert greater control abroad, like the attempt to exert greater control at home, has coincided with the consolidation of Xi's own personal and political power. One China expert writes, "The prevailing narrative in the United States is that President Xi is determined to take China in a new direction, a direction that many experts on China describe as increasingly illiberal at home and aggressive abroad."[72] Another one opines, "Xi's efforts to assert China's growing power have been so bold and persistent that it is fair to say they indicate a new and offensive-oriented mindset."[73] In other words, by the third decade of the twenty-first century everything that China does do, and everything that China does not do, is traced directly to the desk of Xi Jinping. His lust for power has got to the point where he rules with an iron fist.

These conclusions, then, can be drawn with certainty:

- Since he came to power in 2012, Xi Jinping's lust for power has been in evidence at every turn. The more power he got, the more he wanted. It has never been enough. It is still not enough. The evidence that his iron grip extends now from within China to without is at every turn – including in 2019 becoming embroiled in a high-stakes fight (high political stakes, high financial stakes) with Adam Silver, the Commissioner of America's National Basketball Association.[74]
- Xi's grip on power over the Chinese government, over the Chinese Communist Party, over the Chinese military, and over the Chinese people is now so tight that his leadership can accurately be described as having evolved from authoritarian to totalitarian. Of course, while totalitarian leaders are, by definition, all-powerful, they are never fully secure. Therefore, the fight to retain power, as well as to gain still more power, must be, and is, ceaseless.
- Totalitarian states are characterized by terror; by the intrusion of the state into everyday life; by a strict nationalist ideology; and by single individuals who exercise near total control. Because their lust for power remains indefinitely unsatisfied, these single individuals, totalitarian leaders such as Xi, nearly never relinquish power voluntarily.
- All totalitarian leaders employ whatever available technologies there are to increase their level of control. Xi is no exception. But, given the sophisticated, advanced technologies now available, not least in China, unless Xi is stopped he will exercise more control over more people than any other leader anywhere at any time in history.
- Past is not always prologue. It is impossible to foretell the future – cracks in systems do happen. And Xi is hardly invulnerable or impervious to the existing, or for that matter, gathering storms. The protests in Hong Kong presented the government in Beijing with challenges it has yet successfully to address. A trade war with the United States poses a threat to China's economic engine. Xi's

internment of Muslims met with worldwide opprobrium. And, of course, the coronavirus exposed the vulnerabilities of a totalitarian regime faced with an unprecedented crisis – a public health emergency – that necessitated timely, accurate, and complete information, *both* nationally and internationally.

- Past is usually prologue. Notwithstanding the various, some serious, challenges to his regime, seven years after Xi became president of China he remained still at, or near the top of his game. And for the indefinite future it is unlikely that his followers will force him from his perch. For the next several years, then, China will probably be what it has been for the last several years: a dictatorship.[75]

Moreover, Xi's draconian ways have revealed his regime for what it is, which for the Chinese people has created its own set of problems: backtracking on reform has contributed to China's economic slowdown; near total control over modern technologies has alienated much of the global tech sector; protectionist trade policies have incentivized the United States to retaliate; and China's increasingly assertive foreign policy has unsettled liberal democrats worldwide.[76] So far as we are concerned, then, what we do not know rivals that which we do know. As Elizabeth Economy has pointed out, "Xi's centralization of power and growing control over information make it hard to assess how much consensus there really is in China about the direction in which he and the rest of the Chinese leadership are taking the country. There may be more pushback against Xi than is commonly thought" – especially given the coronavirus global pandemic.[77] Moreover, in general, history is cyclical. Whoever goes up, goes down. But whatever the future, even now this much is clear: Xi will forever be remembered as an all-powerful leader who, in most of the important ways and for an extended time, largely controlled the lives of more than a billion people. While his lust for power will, by definition, never be fully satisfied, it has been realized to an extent that by any measure is singular.

Coda

Both Roger Ailes and Xi Jinping had – in Xi's case still has – a passion for domination. Their lust for power was relentless and it was ceaseless.

Theirs was not a lust for power as autonomy. As the phrase "passion for domination" would suggest, theirs was a lust for power over others. They needed desperately to wield control not just over themselves, but over as many others as they could muster. Both can be thought of as narcissists who, the more power they had, the more they needed to have. They not only wanted, they *needed* to keep looking for new recruits, for new people, followers far less powerful than they.

Neither the enormous literature on leadership nor the leadership industry generally address, not to speak of seriously study, leaders who lust for power – leaders who seek to dominate. Nor do they generally address, or seriously study, followers who are being dominated. Ironically, the dean of contemporary leadership studies, the late historian and political scientist, James MacGregor Burns, did look at leaders who dominate, but he refused to refer to such people as "leaders." Instead he called them "power wielders." Power wielders, he wrote, are out to satisfy themselves, to attain their own goals, "whether or not these are also the goals" of their followers. Leaders in contrast are not so self-involved, so self-interested. As Burns conceived of the word, "leaders" consider, and are considerate of, their followers. Leaders take account not only of what they themselves want and need, but also of what others, their followers, want and need. Leaders "arouse, engage, and satisfy the motives of others," Burns wrote.[78] But, his distinction notwithstanding, no one uses the term, "power wielder." Everyone uses the word *leader*, no matter saint or sinner. Which returns us to the connection between lusting for power and being a leader. While having an overweening need to control others is generally to be condemned, those of us with more than a passing interest in leadership as a whole – the range of leadership, from dictatorial to democratic – must not make the mistake of dismissing lusting for power simply as repellent.

To be sure, at the start of this chapter we acknowledged that leaders who lust for power are prone, once they have power, to behave badly, sometimes increasingly badly. Such leaders must be watched, carefully, so that, if necessary, early in their lives as leaders their wings get clipped by followers wise to their ways – followers clever enough to understand the dangers of despots, and of bully bosses, and courageous enough to intervene to preclude it. Meantime though let's be clear-eyed, let's see things as they are, not as they ought, ideally, to be. The fact is that Roger Ailes and Xi Jinping's lust for power goes a long way toward explaining their extraordinary ascent to the top – and their equally extraordinary tenure at the top. Their exercise of leadership was – is – in most ways contemptible. But it was – is – also remarkable.

2   LUST FOR MONEY

Prelude

> "Leaders who lust for *money* have a limitless desire to accrue greater, and then still greater, wealth."

The lust for money is no more, and no less, than the insatiable desire for more money. Some people want to accrue enormous sums of money for a larger purpose such as, for example, improving schools, enhancing the arts, or sending a spaceship to Mars. Other people want to accumulate money, and then more money, absent any larger intent. Either way, however high the pile of money, it is never high enough.

Sometimes the lust for money is deemed a virtue. In the 1987 movie *Wall Street*, the lead character, Gordon Gekko – a lustful, powerful, Wall Street financier – famously insisted, "Greed, for lack of a better word, is good. Greed is right, greed works."[1] Similarly, Ivan Boesky (one of the real-life investors on whom Gekko is based) told a graduating class at the University of California's Berkeley's School of Business Administration, "Greed is all right, by the way. I want you to know that . . . greed is healthy."[2] The audience – which included family, friends, and faculty – clapped and laughed enthusiastically and, to all appearances, approvingly. Then there's Donald John Trump who, when he was running for president of the United States in 2016, gleefully boasted, "My whole life I've been greedy, greedy, greedy. I've grabbed all the money I could get. I'm so greedy. But now I want to be greedy for the United States. I want to grab all that money. I'm going to be greedy for the United States."[3]

What makes any defense of money-lust so striking is that while sometimes it is thought to be good – to wit, Trump, who took pride in his greed – other times, most times, it is thought to be bad. Signs of greed, of money-lust, have been a target of spiritual teachings of most major religions for millennia.[4] For example, in the Book of Isaiah, Christians are warned against leaders who are rapacious, for they are "like ravenous dogs, they are never satisfied. They are shepherds with no discernment; they all turn to their own way, each one seeking his own gain."[5] In Hieronymus Bosch's masterpiece, *Death and the Miser*, the miser, who "stands for the temptation of avariciousness," lays dying, while his attending angel hovers nearby, looking to the crucifix in the upper window.[6] No surprise then that greed remains to this day a target. In 2015, Pope Francis called unbridled capitalism and its apparently attendant avariciousness, the "'dung of the devil.'"[7]

Among the most influential critics of greed ever, especially its association with capitalism, were Karl Marx and Friedrich Engels. Their 1848 polemic, *The Communist Manifesto*, remains to this day the classic anti-capitalist screed. It attacks those who seek to accumulate far too much money at the expense of those who have far too little. Though it has long been argued that *The Communist Manifesto* was distorted and exploited, by, among others, Lenin, Stalin, and Mao, there can be no doubt about the extraordinary impact of what originally was seen simply as political pamphlet. It was not long ago when anti-capitalism incarnated as communism dominated large swaths of the Earth's surface, from the 1950s to the 1980s, in China and the Soviet Union.

Greed has also been held directly responsible for war. In a poignant essay in *The Atlantic*, written during the First World War, L. P. Jacks, the noted English educator, writer, and Unitarian minister, explained, "Poor nations didn't plunge the world into war. Rich nations that coveted even greater riches did." Later he elaborated: "The possession of great riches acts upon nations in the same way that we sometimes see it act upon individuals. Instead of making them contented with what they have, it makes them covetous to get more."[8]

More recently, our ethical ire has been directed at corporate leaders so focused on the bottom line that they exclude other concerns, such as the well-being of employees and the perils of climate change. The CEO of a London investment group admitted that the financial community consisted of "many selfish people who are encouraged by management ... to develop a culture of greed."[9] In 2019, in response to the growing criticisms, a group of business leaders got to the point of feeling the heat and taking modest action. The Business Roundtable, among the most prominent associations of American executives, decided it was past time to issue a new statement of purpose. Instead of having just one priority, profits, and only one constituency, shareholders, the group committed to other concerns, the environment among them, and other constituents, including workers, suppliers, customers, and communities.

Social scientists have also cast an increasingly jaundiced eye on greed. As Nobel Prize-winning economist Paul Krugman put it at one point early in this century, "Greed Is Bad."[10] His argument was based not on moral grounds, but on economic ones. His concerns centered on the excessive temptations of excessive financial incentives. Concerns that were borne out in 2008 when it appeared that as much as anything else, it was the lust for money that had triggered the financial crisis. Greed, then, is criticized not only on moral grounds, but also on empirical ones. The lust for money has come, certainly in some circles, to be seen not only as decadent but as destructive and disastrous.

Since the time of Adam Smith – the great eighteenth-century theorist widely known as the "father of economics" – there has been a widespread view that some level of greed is inherent, endemic to human nature. Not only that all people are greedy to some extent, but that to some extent greed is, indeed, good. That it is an essential evolutionary impulse, one that properly, appropriately, promotes self-preservation. The claim is that people who are predisposed first to gather and then to hoard as many resources as possible have an evolutionary advantage.[11] Along separate though parallel tracks was the growing understanding that the avid pursuit of money should be credited with stimulating economic growth; for instance, with encouraging innovation that leads, in turn, to the development of new industries that increase employment, promote well-being, and support political, economic, and social stability not just for a few, but for the many.[12]

Surprisingly – given the enormous interest in the importance of greed, given the enormous differences in dispositions toward greed, and given the consequences of greed both for individuals and for the communities in which they reside – empirical research on greed, on the lust for money, has been scarce.[13] There is, however, one finding of special interest here – given our focus on the intersection between lusting and leading. It is that people who lust for money tend to land on what is called a "hedonic treadmill."[14] That is, they anticipate that they will be happier in the future if they have more money. But, as soon as they have more money, they change. They adapt their ambition to want still more money.[15] Their goalpost is, in other words, forever being moved, moved just beyond reach.

This explains why the pursuit of wealth can develop into something akin to a compulsion or an addiction. More specifically, chasing money can become a "behavioral addiction," which contrasts with a physical addiction to, say, alcohol or drugs. It turns out that behavioral addictions can, like physical ones, lead to changes in brain chemistry. Behavioral addictions can kick-start the release of chemicals such as dopamine which, in turn, produce "highs" resembling those produced by alcohol or drugs. Therefore, when someone is addicted to money and then is able, somehow, to get money, or to get more money than they already have, their brain chemistry "rewards" them in ways experienced as pleasurable.[16]

The precise genesis of a lust for money – a lust that extends well beyond ordinary self-interest – remains, however, unclear. It is possible that we lust for money – or for that matter for anything else – because we feel deprived. For some reason we feel that something is missing which leads us to, on some level of consciousness, conclude that in this instance money, a lot of it, will fill the gap. Which, of course, it does not. It cannot. Another possibility is suggested, that the lust for money is part of our genetic make-up, part of who we are as human beings. It is certainly the case that from an evolutionary perspective, we benefit, we increase our chances of survival, by accruing as well as achieving. It is not, however, clear what is the evolutionary advantage of a drive to keep acquiring well beyond any needs we might have, and well beyond any returns that can possibly be to our direct advantage.

The origins of the lust for money might, then, be uniquely human. Animals can, of course, be gluttonous and territorial. But we – we human animals – concern ourselves also with *relative* wealth. We concern ourselves not just with how much we have, but also with how much everyone else has. Especially everyone else to whom we directly relate. Do our friends, heaven forefend, or our neighbors, have more money than we do? Among human animals, greed is, moreover, contagious. Specifically, notably, it spreads more easily from one to another than does generosity. In fact, there is research to suggest that while we tend to be more generous when we witness or benefit from generosity ourselves, the impulse is stronger when it applies to greed. Simply put we are more likely to be greedy when we see someone else behave greedily, than we are to be generous when we see someone else behave generously. Greed, it turns out, is especially socially contagious.[17]

We should not be surprised when people who successfully lust for money – especially people who have earned a lot of money as opposed to, for example, inheriting it – become leaders. Though they were not initially motivated by the lust to lead, their ability initially to acquire large amounts of money, and then later to accumulate even larger amounts of money, inspires others to emulate them. It inspires others to become their followers. Why does a man who works money magic – a man like Warren Buffett – have legions of followers? Because he has gratified – not satisfied, but gratified – his lust for money beyond most of our wildest imaginings. And because he has got to the point of wearing his lust loudly and proudly. Buffett's followers do not generally expect to rival his genius for making money. But they do generally think that some of his fairy dust might just blow their way.

Warren Buffett

Warren Buffett is one of the world's savviest investors, ever. His company, Berkshire Hathaway, has a current market capitalization of nearly $532 billion. Beginning in the year that Buffett took control, 1965, through 2017, the compound yearly gain in Berkshire's book value was 19.1 percent per share, and the yearly gain on an investment in Berkshire's stock was 20.9 percent.[18] Buffett himself is the third richest person in the world, with, in 2019, a net worth of $78.8 billion.[19]

Buffett is, of course, not only rich, he is famous for being rich. And he is a leader in the business of giving advice on how to get rich, specifically through the financial markets that long ago he mastered. Buffett is a thought leader, someone who is a "widely recognized authority in a specialized field and whose expertise is sought and often rewarded."[20] People want to know how Buffett does it so that they can try to do the same. Buffett, in turn, usually seems perfectly delighted to oblige the legions of his followers who have come to believe that if they go where he leads, they are more likely to have more money than if they do not. Alice Schroeder reportedly received a $7 million advance for her 2008 biography of Buffett – for good reason. As soon as the book was released, it rocketed to the top of the bestseller lists of both the *New York Times* and *Publisher's Weekly* – and it stayed there for more than three months. Interest in Warren Buffett was then and remains still that high.

Buffett does have, and he always did have, a personal life. He has had two wives and three children. But, overwhelmingly, his fixation has been on making money and then making more money – beginning in his childhood. At the tender age of six, Buffett is said to have purchased six bottles of Coca-Cola from his grandfather's grocery store for a total of twenty-five cents. He then sold the six bottles, each for five cents, enabling him without breaking a sweat to make a 5-cent profit. Not bad for a boy – a 20 percent return on his investment. Notice Buffett did not share his bottles of Coke with his friends, nor did he drink those Cokes all by himself. He resold them. In other words, while other children his age were chasing jackrabbits, Buffett was chasing money.

Context

Warren Buffett was born in 1930 in Omaha, Nebraska. His mother was a "model housewife to the outside world," but she was disposed to "verbally lash" Buffett and his siblings "for hours, until the children wept." Buffett has said that when his mother died, "he cried not because he was sad but 'because of the waste.' She had her good parts, but the bad parts kept me from having a relationship with her." His father, Howard Buffett, was a four-term United States congressman from Nebraska – and he was a stockbroker. Buffett reports having "revered" him.[21]

Because of his father's profession and prominence, beginning when he was young Buffett was in a position to rub elbows with people who had power both in government and business. It was a context suited to a boy with his special talents – early on he was considered exceptional at math – and singular ambitions. When he was ten, he visited New York City with his father.

Together they had lunch with At Mol, a Dutchman who was a member of the New York Stock Exchange. Years later, Buffett described this manifestly memorable occasion as his "road to Damascus" moment – the moment he knew that what he wanted above all else in life was to make money. To make money by becoming an investor. No surprise then that even as a child Buffett regularly visited his father's stockbroker's office, apparently completely content to chalk stock prices on the blackboard while listening to what professional investors said and watching what they did. Given the experiences that his father provided, along with his own early passions and proclivities, Buffett was poised to make his first remembered investment at the age of eleven: he bought three shares of Cities Service preferred stock, each of which cost $38 per share. The stock quickly dropped to $27, but Buffett was tenacious even then. He held on until the price climbed back up to where it had been – and then some. When the stock hit $40 a share, he sold.[22]

Buffett graduated from the University of Nebraska at age 19. He was rejected by the Harvard Business School, but accepted by Columbia, which he since has described as a blessing. For it was at Columbia Business School that Buffett studied under two members of the faculty, Benjamin Graham and David Dodd, both well-known and highly respected securities analysts, whose impact on him was lifelong. Buffett's connection to Graham – now widely regarded as one of the greatest investment gurus ever – was especially strong. While it was Dodd who taught Buffett that he should assess the "intrinsic value" of a business rather than its stock prices, it was Graham, the "godfather" of value investing, who taught him the fundamentals of his investing system. Later in his life Buffett credited Graham's book, *The Intelligent Investor*, with changing forever his approach to making money. He maintained that his own way of investing was "85 percent" shaped by the great Graham.[23]

Notwithstanding his several years in the East, it is Omaha, Nebraska – where he was born and raised – where Buffett chose to live full-time. It is, then, Omaha that constitutes the context within which Buffett's lust for money not only originally emerged, but ultimately was sustained lifelong. Over the years, many Buffett-watchers have found his choice of a place to live and work curious, counterintuitive, maybe even somewhat strange. After all, neither Omaha the city nor Nebraska the state is thought of as a hotbed of high finance. Additionally, neither the one nor the other is where most of us would think to find the third-wealthiest person in the world. Buffett, though, has long maintained that Omaha is his rock, his source of stability in a world that inherently is unstable. It appears he was never seriously tempted either to remain in the East or to return to the East. Omaha is now and always has been the context most conducive to his quest for money – in part because of what it is *not*. "In some places it's easy to lose perspective," he has explained. "But I think it's very easy to keep perspective in a place like Omaha." He went on: "It's very easy to think clearly here. You're undisturbed by irrelevant factors and the noise generally of business investments. If you can't think clearly in Omaha, you're not going to think clearly anyplace."[24]

Finally, there are the macroeconomic contexts within which Buffett accumulated his fabulous wealth. The first of these contexts are the 1930s, during which Nebraska, like virtually everywhere else in the Western world, was hard hit by the Great Depression. Like many who lived through the Depression, Buffett grew up with a deep respect for the value of a dollar. He became *frugal*. Not just frugal, but famously, legendarily frugal. He became so frugal that when he moved to New York to attend Columbia, he chose to live at the YMCA. He became so frugal that he has continued to reside, to this day, in the same Omaha house that has been his home for over sixty years. (He and his first wife bought the house in 1958, for $31,500.) He became so frugal that to this day he prides himself on grabbing breakfast at McDonald's.

But while Buffett was born into the Depression, he came of age during America's ambitious and optimistic postwar expansion. Buffett was, of course, intensely aware that times had changed – dramatically. The burgeoning economy of the 1950s was in most ways altogether different from the depressed economy of the 1930s. Industrial companies still dominated the Dow Jones average, but the Dow had come to include new types of companies: those that specialized in consumer goods. Companies like Procter & Gamble, Sears Roebuck, and General Foods. The value of these companies had little to do with hard assets. Instead, their primary asset was the brand they boasted – the loyalty that customers developed for their brand particularly. A few of these became so familiar that the most successful among them became "household names" – think Jell-O and Ivory Soap. All this familiarity – all the connections between consumers and the products they had come to trust – was initially encouraged and ultimately cemented by mass marketing. It was mass marketing that gave these businesses license to charge relatively high prices for relatively mundane goods. All of which enabled shrewd investors, Warren Buffett most prominent among them, to reap major financial rewards for relatively minor financial investments.

In the 1960s, Buffett acquired Berkshire Hathaway, which years later became the holding company for all his investments. In the late 1970s, he made an additional acquisition: he convinced then 35-year-old Charlie Munger to leave his law practice to become, in time, Buffett's indispensable business partner and close friend. In retrospect it's clear that both men – who reportedly never had even a single argument – not only understood but were able to navigate to their advantage the new economic ecosystem, which explains in large part why during the next several decades they made exceptionally lucrative investments in companies that featured well-known brands.

The irony is that while no one understood better than did Buffett and Munger the contexts within which they operated, Buffett has long sought to distance himself from the contingencies of context. He has tried to ignore the noise of the news, the day-to-day gyrations of what was happening in the world and in world markets. Instead he has been intent on keeping a level head, on dismissing the anxieties associated with short-term investing in favor of the settled strategies of long-term investing. For example, in Buffett's 1988 letter to Berkshire Hathaway shareholders, he wrote that his "favorite holding period is forever."[25] Similarly, years later, in 2016, in response to wild market fluctuations, he told CNBC that "buy and hold" was in the past and remained in the present the best single stock market strategy. Almost always Buffett suggests that investors should hold steady, that they continue to be long-term buyers of equity index funds, and not be distracted by whatever histrionics are unsettling the markets. "Don't watch the market closely," he advised during a particularly volatile time. "If [investors are] trying to buy and sell stocks and worry when they go down a little bit … and think they should maybe sell them when they go up, they're not going to have very good results."[26]

Buffett, it should be added, follows his own lead. He puts his money where his mouth is. During the financial crisis of 2008, when many investors panicked and sought to sell some or even all their stocks as fast as they possibly could, he wrote an editorial for the *New York Times* in which he announced he was a *buyer* of American stocks. He suggested, moreover, that other investors should do the same. His piece was titled, simply, "Buy American. I am."[27] This is an example of a leader telling his followers, in no uncertain terms, what to do and when to do it.

Of course, when an investor lives as long as has Warren Buffett – at this writing he is well into his eighties and Munger well into his nineties – the contexts within which he makes his decisions inevitably change. And then they change again. Key to his past investment strategy was that certain companies were so dominant, and their earnings so secure, that current profits were not only near certain to continue but likely to increase. This explains in part why Buffett avoided buying technology stocks – including highflyers that since have soared, such as Amazon and Facebook – not just for years but for decades. It took time, in other words, for Buffett to recognize that the world had changed and the markets along with it. But, eventually, his lust for money trumped his search for security. Which explains why, finally, it was Apple that became Buffett's largest single investment.

Evidence

We saw that even as a boy Buffett was both industrious and intent on making money. Later, when he was a teenager, he took a series of odd jobs including washing cars and delivering newspapers. These did not suffice; they did not satisfy an already very ambitious young man with, to all appearances, an already outsized appetite for making money. So, once he had saved a bit of cash, young Buffett bought several pinball machines which he proceeded then to install in local businesses. Why? To make more money than he was making already. Imagine then, if you will, a snowball rolling down a snow-covered mountain, accumulating more and more snow as it rolls, growing larger and gaining more momentum with every passing moment. Unless something, say an immovable object of some sort, happens to stop it, the snowball continues to grow. And to gain speed; every second it becomes that much more powerful, that much more impactful. The previously mentioned Alice Schroeder, Buffett's chosen biographer, elected to title her chronicle of his life *The Snowball*, because just like that snowball, Buffett was unstoppable. Just like that snowball, Buffett had a momentum, a money-momentum, that was so strong and so steady that he kept accumulating more and more. So much money that if you had invested $100 in Berkshire Hathaway's stock in 1965, it would have been worth $2.4 million in 2017.[28]

But the snowball parallel, or parable, misses something critical. The snowball rolls downhill in consequence of gravity. Buffett, in contrast, has had to propel himself, get himself to accelerate his own trajectory. He was always unusually determined, always eager to keep score, and always focused, laser-like, on growing his pile of money faster and higher. Most Americans retire at some point during their sixties or maybe early seventies, and when they retire their net savings are, on average, somewhere around $107,000. Warren Buffett, in contrast, is in his late eighties and his net worth is around $86 billion. Still, in 2018 he announced that he would be "delaying retirement."[29] His lust for money is such that his primary purpose in life is to keep on making more. Logic be damned.

Schroeder delves into Buffett's obsession with money, pointing out that he views it less as a unit of exchange than as a store of value. In telling the tale of Buffett's rise, she returns over and over to his almost pathological reluctance to part with money. Otherwise known as stinginess. As rich as Buffett has become, it appears he has never stopped measuring himself by how much money he has. He told Schroeder that he assesses his own self-worth according to Berkshire Hathaway's book value. "He was preoccupied with money," Schroeder wrote. "He wanted to amass a lot of it ... If asked to give up some of his money, Warren responded like a dog fiercely guarding its bone, or even as though he had been attacked. His struggle to let go of the smallest amounts of money was so apparent that it was as if the money possessed him, rather than the other way around."[30] Katharine Graham, the pioneering publisher of the *Washington Post*, once asked him for a dime to make a phone call. Buffett, finding only a quarter in his pocket, strode off to make change.

As he approached old age, Buffett finally gave away enormous sums of money. But – and this is key to understanding his lust for money – he never for even a moment turned his time or energy away from his own money-making endeavors. He never showed any sustained interest in, or involvement with, even those causes his money supported. Nor does he himself seem to have any causes that particularly arouse his concern or stimulate his curiosity. To all appearances, he just gives his money away, leaving it to others to figure out how best to use what he gave them. Then he goes back to doing what he loves and does best: to gratifying if not satisfying his lust for money.

All this was on dramatic display when in 2006, at the age of 75, Buffett made the decision to donate the bulk of his then $44 billion fortune to the Bill & Melinda Gates Foundation. He calculated that since they both had become by then deeply informed and entirely impassioned philanthropists, they would be far better equipped than he to steward his enormous gift with insight and intelligence. He also gave billions to foundations run by his children and to one created by his late (first) wife, Susan.[31] Buffett's decision made sense. He was never in the least inclined to do what Bill Gates did – to pivot from making money and running a company full time to philanthropy full time. So far as Buffett was concerned, all he wanted to do, all he thought he ought to do, was to carry on toward the end of his life as he had at the beginning – growing his fortune.

Buffett cannot possibly need any more money than he already has. He is so legendary a figure in part because instead of living extravagantly, he lives extravagantly *below* his means. The reason for his extreme, almost weird frugality is not completely clear. What is clear is that it enables him to salt away even more of the astronomical amounts of money that he earns. Buffett has used the same wallet for over twenty years. He spends no more than $3.17 on breakfast, usually fast food which he professes to like and which he praises as "cheap."[32] He drives a modest car and lives in what we already described as a modest house bought well over a half-century ago. And his pastimes are similarly self-effacing: mainly he reads and plays bridge with friends, one of whom, Bill Gates, has become a longtime partner.

Warren Buffett has said that he has "never had any great desire to have multiple houses and all kinds of things and multiple cars."[33] In 1971, he did finally buy a second home, a vacation house in Laguna Beach, California, which cost $150,000. He said he considered it a "splurge."[34] But even this inordinately modest indulgence – inordinately modest because of what he could have afforded if he had wanted to afford it – was noteworthy on account of its rarity. While Buffett's passion is to accrue more and more money, his extreme avoidance of spending it is, to him at least, the logical counterpart. One way to have more money is to spend less.

Buffett, then, perfectly exemplifies a leader who lusts for money. Amassing money is its own reward – not what the money can provide. Nor has he ever expressed the least interest in creating a family dynasty. Quite the opposite. While his three children have been generously taken care of (a fraction of their father's fortune will put them in the top tier of the nation's wealthiest people), Buffett has repeatedly said that passing his own enormous wealth on to his progeny never was, and never will be, what he wanted or intended. In 1986, he told *Fortune* that he felt that the "perfect" amount to leave children was "enough money so that they would feel they could do anything, but not so much that they could do nothing." He has long believed that bequeathing to one's offspring "a lifetime supply of food stamps just because they came out of the right womb" can be "harmful."[35]

Berkshire Hathaway itself reflects Buffett's lust for money. Interestingly, tellingly, Berkshire is a holding company – a company created to buy and control shares of *other* companies. Such companies are conglomerations of holdings in companies that have no unifying theme other than that they make, or are anticipated to make, a lot of money. Berkshire Hathaway was once a textile company with roots in the 1800s, created through a merger of the Hathaway Company with Berkshire Fine Spinning Associates Inc. Buffett had no special affection for textile production, or the slightest expertise in textiles. Rather he began buying shares in the company because he judged it undervalued. It was. Just a few years later he owned so much Berkshire stock that he was able to take control; the company became, in effect, his. Buffett held onto the textile business until 1985 but beginning in 1967, he had also begun aggressively to diversify, first into insurance, a relatively safe industry with plenty of available cash that he was able to use to invest in other companies.

So began Buffett's career as one of if not *the* single most successful investor of our time. Today, Berkshire Hathaway has grown to include such well-established American businesses and brands as Fruit of the Loom, Acme Brick, Justin Boots, Benjamin Moore, Dairy Queen, Geico Insurance, See's Candies, Helzberg Diamonds, Nebraska Furniture Mart, Burlington Northern railroad line, and Precision Castparts. It also holds huge stakes in companies such as American Express, Coca-Cola, IBM, and Wells Fargo. While these all have very different businesses, they have one thing in common. They generate cash for Berkshire Hathaway, and for its premier and most prominent investor, Warren Buffett.

A mountain of evidence supports our primary point: Warren Buffett has a lust for money and he always has had. While his famous friend, Bill Gates, focused from an early age on computers, Buffett never engaged in any undertaking in which making money was not the primary purpose. When Gates was a boy, he was furiously coding for the sheer love of coding. When Buffett was a boy, he was delivering newspapers, starting a pinball leasing business, working as an editor for a horse-racing tip sheet, and selling Cokes, magazines, stamps, and golf balls for the sheer love of making money.

Followers

Warren Buffett has long been known as "the Oracle of Omaha." He is also near revered as a "wizard" and a "sage." However, notwithstanding his eminence, he and Charlie Munger have always made it a point to treat those who, on paper, are their subordinates, with decency and dignity. Buffett has said that the "care and feeding" of his managers is, after asset allocation, his most important task. He and Munger have been determined to "create a climate that encourages [their managers] to choose working with Berkshire over golfing or fishing." They have been intent, in other words, on being leaders who themselves were civil and respectful, and who valued their followers "as human beings." Of course, Buffett and Munger are not saints: they act in their own interest. So, while they appear from a distance to be the leaders, the bosses, we all wish we had, they also no doubt know that followers who are valued will "want to give their best effort." More precisely, employees who are valued will, naturally, be as their, or at least these, employers would wish – "more energetic, optimistic, trusting, and cooperative."[36]

Buffett's spectacular professional performance over a long period of time, along with his unusually engaging personality, have brought him a large cadre of devoted followers not only from among those who know him up close and personal, but from among those who know him only at a remove. Buffett's followers are legion, and they are found across the United States and around the world. They range from the rich and famous to ordinary people such as Terry Zhao, an electrical engineer from China, and Thijs Bakker, a Dutch chemist, both of whom follow Buffett's lead earnestly and eagerly.[37] Over seventy-five books have been written about Buffett and his investment principles, as well as a number of others about Munger. The media meanwhile seem unable to get enough of either of them, Buffett, being something of a ham, especially. He appears to relish the attention – no great surprise as when he speaks, people listen. Buffett's audiences hang on his every word. And even when he plays his ukulele, which on occasion he does, he is thought endlessly entertaining, his listeners in this case hanging on his every note.

Buffett has plenty to say, though some have argued that his principles and pontifications do as much to promote his own interests as those of his followers.[38] But, bearing in mind the usual caveat, "buyer beware," the legions who follow the Oracle from Omaha presumably benefit some if not most of the time from thinking that one of the world's richest men is genuinely interested in giving them tips for getting rich or, at least, richer than they would be absent his advice. Buffett's most famous investment principles include: (1) Invest in companies that you understand; (2) Invest in companies that have a sustainable competitive advantage; (3) Invest in companies that have a management team you can trust; (4) Invest in companies when their stock is on sale. None of these is rocket science. Still, coming from the mouth of a man considered as good an authority on investing as there is anywhere in the world, each of these principles is taken with the utmost seriousness both by experts and financial advisors, and by Main Street, ordinary investors hoping to make an extra buck – or maybe to strike it rich.

The most fervent among Buffett's followers don't just follow him metaphorically, they do so literally. They make actual pilgrimages to see him with their own eyes and to hear him with their own ears. Berkshire Hathaway's annual meeting, held in Omaha, is so popular it's been called the "Woodstock for capitalists." For three days, in early May, over 40,000 investors and some spectators "flock" to the great gathering.[39] (The Chinese contingent alone has grown to some 5,000 people. No wonder: Buffett's face has graced bottles of Cherry Coke in China, along with objects such as mouse pads and phone cases.) The meeting's growing popularity has inspired its own underground economy. To attend, you can own as little as one share of Berkshire Hathaway stock which, on May 3, 2019, would have been worth $328,200 for a single Class A share, or $215.93 for the more affordable Class B option. Or you can do what many people do who want to get up close and personal to the Oracle, but who are not themselves Berkshire shareholders – which is to buy a shareholder pass on Craigslist or eBay.

This pass is required to get into any of the shops that offer shareholder discounts on products made by any company owned by

Berkshire Hathaway. Much more importantly, the pass is needed to enter the famed, by now legendary, question and answer session featuring the two superstars: Buffett and Munger. This session consists of some six hours of entertainment, ranging from easy listening to folksy banter, to detailed expositions on smart investing. His followers eat it all up. Whatever their leader says or does, they're disposed to love, even to emulate. Once in Omaha they fight to eat at Buffett's favorite steakhouse (it's Gorat's). Once in Omaha they aim to get their hair cut at Buffett's favorite barbershop (it's 18 bucks a pop). Once in Omaha they seek to pose for photos with oversized pop-ups of none other than the great man himself. And, once in Omaha, if they have money, real money, a handful are ready, willing, and downright hungry to pay big money to buy a meal with the sage himself. For the past twenty years, Buffett has auctioned off lunch with ... Warren Buffett. In 2019, the winning bid was $4.57 million.[40] If that seems steep, not to worry. You can bring seven friends to lunch with you. Besides, the money goes to charity.

All this reverence, directed from followers to their leader, can seem sometimes a bit much. There are, after all, questions about how applicable Warren Buffett's experience and expertise is to average investors. Among the countless differences between the leader and his followers is that Buffett has been exposed to stocks effectively all his life. This gives him a familiarity with markets that most investors can never even dream of replicating. To most of Buffett's followers investing is a sidebar; it is not central to their lives. No tracking of companies, no sifting through reams of financial reports, no fastidious assessing of a company's competition or even of the markets overall. Buffett, in contrast, has access to all the available information as well as to a stable full of underlings to help him make sense of the worlds in which he operates. Additionally, when you are as wealthy and well known as Buffett, information has a way of finding you. The rich get richer, in part because of the networks of which they are a part.

To be sure, most of the advice that Buffett provides is not much more than simple common sense, relatively easy even for average investors to understand and generally safe for them reliably, even religiously, to follow. But the important point is that it is not what Buffett has said that has made him so admired a man, so venerated a leader. It is what he has *done*. His lust for money – lived out lifelong with singular success – explains his unwavering appeal to those who follow where he leads. There is something about Warren Buffett that is refreshingly simple. He never made any bones about the fact that while he loves his family and cares about his friends, his overriding lust in life has been and always will be to make money.

Hindsight

Warren Buffett in hindsight looks very much like Warren Buffett in foresight. His modus operandi has been *not* to change – or at least not much – even as much of the world around him does change. He has, for example, explained many times over why he and Berkshire Hathaway will not be leaving Omaha anytime soon – read anytime ever. Similarly, he continues to take pleasure in searching out quality businesses to invest in, especially those that have fallen out of favor. And though along the way he has made investment mistakes, mainly he thrives on personal and professional continuity.

Despite his now decidedly advanced age, Buffett's leadership – his capacity to enlist and engage followers – shows no signs whatsoever of ebbing. That lunch with Buffett that went for $4.57 million in 2019? It went for $3.3 million in 2018. And for $25,000 in 2000. That's quite a price hike over the years – a price that buyers nevertheless are willing, eager, to pay. That lunch incidentally is not in Omaha. It takes place at a famous steakhouse in New York City, Smith & Wollensky's, which is Buffett's go-to place when he's in the Big Apple. There's a plaque there that bears his name because people like to be in his proximity – even if only vicariously.

Celebrity culture and cult of personality are endemic to the human condition. At the same time, beginning in the 1970s and since then enormously enhanced by social media, the frequency and intensity with which ordinary people follow famous people has skyrocketed.[41] Buffett's leadership flows naturally from his lust for money because he happens to be a genius at making money. But it also follows from his status as a near-perfect celebrity. He has the virtue of consistency. The world seems to change, people seem to change, but Warren Buffett seems not to change, or to change only very little. The man and his gospel have remained essentially the same for years, for decades.

Buffett also has the virtue of authenticity. To all appearances the man you get on television is the man you read about in books and articles and the man you get when you go to Omaha to attend one of his annual shareholders' meetings. He is what he is, plain looking and plain spoken, no airs, no fancy trappings, Midwestern, quintessentially American. From everything that we can tell he is endearingly old-fashioned, simple in his tastes, and invariably modest in his demeanor.

Equally Buffett has the virtue of capacity – he lifts his followers out of the ordinary and into the extraordinary. Follow him and you too will enter the promised land of money. Follow him and you too will enter the promised land of milk and honey, a land more akin to America's fabled past than to either its complex present or its uncertain future. More akin to Omaha, somehow a throwback, than to New York and Los Angeles.

Finally, Warren Buffett comes across as being remarkably, atypically, accessible. Not only does he make himself occasionally literally accessible – he is also metaphorically accessible. Just like us he saves money by eating fast food. Just like us he lives in the same house he has lived in most of his adult life. Just like us he treats himself to an occasional steak, usually at Gorat's, that favorite Omaha haunt of his that Google describes as a "local fixture with roots in 1944 offering steaks, salads & sandwiches in an old-school environment." Buffett brings us into his orbit by making us believe that for all his billions, he and we are little different.

Charles Koch

Charles Koch – "a secretive kingpin surrounded by lawyers, public relations retainers, and security guards" – has lived most of his life in a walled compound in Wichita, Kansas.[42] But in recent years especially, he has become both famous and infamous: as a businessman; as a major political donor and significant political activist, especially for conservative, specifically libertarian, causes; and as a philanthropist. Moreover, for plying the far right with his seemingly never-ending supply of "dark money," money from undisclosed sources, Koch has become, to some, Public Enemy Number One. First and foremost though, he is a businessman. While his political contributions are directed toward propagating a political philosophy in which he deeply believes, their primary purpose is to support his money-making machine – Koch Industries. Charles Koch has transformed what once was a $70 million company into a - $115 *billion* industrial behemoth. Since 1960, the book value of the company has grown 4,200-fold, "26 times faster than the S&P 500."[43] Additionally, in 2019 he personally had an estimated net worth of $42.7 billion, making him the eleventh richest person on the planet.[44]

Though he has long been phenomenally wealthy, Charles Koch's lust for money remains undiminished. He is tenacious and tireless as ever, his wife remarking that he still has, in his eighties, "a drive and a relentlessness that sometimes scare her." Koch meantime has no plans to retire. His intention is to ride his "bicycle until I fall off."[45]

Context

Charles Koch was born in Wichita on November 1, 1935, the second of four boys of Mary and Fred Koch, Sr., a successful industrialist. Fred Sr. was an emotionally distant, hard taskmaster of a father, urging his sons to work hard, to be tough, and to be competitive, even with each other. He told them, "I want all you boys to grow up to be great men."[46] Did young Charles internalize his father's admonitions, or was he driven from within himself from the start? No way of knowing, of course, but by all accounts, Charles Koch was determined from a young age to work exceptionally long and unusually hard.

Early in his career, Fred Koch had a small oil-refining firm. In 1927, he devised a new and more efficient process for converting oil to gasoline, which for various reasons obliged him to work abroad. A detailed account of Fred Koch's trajectory can be found in Jane Mayer's book, *Dark Money: The Hidden History of the Billionaires Behind the Rise of the Radical Right*. Suffice here to say that in his determination to save his company and make his fortune, in the 1930s he built refineries along with both the Soviets and the Nazis.

His experiences made a millionaire of Fred Koch – and an ideologue. "What I saw in Russia," Koch later wrote, "convinced me that communism was the most evil force the world has ever seen and I must do everything in my power to fight it." In 1958, he became one of the founders of the right-wing John Birch Society, which was as fiercely committed to opposing socialism as it was fervently dedicated to supporting small, limited government. It was this worldview, his father's worldview, a libertarian worldview, that Charles Koch came effectively wholly and wildly enthusiastically to adopt.

Father Fred also pulled son Charles into the family business. As he later recounted, "After I finished at MIT, I went to work for Arthur D. Little, a consulting firm. After I'd been there for two years or so, my father called me and wanted me to join the firm. I turned him down." Charles enjoyed being outside his father's orbit, an independent young man with a passion for reading and dating. Fred soon called again. This time he said, "Son, my health is poor … I don't have long to live. Either you come back to run the company or I'm going to sell it." So Charles dutifully went home and took over Koch Engineering.[47]

Fred Koch's impact on Charles continued even from beyond the grave. Years later Charles discovered a letter that his father had written in 1936 to him and his three brothers. He wrote how fortunate they were to have been born into a wealthy family, while at the same time he charged them with doing more. "If you choose to let this money destroy your initiative and independence," Koch Sr. intoned, "then it will be a curse to you and my action in giving it to you will have been a mistake."[48] Fred's instructions were clear. His sons were told not to revel in their inheritance. They were tasked instead with demonstrating "initiative and independence" – lest they "be cursed."

Fred Sr. was the most consequential man in Charles Koch's early life. His three brothers though were also part of the equation: Frederick and twins David and Bill. In the 1980s and 1990s, three of the four clashed in an ugly and long-running legal battle for control of the family company. Charles and David prevailed: they ended up owning what in time they transformed into one of the country's largest industrial empires.[49] Together they controlled the business. Together they had overlapping investments and philanthropic projects. And together they pursued their shared deep and abiding political passions. It's why for a good part of their lives they were referred to not as individuals, but as the "Koch Brothers."

All along, though, it was Charles who was "the brains behind the brothers' vast corporate and political operations." In an obituary for David Koch, who died in 2019, it was Charles who was described as "the major decision maker" and the "dominant voice in Koch enterprises."[50] Still, the fact that he and David were close and compatible was important, very important. It made it possible at every turn for them to apply their joint, joined, means to accomplish their joint, joined, ends. On his own, Charles Koch would have been formidable, a force to be reckoned with. But with his younger brother alongside, their shared resources were in many ways multiplied.

Charles Koch's passion for libertarianism – his abiding political and economic philosophy – has been inextricably entwined with his lust for money. The more money Koch makes, the more he can, and does, contribute to libertarianism. Conversely, the more libertarianism prevails, the more money Koch can make or, at least, keep. Keep, that is, in *his* pocket as opposed to Uncle Sam's. A review of modern-day libertarianism is beyond the scope of this discussion. Here, though, are four of its core precepts: first, the redistribution of wealth hinders progress; second, the key to prosperity is unfettered private enterprise; third, income taxes should be repealed and the Internal Revenue Service should be eliminated; and fourth, nearly all federal programs and agencies, such as the Food and Drug Administration and the Environmental Protection Agency, should be abolished.[51] It is easy enough to see how these relate to Koch Industries, and to how much money Koch Industries can make – and keep.

Libertarians are a minority in the United States, but they are not a tiny minority. According to Pew, in 2014 roughly 11 percent of Americans were libertarians.[52] Thus, Charles Koch is an ideologue, but he is not an outlier. He believes that if we give the poor what they need – if we guarantee that they will never be very needy or hungry – they will fail to "produce" and be forever consigned to "extreme poverty."[53] In contrast, Koch believes that wealth accumulation, even extreme wealth accumulation, is not, nor should it be, an aberration or abomination. To the contrary, Koch is convinced the more money, the more virtue.

Charles Koch has compared himself to one of history's great leaders, Martin Luther, the German reformer, or revolutionary, who was the seminal figure in the Protestant Reformation. "The best way to describe it, which may be ridiculous, but is in a way similar to what Martin Luther must have thought when he said, 'Here I stand, I can do no other' . . . I mean, if you believe these ideas are right, and they're going to benefit the overwhelming majority of people, and you have some capability to advance them, how can you not?"[54]

Evidence

Charles Koch is driven by his lust for money. Though he is now in his eighties, and though he is the eleventh richest person in the world, he still works weekends. He still seeks to add to his stockpile of money, to the billions of dollars that already are his. Surgeons have replaced both his knees and his right shoulder – such is the pounding they took from his decades of passionately pursued sports, including tennis, squash, golf, and polo. Commenting on his lifelong habit of pushing himself beyond all apparent reason, his wife said, "Even the things he does for relaxation are ridiculous." In competition especially, "something happens." One day Koch and his wife were playing tennis. Charles "rushed the net and smashed an overhead shot, accidentally hitting their friend in the mouth. 'What the f– are you doing?' Liz screamed, 'This is NOT f–– WIMBLEDON!'"[55] But for Koch, obviously, even a supposedly friendly match *was* Wimbledon.

From the start, Charles Koch's ambitions for Koch Industries "were enormous."[56] By turning his father's $70 million company into a $110 *billion* company, Koch grew it into the second-largest privately held enterprise in America, and one of the largest industrial conglomerates in the world.[57] He "transformed an obscure Wichita oil company into a $110 billion colossus."[58] Initially Koch Industries focused on oil refining and chemicals, but over the years, it expanded and it diversified. It has come to include cattle, commodity and derivatives trading, fertilizers, fiber manufacturing, forestry, fossil fuels, hedge funds, industrial glass production, mineral processing, natural gas, petrochemicals, polymer development, ranching, robotics, and tissue paper. Its brands include Lycra, Dixie Cups, Stainmaster, Quilted Northern, and Brawny.

What is the thread that ties these far-flung business interests together? Each of them makes money, lots of it. Charles Koch has been Chairman and Chief Executive Officer of Koch Industries since 1967 – with David always in a secondary role. But Charles is of course not entirely self-made; his father gave him a very considerable head start. Charles, though, supersized the fortune. It was he who took "his father's company from a 1961 valuation of $21 million to one worth $100 billion in 2014." Put simply, this is a man who is "really, really, really good at making money."[59]

There are three accounts, each different, of how Charles Koch grew his company – and his pile of money. One is his own. Koch claims to have developed a finely tuned and well thought out set of management principles, Market-Based Management (MBM). These include being customer-focused; establishing relatively flat hierarchical structures; ensuring the free flow of information; and rewarding employees for being entrepreneurial. Though none of these is especially inventive or singularly insightful, Koch considers MBM a guide "not just for operating companies, but for operating entire societies."[60]

More objectively, Koch's phenomenal success is a result of his daring, especially his willingness if not eagerness to make very big, smart bets and very bold, smart moves. When Fred Koch thought it prudent to buy only one of two trucking companies, Charles Koch ignored him, going on instead to purchase both. An employee at Georgia Pacific recalled Koch "greenlighting a $40 million investment after a single phone call." Arguably the biggest and most profitable of Koch's gambles was on the shale oil boom. Koch Industries spent "hundreds of millions of dollars on speculative pipelines from south Texas to their refinery in Corpus Christi." It was a roll of the dice.[61] The company could have ended owning useless pipelines to bone-dry wells. Instead, the oil began to flow – and then it flowed some more. By 2017, United States shale oil production had soared, surpassing even that of Saudi Arabia. Charles Koch, meanwhile, along with Koch Industries, was cashing in like crazy.

Charles Koch's critics point to other sources of his wealth, other explanations for how he came to do so exceptionally, so extraordinarily well. Instead of crediting his management principles, or his derring-do, or his business acumen, or even plain dumb luck, they point instead to the rapaciousness of his character. He has been widely accused of engaging in practices, in malpractices, such as ignoring the law, exploiting the environment, and using undue influence (read money) to gain unfair advantage. He has been charged with employing "cutthroat business practices that crushed union rights, sacrificed environmental and worker protections, and legitimized outright theft." Critics have further pointed out that as Market-Based Management was rolled out throughout Koch Industries it wreaked "its own kind of havoc," contributing to "accidents and spectacular business failures ... and, worst of all, a host of criminal charges brought against the company."[62]

Charles Koch's lust for money is evident not only in his spectacular accumulation of wealth, but in his equally spectacular efforts to defend and even expand his company's right to keep making money, as much money as humanly possible. Koch, the libertarian, frames his passion in freedom – in Koch Industries' freedom to rake in profits unfettered by other considerations or concerns, such as, for example, the common good, or the public welfare. To this end, to enable his passion, to satisfy his appetite, Koch has tried fundamentally to change the political system within which his business operates. Starting in 2003, Charles Koch along with brother David realized that in order to do what they wanted and intended – to get richer than they already were – they would have to plunge into politics. They committed themselves to libertarianism – to proselytizing for libertarianism in a big way.

In 2015, the year for which we can find the fullest accounting, Charles and David Koch had a political operation that employed some 1,200 people in more than 100 offices across the country. As *Politico* noted, this made the Koch brothers' political enterprise larger than the Republican National Committee itself – they controlled a "private political machine without precedent."[63] During the 2012 election cycle, a donor network organized by the two men raised more than $400 million.[64] The money went to candidates whose political agendas were consistent with those of the Koch brothers – along with others among the ultra-wealthy who were equally intent on earning as much money as they could and to keeping as much money as they could. During the 2016 election cycle, Charles and David spent $250 million between them, largely on Senatorial races; and in 2018, Charles Koch and his libertarian network spent approximately $400 million on their preferred candidates. This more recent investment in propagating their political agendas represented a 60 percent increase from two years earlier.[65]

We want to be clear here: Charles Koch's political spending is a direct consequence of his lust for money. The libertarian causes that he especially espouses are economic. He has not gone out of his way to advocate for other libertarian ideals or ideas such as, for example, gay marriage, protection of privacy laws, or open immigration. Instead, his investments have been in pursuit of narrower objectives, particularly eliminating rules and regulations that interfere in any way with Koch Industries' money-making machine.

Finally, there is the matter of what many consider Koch Industries' reckless, relentless, ruthless degradation of the environment, mostly in hot pursuit of fossil fuel profits. Some of the largest environmental regulation violation cases in American history are against Koch Industries. These are the result of the company's at best cutting corners and at worst simply ignoring environmental regulations altogether.[66] For example:

- In 2014, a Koch-owned cellulose facility in Taylor County, Florida, was held responsible for two chlorine-dioxide chemical leaks.[67]
- In 2000, Koch Industries was charged with covering up the illegal release of 91 tons of benzene, a known carcinogen, from its refinery in Corpus Christi, Texas – fifteen times the legal limit.[68] A former Koch employee "blew the whistle" on the company's alleged falsification of emissions reports.
- In 2000 Koch Industries paid what was up to then the largest civil fine ever – $30 million – for violating pollution laws after its pipelines sprung hundreds of leaks.[69]
- In 1989, a US Senate investigation found Koch Oil to be "a widespread and sophisticated scheme to steal crude oil from Indians and others through fraudulent mismeasuring and reporting." Thirty-one million dollars' worth of oil was siphoned from Native American lands.[70] The engineers who had been instructed to carry out the over-extraction called it the "Koch method."[71]

As scrutiny of Koch Industries increased – especially scrutiny of the company as one of the nation's worst polluters – Charles Koch (along with David) went on the offensive. Anything to protect the golden goose – especially Koch Industries' chemical and fossil fuel businesses. Koch supported various efforts to counter climate change claims and he funded multiple initiatives to undercut climate science. The environmental group Greenpeace called Charles Koch one of the kingpins "of climate science denial."[72] And in her aforementioned book, *Dark Money*, Jane Mayer wrote, "The Kochs vehemently opposed the government taking any action on climate change that would hurt their fossil fuel profits."[73]

Academicians found the same. A study published in the prestigious *Proceedings of the National Academy of Sciences* in 2016 concluded that climate change had become controversial primarily due to the "hundreds of individuals and organizations funded by energy heavyweights Exxon Mobil Corp. and the Koch brothers."[74] It singled out Charles Koch as a leader in climate change denial, as an "influential funder" who gave money to "a complex network of think tanks, foundations, public relations firms, trade associations, and ad hoc groups."[75] Koch supported climate denial campaigns through donations to, for example, the CATO Institute, the Heritage

Foundation, and the Heartland Institute. In short, on account of his lust for money Charles Koch ended having a "huge" impact on climate change policy in the United States.[76] As recently as 2014 "only 8 out of 278 Republicans in Congress would admit that climate change was man-made" – "an extraordinary development" attributable in considerable part to the "activities of the Charles Koch and his donor network."[77]

Followers

Charles Koch found followers beginning at home. In the first years of his marriage to his wife, Liz, in addition to "demanding" that she learn how to cook he "insisted that she go to economics seminars." She has described these seminars, and this period more generally as "five years of training ... intense training." It worked. She agreed to raise their children in keeping with what he wanted, she defended her husband at every step of the way, and she adhered, at least in public, to his worldview, particularly to his political beliefs.[78]

More consequentially obviously, Charles and David Koch created and continued to support an entire community of followers, consisting of elite, uber-wealthy, libertarian-leaning business, political, and media movers and shakers who formed the so-called "Koch network." This somewhat secretive group is estimated to consist of some 500 donors, all heavy hitters, who, since 2006, have met semi-annually at gatherings organized and sponsored by the Koch brothers. Leaked documents and recordings revealed that participants included "titans of industry – from health insurance companies, oil executives, Wall Street investors, and real estate tycoons – working together with conservative journalists and Republican operatives."[79] They also included prominent public officials, such as members of Congress, state governors, and Supreme Court Justices Clarence Thomas and the late Antonin Scalia.[80]

These meetings focus on fundraising on a grand scale. Regular attendees pay annual dues, and they are additionally expected to contribute at least another $100,000 a year, specifically to Koch approved causes. Estimates based on tax records indicate that fundraising went from approximately $100 million in 2008 to approximately $300 million in 2014. Koch's network has been called "one of the nation's most influential political forces"; it has also been described as a shadow political party, complete with its own field offices and national voter database. From 2016 to 2018, it is estimated to have spent $400 million on "policy and politics" and "millions more on educational and philanthropic initiatives."[81]

Koch's efforts to create dedicated cadres of politically like-minded followers extend beyond the existing elite. He gives out scholarships, sets up think tanks, and funds sympathetic academics. He supports free market-oriented educational organizations, including the Institute for Humane Studies, the Ayn Rand Institute, and the Mercatus Center at George Mason University, and he co-founded the previously mentioned Cato Institute, a Washington-based think tank. Not incidentally, according to a 2017 ranking of the different think tanks and the role they play in government and civil society, the Cato Institute, which adheres closely to Koch's philosophy of a free market society, is ranked number ten in the United States and number fifteen worldwide.[82]

Koch and his network have also been "investing" more in getting college students to adopt libertarian ideals and ideas.[83] His intentions of course are clear. As a report by the Center for Public Integrity confirms, he considers his investments in higher education "fully integrated" into his broader campaign to promulgate libertarian and free market ideals and ideas.[84] Greenpeace, reporting on Charles Koch's "rapidly expanded" giving to colleges and universities between 2005 and 2012, tracked $50 million in donations from him or his foundations to 254 US and Canadian institutions of higher education.[85]

He also invests heavily in political candidates who share (or come closer to sharing than do their opponents) his beliefs on wealth accumulation and wealth protection. Koch's contributions to coffers such as these enabled the Republicans to take control of the House of Representatives in 2010, and of the Senate in 2014.[86] The icing on the cake has been Vice-President Mike Pence's financial ties to Charles Koch and his late brother David, which run "so deep" that even Steve Bannon, right-wing former aide to Donald Trump, worried that if Pence ever became chief executive, "he'd be a President that the Kochs would own."[87]

Charles Koch has sought to get his ideological friends and allies not only into elected positions of political power, but, predictably, into appointed ones as well. The Environmental Protection Agency (EPA) and the Interior Department, for instance – two government agencies especially important to Koch Industries – have key personnel with deep ties to Koch. Scott Pruitt was a case in point. Pruitt – who finally was forced to resign under a cloud of thirteen different federal investigations – was EPA Administrator during the first year and a half of Donald Trump's presidency. The Koch brothers were generous supporters of Pruitt; he in turn backed the administration's decision to withdraw from the Paris climate accord and rolled back key energy and environmental regulations.[88] Daniel Jorjani, a high-ranking official in Trump's Interior Department, also has deep ties to the Koch brothers. Jorjani worked for the Koch's political funding group, Freedom Partners, and at the Charles Koch Institute and the Charles Koch Foundation. Similarly, Marc Short, Pence's chief of staff, joined the Freedom Partners in 2013. And Mike Pompeo – who became Trump's Secretary of State – as a congressman was exceedingly generously supported by the Koch brothers. For her part, Betsy DeVos, Trump's Secretary of Education, is a billionaire member of the Koch network. The big picture is clear: in 2017 fully "one-third of the Trump team [had] ties to the Koch brothers."[89]

Finally, there are Charles Koch's efforts to drum up followers at the grassroots.

"Most power is power to coerce somebody," Koch has observed, while going on to add that he does not "have the power to coerce anybody."[90] Not one to be stopped, instead he has tried to persuade. Documents uncovered by the Center for Media and Democracy show that Charles Koch and his associates have spent large sums of money to develop personality profiles of large swaths of the American people. Why? Because persuading people to follow your lead is easier to do when you have information about who they are; when your messages to them can be customized and targeted specifically at them. Koch and company used their profiles "to launch an unprecedented propaganda offensive to advance Republican candidates in the 2018 midterm elections."[91] While so far as Koch was concerned the results of the 2018 midterm elections were mixed – the Republicans held on to the Senate, but the Democrats gained control of the House – he will not likely cease and desist. He will not likely refrain from using new strategies and technologies to try in the future what he tried in the past: to persuade the American people to see things as he does. Pete Hegseth, CEO of the Koch-funded Concerned Veterans for America, confirms the long-term plan. "This isn't just about a [single] election cycle. What makes this network different ... is that we've been in these communities ... and we're going to be in them [for some time to come]."[92]

Koch casts his net wide. His initiatives have included community organizing through Americans for Prosperity, through
Generation Opportunity (which targets millennials), and through
the Libre Initiative (which targets Latinos). But, of course, not
every one of his efforts to enlist followers has succeeded; some
in fact backfired. For instance, several universities, including the
University of Dayton (in Ohio) and Suffolk University (in
Massachusetts), have stopped accepting any Koch money. More
telling though is Charles Koch's growing reputation and indeed
vilification as a sort of Dark Lord of the far right. He and his family
have bodyguards, day and night. "We get a lot of death threats,"
Koch has said. "We get threats to fire-bomb our facilities. We get
attacks by [the hacker group] 'Anonymous,' trying to break in,
destroy our communications, computers."[93] He has a security
detail and now works behind "a high wall that he erected around
his campus."[94] And in 2019 *Forbes* reported that a new smartphone
app helps people locate Koch products – just so that they can
boycott them.[95]

Given Koch's persona, given his politics, and, especially,
given his militant denial of climate change, growing hostility to
him and his company, and to everything they stand for, can be
expected. They are vivid reminders that the lust for money can,
ironically, incur a considerable cost.

Hindsight

Charles Koch supports efforts to reform the American criminal
justice system. He has been relatively vocal on the issue. And he
has generously supported at least one of the leading organizations
pushing for changes such as drastically reducing or even eliminating mandatory minimum sentences for low-level, non-violent drug
offenders. Nor is prison reform the only example of the cultural and
civic philanthropies in which Koch and his wife have long been
engaged. But philanthropy is not his passion – money is. It was, in
fact, Liz Koch who launched the Koch Cultural Trust and who
remains its public face.

More to the point, perhaps, is that Koch's motives tend now
to be suspect, no matter what he does. An example is his support for
criminal justice reform which, because it includes a new, higher
standard for prosecuting white-collar crimes, surfaces the skeptics.
As it happens, reforming the system would in fact make it easier for
someone like Koch, and for a company like Koch Industries, to

"evade prosecution for destructive behavior," especially if it can be proven that either the CEO or the company "ignored red flags and whistleblowers in the pursuit of profit."[96] Unsurprisingly, this leads some to conclude that Koch's efforts regarding prison reform are "window dressing" at best – pernicious at worst. Even his modest attempts at rebranding are viewed with suspicion, especially as climate change activists are vastly and rapidly growing in number, and as climate change deniers increasingly are viewed as outliers, either ignorant or downright insidious.

In the opinion of David Axelrod, a moderate closely associated with Barack Obama, whatever Charles Koch's good works, they are "part of a very well-conceived strategy" to change his image as a "dark and plotting" oilman ideologue.[97] So are Charles Koch and his allies simply true believers – simply deeply committed libertarians? Or are their motives more nefarious? Is what they are really trying to do is tilt the political system to favor their own companies and line their own pockets?[98] The answer is yes – and yes. These are not incompatible; in fact, they are entirely compatible, wholly complementary. Charles Koch lusts for money. But given he is a libertarian, such a lust is not a vice, it is a virtue.

During the presidency of Donald Trump, Charles Koch's support for the Republican Party has cooled. He has had significant disagreements with the administration on, for example, tariffs, which is why Koch and his network might decide to "sit on the sidelines" during the 2020 presidential campaign.[99] Some have interpreted this as a change of heart, but quite the opposite is true. It is a recommitment to and reaffirmation of Koch's strictly libertarian belief system. In rejecting what has become at least for now mainstream Republicanism, Koch is simply doubling down on his lifelong lust for money – and on the philosophical handmaiden thereof, a "bracingly free-market brand of conservative purity."[100]

Koch has said of himself, "If I [retired], I'd be dead in six months."[101] When his wife tries to get him to slow down, he replies, "Please don't nag me. If I didn't want to do it, I wouldn't do it. It's why I get up in the morning. I love what I do."[102] His lust for money remains, obviously, unabated, as do his politics, and his economics, which remain as controversial, more controversial, even objectionable, than ever. The temper of the times seems to have caught up with Koch. More specifically, the more glaringly obvious and dangerous become the effects of climate change, the more glaringly obvious and dangerous become the effects of any damage that Koch Industries did inflict and might yet inflict on the environment.

Still, there's no teaching an old dog new tricks. Both Charles and David Koch had prostate cancer. After being diagnosed and treated David donated over $395 million to cancer research between 1998 and 2012 alone. He also agreed to sit on the board of directors of the Prostate Cancer Foundation. Charles Koch? No such thing. There is no evidence that he gave any significant sum – or for that matter any significant time – to support cancer research. While the lust for money, like the lust for anything else, is never satisfied, it remains nevertheless all consuming.

Coda

Charles Koch sees the drive to generate and accumulate money as an engine, an engine that propels economic growth and stimulates social progress. Warren Buffett sees the drive to generate and accumulate money as a scorecard, a scorecard for the game of life. Ergo, their reasons for doing what they do, their explanations for being as driven as they are, are different. The two men also differ in how they spent their money. Buffett ended up a philanthropist who gave and continues to give most of his money away to others – to Bill and Melinda Gates – to dispense and disperse it as they see fit. Koch, in contrast, has been and remains determined to give most of his money to causes that coincide with, that align perfectly with, his own fiscal and political interests. Koch has used his philosophy to justify his money, and he has used his money to propagate his philosophy. Buffett is less complicated. His lust for money is, if you will, purer and simpler. Finally, the two men differ in the reputations they acquired and in the admiration they engendered. It is not too much to say that in his old age Buffett is the gazillionaire that most everyone loves to love, while in his old age Koch is the gazillionaire that lots of people love to hate. Sad to say that while history will likely remember the former fondly, it will not likely remember the latter with even a smidgeon of affection. Respect yes, for what he, Koch, has accomplished. Affection though? Not so much.

But, the similarities between Warren Buffett and Charles Koch are at least as if not even more striking than the differences. Both men are approximately the same age. Both men are from the American Midwest. Both men were given a head start in life, especially by fathers that were, albeit in different ways, generous and attentive. Both men have led reasonably balanced lives; specifically they have had families that included children. Both men did not personally take pleasure from flaunting their great wealth, from being in any obvious way ostentatious. Both men are not especially materialistic: Buffett has lived exceedingly modestly, and even Koch has been reserved as opposed to excessive in his acquisitions. Both men cannot conceive of retirement; their plan is to work until, effectively, they drop. Both men have been leaders with large numbers of followers, some of whom became true believers. And both men have been driven by the same impulse: the lust for money, and then the lust for more money than the mountain of money they already have.

Finally, there is this. Once upon a time in the United States of America the lust for money was rather remarkable. It was unusual, it stood out. Now it's not so remarkable, maybe it's become even unremarkable. The 1980s were dubbed "the decade of greed." Many viewed it as "one long consumption binge" characterized by what one pundit called "conspicuous opulence."[103] Perhaps this explains why the lust for money seems less exceptional now than it used to be. We are no longer shocked by how many graduates from the nation's most prestigious universities – all of which claim to train leaders – want to work on Wall Street. Or by how huge our houses have become. Or by how heavy our cars have become. Or by how many devices we have or by how many pairs of sneakers stand stacked in our closets. This is not to say that Buffett and Koch do not stand out. They do, for various reasons, not least of which is that their lust for money is rivaled by their genius for making it. Still, even they are subsumed in a larger context and culture within which individuals who make astronomical amounts of money loom less large in the present than they did in the past.

3 LUST FOR SEX

Prelude

> "Leaders who lust for *sex* go on constant, countless hunts for sexual gratification."

Hardly a month now goes by without some powerful person, virtually invariably male, being nailed for an excessive, or at least inappropriate, display of sexual lust. In the United States certainly, what in the past could be kept covert, now routinely becomes overt. What has changed in recent decades is not, however, the human animal but the jungle within which the animal dwells.

The context has become conducive to extreme information – information overwhelming not only in quantity, but in quality. Like it or not, we get more information than most of us need or want and, like it or not, we get *different* information than most of us need or want. There's no arguing the more: it's become conventional wisdom that we suffer from information overload. We focus therefore on the what: on the substance of the information that we receive, which in important ways is unlike what it used to be. Particularly pertinent to the lust for sex is the nearly entirely eradicated line between information that used to be thought appropriate only to the private sphere, and information that now is thought appropriate, also, to the public sphere. Hillary Clinton had a famous problem in this regard – famous because her husband was infamous for his infidelities, and famous because together the Clintons straddled the line between past and present. Between what in the past was presumed absolutely to be private information, and what in the present is presumed also to be public information. In 1994 Hillary Clinton told a friend that she had "always believed in a zone of privacy" but that "after resisting for a long time," she'd been "rezoned."[1] Four years later her rezoning was tested as never before – inevitably, ineluctably, as she was ensnared in the most notorious sex scandal ever to bedevil an American president, Bill Clinton's relationship with Monica Lewinsky.

The Lewinsky affair was a watershed moment. The president of the United States was publicly humbled and humiliated as never before – for behavior that, as we will see in our discussion of President John F. Kennedy, was previously kept private, hidden completely from public view. Again, it's not that men, presidents, leaders, have changed. It's that the context within which they are situated has changed. This is not, of course, to suggest that every male leader did have or does have a lust for sex which, as we define "lust," is insatiable. Rather it is to suggest that in so far as the lust for sex is concerned, the rules of the game have changed, certainly in the United States. While Americans' tolerance (occasionally even reverence) for lust for power remains high, Americans' tolerance for lust for sex has dropped. During the few years that have passed since the inception of the MeToo movement, and even during the decade or two before, leaders who were caught, so to speak, with their pants down, were regularly pushed from power. A list of tarnished names comes to mind including former governor of New York, Eliot Spitzer; former governor of South Carolina, Mark Sanford; former CEO of Boeing, Harry Stonecipher; comic and actor, Bill Cosby; former Congressman from New York, Anthony Wiener; retired four-star general and former director of the CIA, David Petraeus; and former Chairman and CEO of CBS, Les Moonves, among a good number of others. It is not only, incidentally, that the culture has changed – our conceptions of what constitutes offensive and even aggressive sexual behavior, and what women particularly are willing to do about it – it is also that the technologies have changed. Think surveillance tapes, sexting, and smartphone cameras and you see in an instant how much easier it is now than it used to be to catch a leader in the act – red-handed, *in flagrante*. If you don't believe us, ask Jeff Bezos.

Henry Kissinger famously said, "Power is the ultimate aphrodisiac." His observation – ostensibly based on his experience – can be interpreted in three ways. The first is that people (generally females) are more interested in having sex with people (generally males) who have more power – as opposed to less. The second is that people who have more power are more interested – or feel more entitled to manifest their interest – in having sex than people who have less power. And the third is that notwithstanding Henry Kissinger, when a woman agrees to have sex with a man, sometimes her consent is less about her passion than it is about his power. As the authors of a book titled *Leadership and Sexuality* point out, there is in any case a "strong association between leadership and sexual success." In fact, in some species of animals the ability even to access sex is limited to just one or a small number of alpha males, that is, males who are leaders. Which is precisely why there is a "powerful incentive for males to try to become leaders." At least they get some sex and, from their vantage point, if they get lucky, they get more sex and better sex.[2]

The association between power and sex, leadership and sex, goes way back and is easily explained by evolutionary adaptation. In order to survive, to perpetuate the species, the human animal, like other animals, had to procreate. Procreation, in turn, was more likely to take place between a female and a strong male, than between a female and a weak male. Why? Because a strong male was better positioned than his weaker counterpart to feed and protect the female and her, their, offspring.

The problem of course is that rules that were applicable and acceptable in the distant past – rules that pertain to male prerogative – began in the recent past to be inapplicable and unacceptable. In the *Epic of Gilgamesh*, Gilgamesh is "king." Ergo, he does "whatever he wants ... takes the girl from her mother and uses her, the warrior's daughter, the young man's bride." Herodotus similarly references a tribe that brings all women before the king, "that he may choose such as are agreeable to him." More recently, in medieval Europe, was the well-known French phrase, "droit du seigneur," the lord's right. The lord's right to do what? "To have sexual relations with subordinate women, in particular on their wedding nights."[3] In other words there is a long history – going all the way back to prehistory – of powerful men claiming the right to have sex with powerless women. This claim can accurately be said to have its roots in sociobiology, roots that continue to sustain some sexual patterns and proclivities well into the twenty-first century.

We've already seen, in the case of Roger Ailes, how power and sex, leadership and sex, can and often do become entwined, especially of course when leaders are males which, overwhelmingly, they always were and largely still are. Moreover, in this chapter we focus on two (male) leaders whose lust for sex – which, by definition, was never fully gratified or satisfied – was acted on with an abandon that in the United States in any case recently has become taboo. One could argue, in fact, that in this respect (as in many others) the presidency of John F. Kennedy took place during a time so entirely different from our own that his behavior seems quaint. Put directly, he got away with it. Jack Kennedy got away with living in the White House, and being married to the iconic Jacqueline Kennedy, while at the same time engaging in numberless sexual encounters with women other than his wife.

This could not happen today – too much prying, too little privacy. Which in theory at least raises an interesting question: How to manage a leader's lust for sex in a time when acting on this lust is liable to severe censure? It could even be argued that male leaders who lust for sex in contexts within which this is frowned on now face a significant challenge. Not only are most leaders still men, most men are still more inclined than women to "seek sex and to believe they have a right to it."[4] So given that Americans in any case live in a culture that continues to expect marital fidelity; and given the censure that usually is associated with extramarital sexual relations; and given that technologies have become as intrusive as they are ubiquitous; the rules and regulations governing acceptable sexual behaviors remain exceedingly stringent. This is so even though, as noted, in men particularly power and sex are prone to be twinned. Psychologist John Pryor has gone so far as to claim that they are "two sides of the same coin and so strongly fused that it's impossible to cleave them apart."[5]

Finally, a point worth reiterating. We earlier mentioned that gaining power and then maintaining it can and often does change people. In fact, the evidence suggests that power can "poison even the most intelligent and well-meaning people when they take influential positions." So far then as the lust for sex is concerned, it is quite possible for a man who previously behaved impeccably – say monogamously while married – to change once his circumstance changes. That is, for him to be more sexually aggressive or at least active after he acquires power than he was prior. Scholars have repeatedly shown that "symptoms of power poisoning" include (1) focusing increasingly on your own needs and wants and decreasingly on the needs and wants of others; (2) having less empathy for others; (3) acting as if the rules don't apply to you; and (4) exhibiting less impulse control. For male leaders this is especially evident in the sex scandals of recent years, which seem to confirm that "for male leaders such power poisoning all too often manifests in 'penis poisoning': their pricks stand up and . . . they do inane things that damage themselves, their families, and their organizations."[6]

John F. Kennedy, though, lived and led in a different time. When he was president of the United States, the professional and political price paid by leaders who unleashed their lust for sex tended still to be low. Sometimes, in fact, as in Kennedy's case, it was, or at least it appeared to be, cost free.

John F. Kennedy

In the last twenty years, the American press and the American people have come to believe that they have a right to know – everything. This is not to say that before the impeachment of Bill Clinton (who ultimately was acquitted) no chief executive had ever been surrounded by the stench of sexual scandal. In the late eighteenth century there were rumors about Thomas Jefferson and Sally Hemming. And as historian David Greenberg has pointed out, in the late nineteenth century, before the advent of the high-toned *New York Times*, "a boisterous, unscrupulous press reveled in bawdy gossip." During the 1884 presidential campaign, for example, candidate Grover Cleveland was "famously taunted" about reputedly having fathered a child with an unmarried woman.

But the cases of Jefferson and Cleveland were the exception not the rule. For virtually the entire twentieth century, despite several presidents and presidential candidates being well known among those in the know to have had women in their lives other than their wives, such dalliances, even serious affairs, were kept scrupulously private, away from prying eyes. Restraint prevailed for various political, social, cultural, and even technological reasons. But in the main they prevailed because of the "cozy relationship" that had developed between politicians and the press. Leading members of the press had been embraced by Washington's elite, which explains why someone like journalist Ben Bradlee (later legendary editor of the *Washington Post*), would never have revealed any of the many secrets he kept about his famously close friend, first Senator then president, John F. Kennedy. Which is to say that President Kennedy, his entire family, and every member of his administration in many ways benefited from an understanding with which everyone concurred: a politician's private life was just that, private.[7] Absent that unwritten rule there would have been no Camelot.

Context

John F. Kennedy's presidency preceded the sexual revolution, though not by much. Still, it was enough to preclude the early 1960s from being affected by the changing mores of the late 1960s. By the end of the decade there was a shift in sexual behaviors, away from restraints and constraints, and toward greater freedom and self-expression. Similarly, by the end of the decade there was a shift in sexual attitudes, away from the conviction that a single sexual partner was destined to be lifelong, and toward the view that before marriage and yes, sometimes after marriage, the number of sexual partners just might be greater than one. But the early 1960s, when the Kennedys were in the White House, were years of transition. Away from the widespread sense of contentment and consensus, toward a time of growing frustration and escalating anger. Away from the older, buttoned-up Eisenhower generation, toward a younger cohort that was looser and freer. Away from an America in which issues such as race, gender, and sexual orientation were considered scarcely suitable for public discussion, toward an America in which identities like these were openly embraced and politically defended. And away from a leader, President Dwight David Eisenhower, who was seasoned, paternal, and reassuring, toward one, President John Fitzgerald Kennedy, who was handsome, dynamic, exciting, and, yes, sexy.

Of course, then as now, there was a gap between what was perceived reality and what *was* reality. Such evidence as we do have about Washington DC during the 1950s and early 1960s – Kennedy was elected US Senator from the state of Massachusetts in 1952 – suggests that beneath the prim and proper political veneer was a lot of what in the old days might have been called "hanky-panky." Some behaviors were downright crooked – so what else is new? – but other behaviors could more reasonably be classified as standard vices in nearly entirely male environments, especially heavy drinking and regular philandering. Here is how Bobby Baker, once a close aide to a man who then was the singularly powerful senator from the state of Texas, Lyndon Johnson, later remembered Tennessee Senator Estes Kefauver. Baker described Kefauver – who in the 1950s twice came close to being Democratic nominee for president – as having "a bad alcohol problem and he also had a very bad record of wanting to go to bed with everyone he ever met." Similarly, here is how Baker later evoked New York Senator Jacob Javits. "He was a very, very bright man, but he was another one – like Senator Jack Kennedy – he was a sex maniac. One of the postmen went in and caught him on his couch having a sexual affair . . . He couldn't wait to come and tell me."[8]

Baker's recollection – relevant to this discussion both because of its general tone and its specific reference to then Senator Kennedy as a "sex maniac" – sets the stage for the sexual intrigues that continued during the entire time that Kennedy was in the White House. There is the backdrop, that imperishable if remote image of the careful and conservative Eisenhower generation, and for that matter the Eisenhower presidency, that most Americans did consider and still do consider emblematic of the 1950s. Then there is the play itself, unfolding on center stage: actors playing their parts before the American public, just as they were expected to, primly and properly, especially if they were associated with someone who was intensely politically ambitious.

There is ample evidence that Senator Kennedy was the supreme exemplar. Privately, behind closed doors, he was, though married from 1953 on, well known for being extremely sexually active. But publicly he carried off with perfect aplomb the role of quintessential family man. In fact, he was the first presidential candidate to regularly and repeatedly draw on his family to frame his persona, ostensibly his private persona as well as his public one. First, there was the unusually large, rich, attractive, and inordinately photogenic Kennedy clan, headed by Joseph P. Kennedy and his wife Rose, with Senator Kennedy just one among their many offspring. Second, there was the Senator's own nuclear family: his wife, "Jackie," who looked picture perfect on every occasion and performed impeccably at every event. Additionally, there were in time two small children, Caroline and John, who came to bestow on the White House an ever-present aura of adorableness.

It has been described, accurately, as an irony: in Kennedy's case the enormous disjuncture between his public image and his private behavior. Beginning in the mid to late 1950s, and until the president's death in 1963, photographs of him often along with his family, first as senator, then as candidate, and finally as president "became mainstays." Ultimately, they became "mainstays of the Camelot myth as magazines and newspapers depicted the handsome chief executive at the side of his radiant wife at social events or in the Oval Office playing with his young children as they peeked out from under his desk or romped around the room." But in the meantime, as noted by the author of a book titled *JFK and the Masculine Mystique*, and as we now know, in consequence of evidence that over time became "mountainous," "JFK womanized relentlessly with a staggering array of female acquaintances, actresses, secretaries, interns, call girls, and mistresses both before and during his term as president."[9]

There is another enormous disjuncture as well. The one between the ostensibly prim and proper period during which Kennedy presided as president, and the inordinately promiscuous and highly risky behavior in which he dared to indulge. As already suggested, it is not unusual for men with a large appetite for power also to have a large appetite for sex. But as will be further confirmed below, Kennedy's appetite for sex was outsized, even among leaders who are lusty. It is not for us to venture the reasons why; we leave to others the tenuous business of armchair psychoanalysis. We would, however, point out that in Kennedy's case the extremity of his behavior was not just confined to quantity, it extended to quality. Put directly, some of the women with whom President John F. Kennedy was sexually involved were, of themselves, high risk.

Evidence

"If I don't have sex every day, I get a headache," John F. Kennedy reputedly remarked, "supposedly to anyone who would listen, from British Prime Minister Harold Macmillan to a lowly Senatorial aide."[10] Well, every day is a lot of days. There are three hundred and sixty-five days in a year, and John F. Kennedy was a member of the US Congress (he was first elected to the House in 1946) for fourteen years, and president of the United States for three. So, either he had frequent sex, or he had frequent headaches, or maybe both. The evidence in any case is clear: John F. Kennedy's lust for sex was part of his persona. He boasted about it, considered it critical to his health and welfare, and did what he could, no matter the personal, professional, or political constraints, to engage in sexual activity of some sort whenever and wherever possible. Moreover, as we will see, he was enabled in his relentless quest for sex and more sex by virtually every adult to whom he was close – usually implicitly but, not infrequently, explicitly. The list of followers, enablers, call them what you will, included Kennedy's wife who knew perfectly well – at least she got the big picture – about his countless infidelities. Still, she decided, to all appearances early in their marriage if not before, for her own reasons, to put up with them.

Over the years the evidence of Kennedy's lust for sex has accumulated to the point of becoming incontrovertible. Some of the information was gleaned from repeating gossip and reporting news; other information was gained first-hand, from women who themselves were Kennedy's sexual partners. These women ranged from those who at the time of their involvement with the president were young White House interns, to those who at the time of their involvement with the president were not only older but experienced in the ways of the world. Most had names entirely unfamiliar; some had names that were famous worldwide. Most were women who were then and are now anonymous; some were women whose involvement with the president has been so well known and thoroughly documented that their stories are enduringly entwined with his. Of course, the full truth about Kennedy and his sexual relations with women can never be known. But even from what we do know, the claim that Kennedy was "without a doubt the most promiscuous and sexually active man ever to occupy the White House" appears to be justified.[11]

President Kennedy's appetite for sex was unusually wide-ranging and relatively undiscriminating. As suggested, his extramarital partners ranged from faceless women seemingly satisfied or even delighted to play games with him in the White House swimming pool (where most of the president's sex parties reportedly took place), to women with household names, such as Marilyn Monroe, Angie Dickinson, and, or so she claimed, Marlene Dietrich. Worth noting in any case is that years after his death two of President Kennedy's relatively long-term extramarital partners chose to write about their relationships with America's chief executive.

One is a woman named Mimi Alford – at the time Mimi Beardsley. Alford did the president and his family the considerable favor of keeping her trysts with the president a secret for more than forty years. But, at some point, word got out or, at least rumors began to circulate. So, in 2012, she decided to tell the story of her affair with the president, in a book titled *Once Upon a Secret*.

In 1962 Alford was 19 and just four days into her job as a White House intern when she got a call from one of the president's closest aides, Dave Powers, who asked, "Want to have a swim?" In reconstructing her younger self, Alford describes being befuddled by the question – less than a week into her job she had no idea the White House even had a pool – but she accepted Powers's invitation. Within minutes he appeared in her office to escort her, personally, at midday, to where the fun was.

In no time flat Alford was in the pool with two other young women – and with America's chief executive. (She recalled Kennedy as looking "remarkably fit ... for a forty-five-year-old man.") The party of four apparently had a high old time, Alford returned to her office, only to receive later in the day yet another call from Powers, who extended yet another invitation, this one for a get-together with staff after work. Alford accepted, again had fun, this time downing a few, not many, just a few, drinks. Sometime later the president joined the group and, in short order, walked up to her and asked, "Would you like a tour of the residence, Mimi?" Mimi did – the White House intern did want a private tour of the residence provided by the president. In short order, she was led into what Kennedy told her was "Mrs. Kennedy's bedroom." Alford continues: "The next thing I knew he was standing in front of me, his face inches away, his eyes staring directly into mine. He placed both hands on my shoulders and guided me toward the edge of the bed."[12] Yes, according to Alford, who is widely considered credible, she and Kennedy did subsequently have sexual intercourse and yes, in keeping with the tradition of "droit du seigneur," she was on that night, at least at the start of the night, a virgin.

Kennedy and Alford soon spent "more and more time together," to the point where both apparently were entirely comfortable with the arrangement. There were baths. There was music. There was the full run of the second floor. Sometimes she would sleep over, sometimes not. He taught her how to make scrambled eggs. Alford writes that she was blissfully unaware at the time that she was one among a number of other women with whom the president was, simultaneously, also having extramarital relations. "It wasn't until much later," she recounts, "that the full extent of his philandering began to dawn on me."[13] It was just as well for

Alford that by the end of 1962 she was engaged to another man, and that her affair with the American president had come to a gradual end.

Of the many other women in President Kennedy's extramarital life, one of the most important, and among those that put the president at highest risk, was Judith Campbell Exner. Some fourteen years after the president's death, Exner also told her tale, this one in a book titled *My Story*, which, notwithstanding what subsequently were deemed its insufficiencies and inaccuracies, still approximately chronicled Exner's relationship with America's chief executive. Exner and Kennedy met in a glitzy setting, in Las Vegas, and they met through a couple of glitzy guys, actor Peter Lawford (also Kennedy's brother-in-law), and the famed and fabled singer and actor Frank Sinatra. It was early 1960. The relationship between Exner and Kennedy – who immediately impressed her as "so handsome" with "strong white teeth and smiling Irish eyes" – lasted some two and a half years.

Once again, Kennedy let no grass grow under his feet. Virtually immediately after they met, he and Exner became involved in a relationship that probably was the most consistent and longest lasting of Kennedy's extramarital life. All this occurred during the year he ran actively and aggressively for president; and during the subsequent year, his first in the Oval Office. To take just a single example, on the eve of the New Hampshire primary Exner and Kennedy were together, in bed. "We lay in each other's arms for a long time. Mostly we talked about ourselves, but he did relate anecdotes from the hustings ... I loved the wonderful airy, light side of him. It was amazing to me that he could be so relaxed on the eve of the first important primary. Not once did he mention New Hampshire. He had an air of confidence that was unshakable. Come hell or high water he was going to win."[14]

What Exner did not mention in her book – she confirmed this only years later – was that simultaneous to her involvement with the candidate and, later, the president, was her involvement with a man by the name of Sam Giancana. As Giancana was head of the Chicago mafia, this was not, however, just another story of one woman sleeping with two men at the same time. It was, additionally, a story of a woman who served as courier between them, with Exner ferrying envelopes from JFK to the mob, envelopes that included "alleged payoffs or instructions for vote-bullying in elections and plans to kill Fidel Castro."[15] Years after the fact it seems that Exner more fully understood that her several attractions to Kennedy – initially clearly centered on her physical charms – came to include her connection to Giancana. "I feel like I was set up to be the courier. I was a perfect choice because I could come and go without notice, and if noticed, no one would've believed it anyway." Exner went on to say that she never told anyone until much later, "because I thought I'd be killed. Look what happened to Jack, and to Sam, who was murdered in his house while under police surveillance."[16] Again, Exner's testimony on this should not be taken as gospel. But so far as we are now able to determine, what she told was far closer to fact than fiction,

The evidence that John F. Kennedy's appetite for sex was "unrestrained" is as overwhelming as it is by now glaringly obvious.[17] But, this "philanderer," this man "whose passion for women was exceeded only by his passion for politics," also had an extreme and equally unrestrained appetite for excitement.[18] This is testified to by the number of his relationships with women – and further confirmed by his choice of women such as Exner, women who already were, or who were placed in, situations that were risky or even reckless. Ellen Rometsch – described as "a sultry 27-year-old brunette … with an hourglass figure, a beehive hairdo and a Cindy Crawford mole" – similarly fell into this category. She reputedly was a lover of Kennedy's – and she reputedly was an East German spy. In any case, in July 1963, FBI director J. Edgar Hoover warned Attorney-General Robert Kennedy (John's bother) that he knew about the president's relationship with Rometsch, a woman who was said among other things to have "supplemented her income by turning tricks for Washington's best and brightest." Not long after, in August 1963, at the behest of the State Department, Rometsch was flown back to Germany on a US Air Force transport plane. Years later, the University of Virginia's Professor Larry Sabato confirmed that "records related to Rometsch's deportation have either vanished or were never created in the first place."[19]

Followers
The cast of characters composing Kennedy's followers – the cast that followed where he led, in this case to people and places that enabled him to satisfy his lust for sex – was surprisingly large. While the general public had no idea what was going on, there were many people who did. Either they did nothing to restrain or intrude on the

president's licentiousness, or they actively supported his tireless efforts to get many different women into many different beds.

To begin with there was his family. There is no question that most of the adult members of President Kennedy's family knew about – and did little or nothing to stop him from satisfying or trying to satisfy – his lust for sex. As indicated, they included his wife, who acquiesced in her husband's infidelities long before they ever moved into the White House and during the years thereafter. They included the president's father, Joseph P. Kennedy, who himself had been a well-known bounder, and who would do anything to keep his son's preternatural interest in sex from interfering with his run for, and later tenure in the White House. And they included his adult brothers, Robert and Edward, especially the former to whom the president was personally and politically extremely close, and who was as indispensable to the president's administration as he had been to his campaign.

Those who enabled the president's sexual conquests also included his closest aides. The previously mentioned Dave Powers, known as "First Friend," was highest on the list of enablers. "He placed his mischievous charm at the President's disposal. No one was more loyal to the President or more in his thrall ... Above all, Dave Powers's job was to make the President happy."[20] But if Powers was the most obviously deeply devoted of the president's White House aides, he was by no means alone. There were others who had long been associated with Jack Kennedy, such as Lawrence O'Brien and Kenneth O'Donnell, and who would have done almost anything to protect him from harm. Additionally, there were those much newer to the president's circle, but no less devoted to keeping if not enabling his secrets. They included, for example, the Secret Service. Within the larger Service, the president was said to have "his own group of agents and, instead of using them primarily for the protective and business purposes for which they were intended, he organized them into a high-living fraternity devoted to partying." According to one of JFK's Secret Service agents, the chief executive "didn't want to know about security but about broads."[21]

Additionally, there was the ubiquitous, the reliably decorous, and the unfailingly discreet Evelyn Lincoln, the president's personal secretary. Lincoln was a woman with a remarkable career, but, as was typical of her generation, it was entirely subordinate to that of a man, her boss, who in this case became president of the United States. In writing Lincoln's obituary, British journalist

Godfrey Hodgson described her as follows: "Lincoln used to sit in the small secretary's room next to the Oval Office in the West Wing of the White House, a cool figure who often dressed in grey and never seemed flustered by even the maddest day of overcrowded schedules and outsized egos. It was possible to wonder at the time, when the White House rustled with rumours about the President's private life, and later, when so many of those rumours were confirmed, how much the impeccably proper Lincoln knew what was going on." But, Hodgson continues, late in her life Lincoln made it plain that she had been "very well-aware," of the president's secret life, "indeed that she helped to facilitate the amorous President's rendezvous." Half her time, she revealed years after the fact, "was spent with women calling to find out about him."[22]

The Washington press corps was, of course, also in the know, but for all practical purposes it was committed to keeping quiet. Of course, many members of the press were themselves star struck, only too happy to be in the presence of a president as dashing as Jack Kennedy. Kennedy was, no doubt about it, a star. Seamlessly dazzling in his appearance and endlessly charming in his countenance, he was also inordinately interesting – clever and informed, lively and witty. He along with his fabulous family were all great copy. Moreover, his appeal was not only *not* at odds with his lust for sex, it was of a piece with it. For his attractions were deeply, deliberately, masculine. As *Life* magazine put it at the time, there was a "new breed of American man that ... at this moment in history was starting to take over our destiny."[23]

America's preoccupation with maleness was not limited to *Life*. During the Cold War, liberals were prone to being criticized for their "psychological and intellectual timidity."[24] Not by accident, then, a 1958 article appeared in *Esquire* titled "The Crisis of American Masculinity" and, that same year, an article in *Look* (then another well-known magazine) titled "The Decline of the American Male."[25] By the same token, it was also not by accident that Kennedy purposely positioned himself as the perfect antidote to the "dread that American men had grown soft."[26]

His administration was tagged the "New Frontier." The appellation was first used at the 1960 Democratic National Convention, intended to convey a bold, bright future with bold, bright, and innovative public policies. "We stand today on the edge of a new Frontier," Kennedy declared, "the frontier of the 1960s."[27] But, again, the New Frontier was not just about substance, it was also about style – specifically a style that was traditionally, unequivocally, masculine. Here is an example. Shortly after being elected president, Kennedy wrote an article for *Sports Illustrated* in which he identified what he described as a significant problem: "a decline in the physical strength and ability of young Americans." While he did not say that he was writing about men only, his target audience, readers of *Sports Illustrated*, was obviously overwhelmingly male. Kennedy lamented the "increasingly large numbers of young Americans who are neglecting their bodies – whose physical fitness is not what it should be – who are getting soft. And such softness on the part of individual citizens can help to strip and destroy the vitality of a nation."[28] Setting aside the telltale imagery – soft is bad, hard is good – it was an instance of Kennedy's conscious association with vigorous physicality and masculine sensibility. He fully intended to appeal to and attract not only followers who were up close and personal, but also those at greater remove, the American people.

Finally, there are those followers that leaders must have if their lust for heterosexual sex is to be at least temporarily satisfied – women. The evidence we have confirms what we might suspect: this was at the bottom of the list of John F. Kennedy's problems. During the more than a decade and a half that he lived mostly in Washington DC numberless women were only too glad to follow where he led – to bed.

Hindsight

In the almost immediate aftermath of President John F. Kennedy's assassination, his wife Jacqueline and brother Robert began scrubbing the historical record. Specifically, in so far as they could, they erased anything that threatened to tarnish the image of the slain president. And, in so far as they could, they surfaced anything that promised to burnish it. Camelot especially – that fantasy land in which idealism reigned and good men ruled – was Mrs. Kennedy's contribution to the cause, the cause of her husband's legacy which was to remain as pristine as possible for as long as possible.

Arguably, then, it was the more shocking when it gradually came to light that Kennedy was more complicated a man than Americans had generally understood, that he was more imperfect than they had appreciated, and that, so far as his private life was concerned, a more, much more, sexually promiscuous man than they had realized. It turns out, in fact, that so far as the historical record allows, there's no contest. Kennedy was the most promiscuous man, the most unfaithful husband, and the most audacious president ever to occupy the White House – especially in the service of sex. Which raises these questions: Does this specific lust – a lust for sex – matter? Should Americans care what their presidents, or for that matter, any other of their other leaders, do in private so long as it doesn't impinge on how they perform in public? Should followers care what leaders do inside the bedroom so long as it does not affect how they lead outside the bedroom?

Inevitably, answers to questions like these depend to an extent on the context within which they are asked. There is no evidence that, say, the presidency of Franklin Delano Roosevelt was negatively affected by his long, secret (from the public) relationship with Lucy Mercer Rutherford. (Their amorous friendship was first forged years before Roosevelt became president; at his death, which happened away from the White House, it was Mrs. Rutherford who was with him, not his wife Eleanor.) But there is ample evidence that when a half century later President Bill Clinton chose to dally with a White House intern, and the American people found out about it, the ensuing scandal derailed the nation's business for fully a year (1998). Similarly, now, post the MeToo movement, Americans certainly seem to have little tolerance for male leaders in particular who harass women, or even who engage in consensual sexual relationships if these relationships are in any way considered either unacceptable (for example, a workplace superior with a workplace subordinate), or unseemly (for example, a husband with a woman who is not his wife). One could even make the case that in some ways, so far as sex is concerned, Americans are living in a time that previously would have been described as puritanical.

In President John's Kennedy's case, context was critical. The times in which he lived enabled him to keep from prying eyes a lust for sex that was atypical. It was atypical because it was extreme and because he had no apparent want or need to rein it in. On the contrary, Kennedy used his position further to enhance his already strong sexual appeal. To countless women his was an irresistible combination: the power of his public position wed to the power of his private persona. It enabled him over and over (and over) again to let his lust for sex run rampant. President Kennedy saw no need to hide his appetite from his closest aides; he seemed in fact, to some at least, to revel in it, to be proud of it, to consider it a sign of his unusual virility, his singular manhood.

In hindsight, from the vantage point of more than a half century later, Kennedy's lust for sex was, occasionally, downright dangerous. One could reasonably argue that his sexual behaviors were not always only private encounters; sometimes they had, potentially at least, public implications. His relatively long relationship with Judith Exner, and his brief encounters with Ellen Rometsch, are examples of entanglements that could have – maybe they did – impinged on the national welfare. In engaging with women like these the president was, then, putting at some risk not only himself, his family, and his administration, but also the American people.

Finally, a sidebar. In matters of sex, it's clear that while some things change – most obviously the contexts within which the lust for sex manifests itself – other things do not. Other things stay the same. Since he entered politics, the previously randy Donald Trump seems to have conformed to the prevailing norm, to monogamy. However, we do now know that even during his third marriage, to Melania, Trump was sexually involved with a stripper or, if you prefer, an exotic actress by the stage name of "Stormy Daniels." We similarly now know that during his marriage Kennedy was also sexually involved with a stripper or, as one might say, an exotic actress. What was her stage name? "Tempest Storm."

Silvio Berlusconi

Since the end of the Second World War, Italy has stood out among Western European nations for its turbulent politics. And, in that period, Silvio Berlusconi has stood out among Italian politicians for his turbulent life – both his public life and his private one.

The numbers can only hint at his operatic extravagances. Berlusconi is a self-made man who in 2018 was ranked by *Forbes* as the 190th richest man in the world. He originally made his fortune mainly in media, and he still held, aged over 80, significant stakes in, among other assets, television, publishing, film, finance, insurance, and sports. Berlusconi served as prime minister of Italy on three separate occasions, for a total of about nine years (between 1994 and 2011), making him his country's longest-serving postwar prime minister. Notwithstanding his enduring domination of Italian and to a lesser extent European politics – in 2009 *Forbes* named him 12th among the world's most powerful people – Berlusconi has often been in trouble with the law. In 2013, for example, he was convicted of tax fraud, sentenced to four years in prison, and banned for two years from public service. (By then, though, he was over 70, which exempted him from being incarcerated.)

Whatever his singular strengths and weaknesses, Berlusconi remained even into old age a controversial figure. He has been envied and admired by some Italians for his overarching and all-consuming outrageousness – in business and politics, and in his private life. He has also been reviled and derided by other Italians for the same reasons. For decades Berlusconi was, in any case, among the most newsworthy, and tabloid worthy, of all Europeans: famous for his various accomplishments, and infamous for his various appetites, with lust for sex highest on the list.

Context

Italy is widely considered the only West European country that subsequent to the First World War failed to develop a reasonably effective and enduring political system. The reasons for this are, of course, as complex as they are various. But arguably the most prominent among them was the Italians' unwillingness and/or inability to cooperate and compromise with each other – for instance the old ruling liberal elites with the newly empowered socialists – in order to forge a governing coalition that was workable and stable.

Though under the dictatorship of Benito Mussolini Italy's fractious factions were forced to merge into a coherent whole, once Il Duce left the scene – in 1945 he was summarily executed by Italian Communists – their previous proclivity toward extreme divisiveness resurfaced. To give an idea, Italy has had sixty-five governments in seventy-three years – equal to one every thirteen months. Moreover, if anything, Italians are getting more contentious, not less. After another government collapsed in the summer of 2019, an Italian journalist described "bickering, confusion, and inefficiency" that "were unusual, and spectacular. Even by Italian standards."[29] At the same time there was an American headline that read, "Italy's Government Seems to be at Breaking Point – Here are 5 Reasons Why."[30]

So, again, why for nearly three quarters of a century has Italy had such a high turnover at the top? It is best perhaps to think of the volatility as a manifestation of Italy's political culture. Italians have a high tolerance for political disorder. They have a strong tendency toward political factionalism. They never had much use for their central government. And they tend toward anti-authoritarianism, except, that is, when their leader is an author-itarian. Assertions such as these have been made for years. For instance, the author of a book on contemporary Italy, who himself is Italian, wonders why Italians are "inept at preserving liberty." He writes they lack a sense of "moral liberty," and maintains that educating for democracy in Italy is work that remains to be done. "Centuries of serfdom got the average Italian to oscillate between servile habit and anarchic revolt. He lacks the . . . notion of liberty as moral duty." Without getting into the details of a debate such an assertion might provoke, it seems safe to say that in the twentieth and twenty-first centuries Italy has been relatively fertile soil for a leader "who believed himself to be omnipotent," and who further believed that he should be "allowed to do what normal mortals can only dream of, including possessing all women, the younger the better."[31]

Silvio Berlusconi dominated Italian politics either as *the* leader or as a leader of the opposition for the better part of two decades. This was despite his regular run-ins with the law and his regular displays of bad behavior – behavior more suitable to a Rabelaisian outlaw than to a proper head of state. It was also despite his affection for domination – personal, professional, and political domination antipathetic to what typically is associated with democratic governance.

Of course, Berlusconi was so exceptional a leader also *because* of a number of things. First, he was unusually bright and entrepreneurial, having become even as a relatively young man immensely rich. By the early 1990s he was so well situated he could use his fortune initially to obtain political power and subse-quently to sustain it. Second, his timing was right – many times over. After the fall of the Berlin Wall (1989), for example, and after the collapse of the Soviet Union and the end of the Cold War, Italy's political landscape naturally shifted. Berlusconi had the political brains and economic brawn to seize the moment: he forged a fresh coalition and a new political party that enabled him to gain political stature, even though he had no political or governmental experi-ence. Third, Berlusconi was something of a genius at tapping into Italy's popular culture. His media money and savvy enabled him to be "present in everyone's home through his popular TV channels." He shamelessly used his television empire to "reshape" the social order and, in turn, to "create fertile terrain for his electoral and political successes."[32] Somewhat similarly, for three decades and more he was heavily involved in what by far is Italy's most popular sport, football (soccer). Berlusconi owned a prized team, AC Milan, which during his long reign won no fewer than twenty-nine trophies.

Finally, he was and remained for so long a dominant figure because among his many unusual traits which Italians apparently admired was his unabashed shamelessness. There was little or even nothing that seemed to embarrass the man, to faze him, or to inhibit – or indeed to satisfy – his multiple lusts. To prove the point, here's how one close observer characterized Berlusconi's ownership of AC Milan. While a score and more trophies "would make their way to the Mondo Milan Museum during his reign, so too would a litany of sexual controversies, bunga-bunga-parties, corruption, racial remarks, homophobia, tax evasion, and mafia association."[33] No matter. Berlusconi seemed not to care one whit about playing by the same rules as his European peers. To the contrary, he seemed almost deliberately to present an alternative to the "serious, factual, and moral Northern European leadership style."[34] Which is especially striking given that he was the most prosecuted leader in Italian history, enduring and by and large surviving a long string of allegations including abuse of office; defamation; extortion; perjury; mafia collusion; false accounting; embezzlement; money laundering; tax fraud; witness tampering; corruption; bribery of police officers, judges, and politicians – and sexual abuse of children.[35]

It is generally difficult to explain on anything approaching rational grounds just what it is about some apparently awful leaders that enables them not only to be tolerated by their followers, but sometimes even to be venerated by them. Venerated for precisely those traits and behaviors that others find contemptible. Berlusconi's long period of power in Italy has some roots that are easy to grasp, for example, his control over the media, especially television; his particular personalization of leadership; his capacity to build new and attractive electoral coalitions; his long and close relationship with the Catholic Church; and Italians' longstanding ambivalence toward republican institutions generally and the central government specifically. But there are other aspects of Berlusconi's persona and politics that defy comprehension as it pertains to public perception, including his lust for sex. For not only was it on open display, it violated some of Italy's most traditional, most conventional norms. Unlike John F. Kennedy, who kept his private life private, hidden completely from public view, many if not most of Berlusconi's sexual antics, misdeeds, and wrongdoings seemed almost deliberately to be played out in public. Moreover, they frequently involved partners that most of us would deem off-limits, especially underage girls – though in Italy the age of consent is 14.

Berlusconi's sexual proclivities were not practiced or evidenced in a political vacuum. Among the relevant contexts was the European Union, most of whose members tolerated the Italians generally and Berlusconi particularly, though they were hardly in love. For years commentators remarked on the "corrupting influence on Italian politics of the monopolistic Berlusconi media empire." But in the end no one did anything about it. "Why did Silvio Buffoon last so long?" asked one expert on European politics. "In part because the apparent security of the euro bloc allowed it. Italian politics was a joke. Everybody shrugged. Most people laughed."[36]

As to Italy the country, the country as context, while it was and remains behind the United States in the politics of sexuality – for example, abortion was legalized in the United States in 1973 and in Italy only five years later – it is also the case that by the twenty-first century even in Italy debates over sexual practices and identities had become more open and common. In fact, toward the end of Berlusconi's tenure, sexual scandals involving him, and his entourage, were starting to catch up with him, to hurt him politically, precisely because what previously was considered his private preserve was now considered of public consequence. It took a long time. But in time, "despite attempts to reduce the so-called Berlusconi-gate to an issue of a private matter, and its frequent characterization by the international media as a laughable Italian idiosyncrasy, it represented a key moment in the re-evaluation of the meaning and importance of sexuality in shaping the dynamics of politics and power in the country."[37]

Evidence

Silvio Berlusconi was born in Milan in 1936 and raised in a middle-class family. In many ways, he continued into his adulthood to live rather a typical, Italian bourgeois life. He married for the first time at age 29 and before long had two children, a son and a daughter. But in 1980, about fifteen years after he married, and after he had become exceedingly successful and wealthy, Berlusconi began a long-term relationship with an actress by the name of Veronica Lario. He and Lario eventually had three children; after the birth of the third, in 1990, they wed. In 2009 Lario filed for divorce. Three years later a settlement was reached in which she received $48 million; he held on to their $100 million home.

For years Berlusconi's sexual predilections – particularly his predilections for having "at his disposal large numbers of women young enough to be his granddaughters" – were to an extent under the radar. As a result, when his scandalous behaviors finally played out in full public view, in Berlusconi's late middle age and even beyond, they were attributed to, among other things, his failing marriage and some sort of mid-life crisis. In truth though, "he'd been playing away from home as long as his friends could remember." Almost a quarter century earlier the man who had become a media and sports mogul was "ordering in girls ... like most people phone for pizza."[38] Notwithstanding, for most of the time that Berlusconi was married to his first and second wives, there was nothing in his personal life that, to Italians at least, seemed especially unusual. Whatever his sexual appetites and activities, proclivities and idiosyncrasies, they were not deemed politically important. They did not, in other words, approximate the ceaseless sexual scandals with which Berlusconi would become associated later in his life when, ironically, he was prime minister.

Berlusconi was in his late 60s and early 70s and at the pinnacle of Italian politics when that which previously had been kept private to an extent, became blatantly public. The period of his greatest extravagances began in the early 2000s. And the period of his greatest embarrassments began some years later, in 2009, when his wife wrote an open letter to the press in which she vented her fury at her husband's choice of young, attractive female candidates (most with zero political experience) to represent his party in elections to the European Parliament. She took the occasion further to state that her marriage was finally and unequivocally over, declaring that she could not and would not "stay with a man who frequents minors."

Again, this is not to say that earlier in Berlusconi's life there was no hint of sexual impropriety. In 2006, for instance, on the eve of an Italian election, the husband of a woman with whom Berlusconi apparently was involved, threatened to sue the prime minister for "abuse of office and maltreatment."[39] (The husband claimed that his wife and Berlusconi had been involved in an "intense relationship" during which the latter gave her expensive gifts, invited her to his villa in Sardinia, and personally promoted her television career.) It is, however, to say that only several years later did the sexual scandals become relentless, regularly entailing not just a relationship with one woman but one-night stands with many women, and that some of these women were very, very young.

When Berlusconi's (second) wife went public to accuse her husband of "consorting with minors," she opened the flood gates. From then on it became impossible for him to disassociate himself from a lifestyle that already had been and was continuing to be licentious. By 2011 writers for Reuters were describing sex parties at the prime minister's "palatial villa" that followed "a well scripted routine drawing in erotic dancers and underage prostitutes." First there was dinner, a meal often composed of foods in the red, white, and green of Italy's tricolor flag. "Then followed what has become known as the 'bung bunga' session which took place in a disco-like room where the female participants engaged in dressing up, striptease and erotic dances, touching each other or touching and being touched in their intimate parts by Silvio Berlusconi. Finally, at the end of the evening, 74-year-old Berlusconi could choose one or more women with whom he spent the night in an intimate relationship, in exchange for money, expensive gifts or rent-free apartments."[40]

Of all the women with whom Silvio Berlusconi consorted during his long and active marital, extramarital, and single sexual life, there was one particularly who got him into trouble. Personal trouble, political trouble, legal trouble. She was called "Ruby" – the scandal became known as "Rubygate" – though her real name was Karima El Mahroug. Born in Morocco to a poor family, Ruby had made her solitary way in the cold, hard world since the age of 14. At age 16 she turned up in a beauty contest in Messina, where she was seen by a member of the jury who happened to be Berlusconi's "talent spotter." In no time, Ruby was moved to Milan, from then on swimming in money, courtesy, it was widely assumed, of the prime minister.

Rubygate dragged on for years. In November 2010 Ruby claimed that she was given $10,000 by Berlusconi at his private parties, or orgies, or "bunga bunga." Later that year it became known that Berlusconi had tried to get Ruby sprung from a shelter for female offenders by claiming that she was related to the then president of Egypt, Hosni Mubarak. In January 2011 Berlusconi was placed under criminal investigation for his relationship with Ruby, charged with having sex with an underage prostitute and abuse of office in relation to her release from detention. In February 2011 Berlusconi was indicted and ordered to stand trial on related charges that carried up to fifteen years in prison. In June 2013 he was found guilty and sentenced to seven years' imprisonment. One year later, after appealing his sentence, the charges against Berlusconi were dropped.[41] To be clear: we're talking here about a man who was prime minister of Italy from 1994 to 1995, and again from 2001 to 2006, and again from 2008 to 2011.

No one doubts that for decades Berlusconi gave free rein to his lust for sex. Moreover, most conspicuously though certainly not exclusively, during the first decade of the twenty-first century he engaged in sexual parties, or orgies, in which sex was as rampant as it was paramount and money was paid for the pleasure. Police wiretaps confirmed that bunga bunga had repeatedly taken place. And young female participants later provided "astonished magistrates" with salacious details, including "nude girls dancing around a giant phallus, chanting Berlusconi's self-aggrandizing theme ... 'Thank goodness for Silvio.'"[42] Showgirls, models, actresses – all participated in what has been called the pleasures of the flesh, mostly in exchange for material benefits such as money and manses, some of which involved their playacting, posing as everything from nurses to nuns. But, one day, the party was over – more or less. By the start of 2011 Berlusconi in addition to charges of paying for sex with a minor and abuse of office, was facing charges of bribery and tax fraud.

Followers

Among his followers – that is, among the legions who went along with Silvio Berlusconi during the decades that he satisfied, and then satisfied again, his lust for sex, was one Patrizia D'Addario. Ms. Addario, who later recalled being with the prime minister in his mansion the night Barack Obama was elected president, turned out to be anything but reticent. Among her other contributions to the historical record was a kiss-and-tell book, *Take Your Pleasure, Prime Minister*, that revealed intimate details about her encounters with

Berlusconi. It was her willingness to tell all – or, at least, a lot – that gave license to "dozens of other showgirls and models to say that they too had attended Berlusconi's parties at this residence, Palazzo Grazioli, close to the Italian parliament." Withal, D'Addario remained a fan, a follower. She continued to praise the now publicly embarrassed prime minister – "Silvio Berlusconi is a strong person, he should continue to fight for the good of Italy" – and to insist that she never had the slightest intention of bringing down either him or his government.[43]

D'Addario is just one of the countless women with whom Silvio Berlusconi had sexual encounters over the course of his lifetime. Mostly these were transactional relationships. No doubt some of the women found Berlusconi admirable and attractive; they genuinely liked or even loved him. No doubt others felt obliged or even compelled either to join the shenanigans or succumb to his propositioning because they were poor or in some other way in need. Still, it's safe to assume that most of the women who consorted with Berlusconi did so freely and willingly, partying and even ending in his bedroom in the reasonable expectation that they had something to gain, personally, professionally, materially, and/or financially. Whatever the objections to being in some way paid for sex in exchange for money or another thing of value, prostitution – women plying their bodies to get something in return, including safety and security – and its various facsimiles are reputed "the world's oldest profession."

More interesting are the rest – all those in addition to the women who for so long went along with Berlusconi's sexual promiscuousness and licentiousness until finally it became too embarrassing or discomforting to continue doing so. Top of the list are the Italian people, who supported the man, the mogul, the politician and prime minister well beyond what others might have considered reasonable limits. For many years there were legions of Italians more admiring of and amused by – or maybe just tolerant of – Berlusconi's extravagances and indulgences, misbehavior and misconduct, than they were incensed or censorious.

Why is it that followers put up with bad leaders – in this case one who was intemperate, so lustful his private appetites intruded on his public performances?[44] It's a critical question – but one impossible easily to answer. Moreover, the answers vary, depending on who is the leader, who are the followers, and what is the context within which leadership and followership are taking place.

Here it's reasonable to reiterate that the history and culture of Italy provide at least one explanation for Berlusconi's strong hold on the Italian people. As one expert framed it, his regime, his reign if you will, resembled nothing so much as an early modern court. In these courts one man was the master; everyone else was a subject. But, unlike earlier courts that governed the lives of several hundred people or maybe several thousand, Berlusconi's control of the Italian media enabled him to exercise his influence over "practically the whole country." Practically the whole country developed a singularly "servile mentality" that was characterized by an "identification with the feelings, the thoughts, and the will of the signore" – not to mention the many women who "offered their services to magnify his splendor."[45] It was a charge leveled not only against Italy's masses but also Italy's elites. "The fact is that these elites failed to prevent the formation of the enormous power of Silvio Berlusconi."[46]

Berlusconi did as much as he felt he could get away with to stifle and even suppress the Italian people. He fed their illusions; played to their basest fears; set them against each other; lied and otherwise misled; and promoted corruption and cronyism. But to be clear: his attractions to Italians were real and remarkably enduring. What was it exactly that Berlusconi bestowed on his followers in exchange for their support? Why did so many stand by him for so long? Because he was "a showman who played with the dreams of individuals and the collective ... He represented the strong leader many Italians crave, and the safe pair of hands they needed when they felt vulnerable ... He provided benefits, cohesion, identity." Finally, not insignificantly, no one else in Italian politics offered "a clear and compelling alternative."[47]

To be sure, not everyone was drawn in. Not everyone was thrilled by what Berlusconi had become – a leader who, by 2009 certainly, if only on account of his now in-your-face lust for sex, was visibly a political embarrassment, not only at home but abroad. Among the prime minister's many longtime and all-important followers had been the Catholic Church, the Vatican, which by then he had put in an especially difficult position. When readers chided a Catholic newspaper for staying silent, when they insisted that the paper had a moral duty to denounce a leader who consorted with teenage girls, hosted naked poolside parties, and was caught on tape telling a prostitute to wait in "Putin's Bed" while he showered, the editor finally felt obliged to weigh in. "People have understood the unease, the mortification, the suffering that this arrogant neglect of sobriety has caused the Catholic Church," he wrote. What was the result, the response? Within days the editor was fired. Within days he was called out by a rival newspaper – owned by none other than Berlusconi's brother – for being "a homosexual known to the Italian secret services." A reporter for *New York Times* summarized the situation: "No one can mess with Silvio Berlusconi," she wrote, "not even the church." Whatever his transgressions, he still enjoyed "wide support." And he was still able to govern "largely unopposed."[48]

Two years later the Church's stance vis-à-vis Berlusconi became even more awkward – one would have thought untenable. Though for decades he had been a staunch political ally, a supporter of the Vatican, by 2011 Berlusconi's personal behavior and public demeanor had turned him from favored friend into significant embarrassment. Notwithstanding, the Church remained a reliable follower. No member of the Catholic hierarchy came out in opposition to the prime minister. And none ever clearly and unambiguously voiced his moral indignation at the wayward actions of the man who for many years was Italy's most prominent politician. Instead the Vatican was satisfied to speak in only very vague terms about how all public officials should "rediscover their spiritual and moral roots."[49]

In the end, the only group of Berlusconi's followers who refused unequivocally to follow him were women. Decidedly not all women, nor, tellingly, most women. But some women, those who might broadly be labeled feminists, and who were politically active. In 2011 some 73,000 people signed a petition on the website of a left-wing Italian newspaper asking women to tell Berlusconi "enough already." At the same time there were protests involving thousands of Italians, many of them women, taking to the streets in coordinated demonstrations against their blatantly sexist prime minister. To rousing applause in Rome, in the "packed to the breaking point" Piazza del Popolo, Susanna Camusso, leader of Italy's largest labor union, declared, "We want a country in which it's possible for women to live in dignity!"[50] Of course this was not only about Berlusconi the man. It was also about Berlusconi the prime minister, the leader of a country that continued to lag significantly behind its European counterparts on equality indicators such as employment of women, and women in positions of leadership. The leader of a country that, according to the 2010 World Economic Forum Gender Gap Index, ranked 74th out of 134 countries.[51]

Hindsight

The impact of the MeToo movement has been substantial. Notwithstanding Donald Trump's pre-presidency history, it is near inconceivable that Bill Clinton, given his scandalous sexual relationship with White House intern Monica Lewinsky, would or could ever re-enter the political fray. But, of course, the impact of the MeToo movement in the United States has been different from its impact in Italy. It is not too much to say that in the United States the movement has changed the context within which women work – at least to some extent. Moreover, the movement is etched in the nation's consciousness: it affects how Americans think and to at least a degree how they behave. In Italy, in contrast, again in keeping with its history and culture, the impact of the movement has not been nonexistent, but it has been minimal. As a correspondent long based in Rome summarized it, while in some countries in Europe MeToo "has been embraced," in Italy this has not happened to the same extent. In Italy "the public has largely reacted [to MeToo] with scorn and skepticism."[52]

A telling contextual comparison was in the wake of sexual harassment charges against world-class tenor Placido Domingo, in 2019. In the near immediate aftermath of the accusations, two American institutions, the Philadelphia Orchestra and the San Francisco Opera, canceled Domingo's upcoming concerts, "citing their need to provide safe environments."[53] In contrast, during the same time frame, not one of Domingo's many scheduled performances in Europe was similarly scratched.

This contrast explains certainly in part how it happened that Silvio Berlusconi had the temerity to re-enter the political fray at age 82. How it happened that he was able to stage yet another political comeback – despite all those sex scandals and all those other transgressions and convictions for fraud. And how it was that he had the unmitigated gall to attack the opposition for having "no experience and no competence" while he successfully ran for a seat in the European Parliament.[54] Is it that Italians' memories are short, or is it that they remain even now, years after his prime, singularly attracted to their former prime minister? Here's one answer to the question – provided by an Italian executive – that's as good as any other. "As a self-made man, a great salesperson, a man of business, and a billionaire, [Berlusconi] has no match in the political landscape in Italy."[55]

In contrast to John F. Kennedy, whose life was cut short, Berlusconi is enjoying a long life, including a long life in politics. His durable appeal is astonishing, his appetites even more so. It's clear of course that Berlusconi had not just one large appetite, but several. He was hungry for power – how else can we explain his becoming prime minister of a major European nation three times over? He was hungry for money – witness his earning enormous amounts of money at a relatively early age. And he was hungry for sex, so endlessly, tirelessly, relentlessly hungry for sex it was a preoccupation, an obsession even – it was a lust. He was in his seventies when he became most infamous for his unstoppable sexual adventurism. He was in his seventies when he proved most prepared to face sexual scandal after sexual scandal, no matter how seamy and sordid, no matter how embarrassing and humiliating. In fact, by the time Berlusconi reached his eighties, his capacity for surviving and surmounting his repeated wrongdoings seemed almost to burnish his image than tarnish it.

No doubt all that drama would have felled many a man less resilient than Berlusconi. Some of the reasons he remained so viable for so long are objective, including media coverage that was less than robust; repeated appeasement by the Catholic Church; the lack of stiff political competition; and, again, Italy's particular political history and culture.[56] But other explanations for his personal and political longevity are subjective, difficult if not impossible precisely to pinpoint. Among them is the real possibility that on some level of consciousness Silvio Berlusconi's very brazenness and shamelessness added to rather than subtracted from his enduring appeal to the Italian people.

Still, it ain't over till it's over. In March 2019 Italian authorities opened an investigation into the death of a young Moroccan model by the name of Imane Fadil. Not long ago, Fadil had been a regular guest at Berlusconi's bunga bunga parties. At a trial in 2012 she was a star witness, describing to the court a party at Berlusconi's home during which young women, "sometimes in pairs, wearing nuns' costumes … stripped off while performing raunchy pole dances."[57] On hearing the news of her untimely death – Fadil was only 33 years old – Berlusconi denied ever having met her. Then he added, "It's always a pity when a young person dies."[58]

Coda

Obviously, there are differences between the lust for sex as evidenced by the two men under discussion, President John F. Kennedy and Prime Minister Silvio Berlusconi. But there are also striking similarities. First, in keeping with poet Nayyirah Waheed's line that "desire is the kind of thing that eats you and leaves you starving," their lust for sex remained relentless.[59] Second, were the contexts within which they were located, which in both cases were conducive to leaders who lusted for sex. Kennedy's context was conducive primarily because it allowed for complete privacy and total secrecy. Berlusconi's context was conducive primarily on account of its culture. Italy's social culture has always included, and still does, though marginally less than a decade ago, a high tolerance for men who have sexual relations with women other than their wives. (Maybe nothing so readily highlights differences among countries and cultures as attitudes toward adultery.) Additionally, the political culture of Italy has long been hallmarked by political disorder and suspicion, especially of the central government.

A second similarity between these two men were their followers who, in both cases, were willing to support their leaders no matter the extremity of their sexual excesses. The cast of characters – of followers who actively or passively enabled their leaders – is in both cases mind-boggling. In Kennedy's case, for example, they included his wife Jacqueline, and his brother Robert Kennedy, who also served in the administration as attorney-general, both of whom clearly knew more or less what the president was up to – but they went along, apparently saying little and doing less to stop him. In Berlusconi's case, the followers included the Catholic Church, several of whose most fundamental precepts Italy's pre-eminent politician regularly violated openly – and without apparent contrition.

An equally striking similarity between the two leaders is their willingness to risk so much given the positions they held. Their lust for sex was so strong, so dominating a demand that they surrendered to it without, evidently, giving much thought to possible political consequences – consequences not only to them personally, but to their people, to the nations they were supposed to lead, presumably reasonably and reliably. Kennedy's long-term relationship with Judith Campbell Exner was by every measure a wager, a bet that his involvement with her would not imperil him or anyone else. Though the full truth about Exner's role in the president's life is unlikely ever to be revealed, what is clear now, as it was some sixty years ago, is that she was anything but the girl next door. Similarly, Berlusconi, who for many years and even into old age behaved so inordinately wantonly that we are left to wonder at his brazenness.

It would not be prudish to conclude the following: first, that leaders with a lust for sex may be at relatively high risk, and perhaps their followers as well; second, that leaders with a lust for sex owe it to their followers to be careful, mindful of what's at stake; third, that followers close to leaders with a lust for sex should protect everyone even remotely involved from the consequences of their excesses; and fourth, that on account of changing mores and technologies, in some countries and cultures, such as the United States, the relationship between lust and leadership is far more fraught in the present than it was in the past.

4   LUST FOR SUCCESS

Prelude

"Leaders who lust for *success* have an unstoppable need to achieve."

To say that someone lusts for sex paints a vivid picture. We know quite precisely what that someone wants, craves, hungers for with passion and without cessation. One could say the same about power and money. To lust for either one or the other is to lust for something specific – in the case of money it's even measurable, quantifiable, though as we use the word "lust," enough is never enough, no matter how much.

Success is more fungible, more malleable a concept. For example, when LeBron James personally attests to his lust for success – "Whatever success I have had is never enough. I always want more" – what is it exactly that he lusts for, that he still wants?[1] It's clear he's never satisfied. His thirst for success, more success, and then still more success is never quenched. What though does he mean when he says he wants even more "success" than he already has? We can probably assume that he wants one of, some of, or all of the following: (1) achievement; (2) attainment; (3) accomplishment; (4) acquisition; and/or (5) acknowledgment, sometimes to the point of adulation. Among these five sorts of rewards, there's some overlap. Moreover, sometimes they work in tandem, to reinforce each other. For example, to be a high achiever can mean and often does to be acknowledged. To be acknowledged by others for achieving something of significance, as in the case of James, whose feats on the courts have garnered him worldwide recognition as one of the greatest basketball players, one of the greatest athletes, of all time. These feats enabled him as well to acquire enormous wealth: in 2018 his net worth was estimated at $450 million; in 2019 his estimated annual earnings were over $88 million. Still, achievement, attainment, accomplishment, acquirement, and acknowledgment do not always work in tandem, and they do not always reinforce each other. As an example, to achieve is often also to be acknowledged. But it is not *always* also to be acknowledged.

While we define success as something of an amalgam – the acquisition of goods and goals that are related but distinct – the literature that's the most pertinent is in the field of psychology, specifically on "achievement." To wit, this observation from fully fifty years ago: "In a discipline characterized by as many fads and fashions as psychology, it is especially impressive that research in the area of achievement motivation has continued for two decades."[2] All along, there has been a single, key question: Why are some people motivated to achieve, even highly motivated to achieve, while others are not? It has been assumed that if the mystery of motivation was solved, it would enable us to improve performance, effectively from the cradle (performance in school) to the grave (performance at work). As one expert wrote in the mid-1970s, "Anyone interested in the effective function of a society, school, organization, and/or the individuals in them must inevitably deal with the question of achievement motivation and its determinants."[3]

While the long history of research on motivation has born fruit, it has not provided the keys to the kingdom. As we will see when we consider Hillary Clinton and Tom Brady, there remains something elusive about those who are driven, in some cases beyond all apparent reason, to keep achieving, to keep succeeding, even after they have achieved much more, succeeded much more, than most of us mere mortals can ever hope to. For those among us who watched LeBron James grow over the years from being an outstanding basketball player to being in the top tier of basketball players who ever lived, his continuing to play could be said to defy logic. What else is left? What else does he need? He has everything that anyone could possibly want – but still he wants more. Still he lusts, by his own testimony, for "success."

In the last few decades the academic literature on the motivation to achieve has, of course, evolved. Among the changes was a shift away from simply accentuating the positive, the wish to achieve, to investigating the negative, the fear of failure. Attention to the fear of failure goes back to at least the 1960s, when a young academic by the name of Matina Horner (she later became president of Radcliffe) found that women especially were plagued by a "fear of success." This was not to say that women did not *want* to succeed; rather Horner concluded that women, many women, maybe even most women, were *afraid* to succeed. Afraid because they thought that being professionally successful would violate traditional, conventional conceptions of what women should be and how they should behave. (Even now more women than men have feelings about succeeding that are ambivalent.)

By the 1990s the relationship between success and satisfaction had come under scrutiny. Instead of assuming automatically that success was essential to satisfaction, questions were being raised about whether success was all it was cracked up to be. As the title of a book on the subject suggested – *The Fear of Sinking: The American Success Formula in the Gilded Age* – the quest for success could be a mixed bag. It could reflect escape from fear as much as, maybe even more than, the search for satisfaction. No surprise then that by the twenty-first century success became, in some quarters, pathologized. Not success per se, nor some success or even considerable success. What became suspect was the constant craving for success – the possibly pathological pursuit of success because of the need to be perfect. As the author of a book about the "chains of perfectionism" put it, "The difficulty can begin with setting extremely high and sometimes unreasonable goals for yourself ... The emotional consequences of perfectionism include fear of making mistakes [and] stress from the pressure to perform."[4]

Predictably, the next stop on the path toward performance pathology was addiction – "performance addiction." What exactly is performance addiction? It is the belief that "achieving status will secure love and respect from others."[5] Interestingly, perhaps even counterintuitively, the evidence on this particular "addiction" suggests that those most likely to be addicted, to need desperately to perform at an extremely high level all the time, are not those who tend otherwise to do badly. Rather it is those who already are capable, exceedingly capable. They already embody "many of the qualities that are highly regarded in professional and public life." They already are "extraordinarily competent" – but they cannot help themselves. They are relentless, tireless "scoreboard watchers."[6]

We do not presume to suggest that people who lust for success are pathological, not to mention addicted. What we do suggest is that people who lust for success are atypical. Their lust manifests itself as an appetite so relentless and extreme it sets them apart from the rest of the pack, from others who want, of course, also to succeed, but whose want is less intense. Moreover, since we are talking here about *professional* success, we can assume some connection between a lust to succeed and a lust to lead. For those who are exceedingly successful in their professional lives are more likely to *lead* in their professional lives than those who are not. Moreover, assuming they continue to succeed they are likely to continue to lead – over time to take on larger and more important leadership roles.

A final note on the contexts within which the lust for success is manifested. We have already seen that national contexts matter. It mattered, for example, that Xi Jinping was a Chinese leader, not a Japanese one, and that Silvio Berlusconi was an Italian leader, not a German one. Similarly, as we turn to Hillary Clinton and Tom Brady, we note that they are Americans, and that their successes were evidenced most spectacularly during the first two decades of the twenty-first century. We draw attention to their Americanness because some have suggested that the need to succeed has historically been particularly, even peculiarly, an American phenomenon. It is true in any case that the success archetype has been threaded through American history since the beginning of the republic, supported by ideas and ideals such as individualism and capitalism, and by the presumed, ingrained, virtues of hard work.[7] Moreover the moment in time matters because until recently Clinton's need to succeed could not have been realized in anything approximating the same way or to the same degree.

Hillary Clinton

It's impossible to discuss Hillary Clinton's lust for success without first stating the obvious: she is a woman. Clinton has stood out for many reasons, including her own exceptional personal, professional, and political strengths. What has, however, assured her place in American history is that she is female. Her lust for success, her quest for success, and her achievement of success were singular in part precisely because she was female. To be clear, leaders who lust are always unusual – whether their lust is for power, money, sex, success, legitimacy, or legacy. For lust is an urge, a drive, a hunger, a passion so extreme that it is not, by definition, the norm. But so far as leaders who lust are concerned, women must be considered separately from men. First, as we observed earlier, there have always been more male than female leaders, many, many more. Specifically, throughout recorded history far more men than women have held positions of authority. Second, while lust of any kind is considered acceptable, sometimes even desirable in a man, it sometimes is, certainly has been, considered unseemly, if not downright repugnant, in a woman. Men can and sometimes do boast of their lust – their lust for power, say, or sex, or, as we will see in the case of Tom Brady, their lust for success. But, mostly, women have not had that option. Mostly, women have had to conceal whatever their lust – lest they be judged voracious.

Women have felt pressured to contain or even conceal their lusts for various reasons, including bias, implicit or explicit. While American attitudes toward women and power, say, or women and success, have certainly changed in the last half century, they have changed incrementally, not radically. Around the time that Hillary Clinton competed with Barack Obama for the Democratic nomination for president (in 2008), a study came out that confirmed what many suspected: the bias against women who were seen to be seeking power was persisting. "Specifically, unlike male politicians ... female politicians are expected to live up to a prescribed level of communality." Their failure to meet such standards "elicits backlash." Moreover, this backlash seems to "occur more often in political roles requiring ... commanding, decisive, and authoritarian styles" – such as, obviously, the American presidency.[8] Again, attitudes like these are changing. But the number of women at the top is still stunningly low. In 2019, only thirty-three women were CEOs of Fortune 500 companies – a measly, puny 6.6 percent of the total.[9]

Context
Hillary Clinton is known for many things – including graduating from Wellesley, an elite college for women, in one of the most

tumultuous years in American politics ever, 1969. Her time at Wellesley was a turning point – for the nation politically and for her personally. In the early and mid-1960s, women in college were still under strict supervision, governed by rules on everything from good morals to good manners.[10] But by the time Clinton arrived on campus, in 1965, things were changing. Indeed, Bob Dylan's iconic, emblematic song, "The Times They Are a-Changin'" had come out just one year before. And Betty Friedan's feminist classic, *The Feminine Mystique*, had appeared one year before that. By the mid and certainly by the late 1960s, then, not only had most of the rules confining female undergraduates evaporated into the ether, the United States more generally was undergoing seismic changes. These included rights revolutions such as civil rights and women's rights. And these included rights rebellions, most prominent among them widespread protests, on campus and off, against the war in Vietnam.

It was a perfect fit – between Hillary Rodham, as she then was known, and the moment during which she transitioned from adolescence to adulthood. The moment enabled her to forge her identity as a leader, a goal she had set even before she went to college. In her senior year of high school, Clinton decided to run, against two boys, for senior class president. While most girls at Illinois' Park Ridge High School could not even imagine such an ambition, she did. Told by one of her opponents that she was "really stupid" if she thought a girl could be elected president, she nonetheless hung in.[11] Clinton never did become class president in high school – but she did in college. Moreover, she was selected to be the first undergraduate ever to deliver a speech at a Wellesley graduation. It was so striking a debut on the national stage that a picture of her appeared in a June 1969 issue of *Life* magazine.

When Hillary Clinton entered Yale Law School in 1970 (the same year as Bill Clinton), only 8.5 percent of students at ABA-approved law schools were women. Moreover, throughout the 1970s women students and faculty had to pressure law school placement offices to compel "law firms to recruit women seriously or face sanctions."[12] Put differently, at the time, for a woman to choose to attend law school was itself a signal that she was unusually ambitious to succeed. As was her choice not long after graduating from law school to go to Washington to join the House impeachment committee, which had been tasked with developing articles of impeachment against President Richard Nixon. Once again Clinton was in an unusual position: of the forty-three staff attorneys who were part of the committee, just three were women.

For the better part of the next two decades (beginning in 1974) Hillary Clinton lived in Arkansas. She went west – in part probably because, shockingly, she had failed the Washington DC bar exam – to join Bill Clinton, who was staking his personal, professional, and above all his political fortunes in his home state. In her autobiography she wrote, "I had fallen in love with Bill in law school and wanted to be with him."[13] And so she moved to a place that was far from home – far from her home state of Illinois and far from the cosmopolitan metropolises within which she had lived since going to college. Clinton also changed from being front and center herself to being the spouse of a man who himself was front and center. Nevertheless, by every accounting, Bill Clinton had met his match. His lust for success was equaled by his wife's – their shared ambitions likely explaining better than anything else their obviously difficult if ultimately enduring marriage.

To say that Hillary Clinton had to navigate her way, carefully, through the Arkansas thicket is to understate it. She was an Eastern fish in Southern waters, swimming upstream. More precisely, she was straddling a difficult line: on the one side playing the part of dutiful political wife, on the other side playing the part of successful legal professional. Again, being a woman in this context was a key determinant of what she could do – and could not do. She continued throughout her time in Arkansas to hitch her wagon to her husband's political star – Bill Clinton first became governor of the state in 1979 – and she continued to further her own career as an attorney at a prominent Little Rock law firm. Though being a woman with a career in the state capital was not easy, Hillary Rodham, as she preferred to be known until 1980, persisted. Along the way were the by now familiar litany of problems – personal, political, professional, legal, and financial – which did not preclude her from continuing to stand out. Testimony to her unremitting ambition was her own professional success – in 1988 the *National Law Journal* named her one of America's 100 most influential lawyers – and her abiding marriage to an errant husband who as time went on became hell-bent on running for president of the United States.

Subsequent to Arkansas there were six stages in Clinton's life: (1) first lady (1993–2001); (2) senator from the state of New York (2001–2009); (3) candidate for the Democratic nomination for president of the United States (2007–2008); (4) Secretary of State under Barack Obama (2009–2013); (5) Democratic candidate for president of the United States (2015–2016); and (6) retirement (2016–). Each of the first five was in a different context, entailing a different personal as well as political dynamic, and different role expectations. And each was at a different point in her marriage to a man whose shadow loomed exceedingly large. All along though was the same overriding theme: Hillary Rodham Clinton as among the first women ever to do this, and as among the first women ever to do that.

Her lust for success must, then, again, be seen in this light. This light continued to shine harshly on any woman who dared to lust for success as ardently as did she. Most of us are familiar with women leaders trapped between being viewed as either too passive or too aggressive; too communal or too remote; too feminine or not feminine enough. Most of us are familiar as well with the media as a mediator, old media and new, that even in the second decade of the twenty-first century remained beset by bias – by "patterns of . . . gender discrimination" that continued to persist.[14] What most of us are less aware of is the iron will it took for Hillary Clinton to get as close to being president of the United States as she did – given that she ran for president during a time when hyper-partisanship had already become endemic and when women so highly positioned remained exceedingly rare birds.

Evidence

Hillary Clinton became a nationally known figure when her husband first ran for president, in 1992. Given everything that happened in the decades that followed, it's hard to recall the earnestness, and the high-mindedness of her original ambitions. We have come to associate Clinton's lust for success with worldly and even material success. To wit: her strenuous efforts to be elected or appointed to the nation's highest political offices, and her obvious interest in being paid large sums of money, especially for giving talks to groups of wealthy people. But in her original incarnation Clinton was very much an idealist, a woman intent on changing the world in keeping with her moral precepts.

While still in New Haven she was associated with the Yale Child Study Center, and familiar as an advocate of the fledgling children's rights movement. Subsequently, she took a job as staff attorney at the newly established Children's Defense Fund. Not long after she moved to Arkansas, during her time as faculty member at University of Arkansas Law School (one of two women on the faculty), Clinton served as the first director of a legal aid clinic – while continuing her work on behalf of child and family welfare and, later, helping to establish a rape crisis center. Clearly Clinton's social conscience dictated many of her early choices – notwithstanding her professional ambitions, her life as a political wife, and, in time, as a new mother. (Chelsea, the Clintons' only child, was born in 1980.) All the available evidence suggests that Clinton's activism grew out of deeply held convictions. That is, her early social and political commitments especially were genuine, ends in themselves, not merely means. It explains why she has been considered by some, including eminent historian Garry Wills, one of "the most important [of recent] scholar-activists."[15]

No surprise then that the author of a *New York Times* profile of Hillary Clinton, written shortly after she became first lady, was struck by her fervent determination to do good. To all appearances she was resolved to succeed not just in the conventional sense. From her perch next to the president, "Hillary Rodham Clinton," wrote journalist Michael Kelly, harbored "an ambition so large that it can scarcely be grasped. She would like to make things right." During two long conversations with Kelly, she evidenced her hopes and dreams, which centered on making the world a better place – as she defined better. America, she had earlier said, suffered from a "sleeping sickness of the soul." Who, she asked, was going to "lead us out of this spiritual vacuum"? It was clear at least to Kelly that she, presumably along with her husband, the president, had every intention of doing what they reasonably could to enable and encourage a politics of meaning, a politics of virtue. Her sense of mission – a product of the Methodist principles on which she was raised and the activist convictions common to her generation – explains her ambition. Her lust for success, she seems to have believed, was not about securing power and influence for herself. It was about securing power and influence to help others, to repair a nation whose cities were "filled with hopeless girls with babies and angry boys with guns" – signs of a country and a culture that were in the throes of a "crisis of meaning."[16]

Increasing age usually is associated with decreasing idealism and, concomitantly, with greater realism. Hillary Clinton was no exception. This is not to say that her early high-mindedness was abandoned so much as it was subsumed and ultimately overwhelmed by a pragmatic push to succeed as success is conventionally defined. From being named chair of Bill Clinton's Presidential Task Force on National Health Care Reform in 1993 all the way through to the presidential campaign in 2016, her focus turned to being appointed or elected to high political office. She, of course, would have argued, indeed she did, that her purpose in trying to procure said office(s) was not self-aggrandizement. To the contrary. It was, she said, to gain power, authority, and influence in order to fix what was broken or, at least, to improve the state of the nation and ultimately the state of the world.

Hillary Clinton's lust for success, however, is impossible fully to grasp without having a sense of what she had to endure to survive her journey. To say that she suffered slings and arrows every step of the way, at every bend in the road, is grossly to understate it. From her first major appearance on the national stage, as the wife of presidential candidate Bill Clinton, to her last, as presidential candidate in her own right, she was victimized (not too strong a word) by attacks that ranged from simply nasty to downright vicious, and from threatening finally to frightening. Most of these were, predictably, grounded in her being a woman. Early on she was tagged, "the Lady Macbeth of Arkansas." And the "Yuppie Wife from Hell." Or, as the previously referenced Roger Ailes once put it, "Hillary Clinton in an apron is Michael Dukakis in a tank."[17] (Ailes was evoking a public relations disaster of a few years earlier when Dukakis, the diminutive Democratic candidate for president, was photographed crouched in a tank, looking ridiculous.)

The attacks on her, personal and political and particularly vitriolic, never let up, not once during her approximately quarter century in the public eye. Her tenure as first lady was, it should be added, marred not only by her humiliating failure as a policy maker (especially on healthcare) – in one 1994 poll 62 percent of those surveyed said they did not want her involved in policy making – but also by her humiliating experience as the wife of a president impeached for lying about philandering. Even her tenure as Secretary of State was grinding, during and for years after, most notably on account of the 2012 attacks in Benghazi, Libya, in which four Americans were killed. Clinton was accused of being responsible for the tragedy not only by Republicans, but also by parents of two of the dead, who filed a lawsuit against her for failing to provide proper security. (In 2017 the lawsuits were dismissed.) For its part, the special committee created by Congress (in 2014) to investigate the terrorist attacks concluded its work only after two and a half years, and after spending more than $7.8 million, and after Clinton personally testified on three separate occasions, the last time for eleven hours straight.

Still the legacy of Benghazi lingered – into the 2016 presidential campaign (and beyond), during which the issue of State Department emails and email servers became of paramount importance and major contention. We cannot prove or even presume motive. We cannot, in other words, prove or even presume that what happened was on account of Hillary Clinton's need to control the narrative – to control the narrative to make more likely her success. But while during her tenure as Secretary of State she should have used official State Department email accounts that were being maintained on secure federal servers, she did not. Instead, she used her own private server to conduct official public business – which when she ran for the White House cost her no end of trouble and, possibly, the election.

After enduring an astonishing, and bitter, loss to Donald Trump, Clinton finally expressed her anger and hurt over the fallout from Benghazi, notably in her book about one of the most controversial, and consequential, elections in American history, *What Happened*. "Here's where the story takes a turn into the partisan swamp," she wrote. "Republicans turned the deaths of four brave Americans into a partisan farce."[18] But *What Happened* is most interesting for what it is more generally: a vehicle for Clinton at age 70 finally to vent. To vent her fury – and to express her pain – about how she was treated during her many years in public service.

Understandably, "on being a woman in politics" is a running theme. In a chapter so named she wrote, "It's not easy to be a woman in politics. That's an understatement. It can be excruciating, humiliating … it can be unbelievably cruel." More broadly she noted that "both sexism and misogyny are endemic in America … People hiding in the shadows step forward just far enough to rip [a woman] apart." Misogyny she continued is "rage. Disgust. Hatred." Misogyny is when "a woman gets a job that a man wanted … he calls her a bitch and vows to do everything he can to make sure she fails." Clinton is not, of course, in the business of deterring women from wanting to become leaders. So, she threw in several bromides, such as how "being a woman in politics" has been "rewarding beyond measure." Still, what rings most true in her book is her unmitigated anger. After bottling up so much for so long, finally her fierce sense of grievance is revealed, in her own words, for everyone to see. "For the record," she writes, "it hurts to be torn apart. It may seem like it doesn't bother me to be called terrible names or have my looks mocked viciously, but it does."[19]

Hillary Clinton's lust for success climaxed in her run against Donald Trump for president of the United States. By everyone's account, including her own, for her it was an occasionally exhilarating experience, but mostly it was grueling and often it was awful. A test of endurance so grindingly trying that it provides the strongest possible evidence of her lust to succeed. By the end of the Republican National Convention in July 2016 the chant had caught on. The by now familiar three-beat chant that ever since has had Republican crowds hooting and hollering, yelling and screaming, "Lock her up! Lock her up! Lock her up." Clinton's take on the continuing hate? Three years after her excruciating loss she told MSNBC anchor Rachel Maddow, "I'm living rent free inside of Donald Trump's brain, and it's not a very nice place to be, I can tell you that."[20]

Followers

For whatever constellation of reasons, as we have seen Hillary Clinton brought out the haters. Brought them out in droves. No one has quite figured out, nailed precisely why, large numbers of people disliked her so intensely for so long. But, even when she was still relatively early in the White House, as first lady during Bill Clinton's first term, observers were struck by the high level of animosity she evoked. In an article titled "Hating Hillary" that appeared in *The New Yorker* in 1996, Henry Louis Gates wondered what was "fueling the furies?" He came up with several answers but, ultimately, they were inconclusive. Clinton's apparently limitless capacity to engender in others not only dislike but distrust remained mysterious, a "large-scale psychic phenomenon" without clear explanation or justification.[21] Moreover the impulse – to hate Hillary – persisted. Fully two decades after Gates's article appeared, there was an identically titled essay in *The Economist*, "Hating Hillary," that raised the same question. Just what is it about Hillary that makes her so hated? *The Economist* found it as difficult to explain the "unbridled loathing" as did *The New Yorker* two decades earlier, though both did suggest that sexism played a part. Still, sexism notwithstanding, the question remained: "What then explains the depths of unpopularity, which on November 8th will drive millions of Americans to justify voting for a man whom they have heard boast of groping women?"[22]

The hostility to Hillary cannot be reduced to single explanation or justification. Nevertheless, the evidence of a connection rooted in sexism – between her lust for success on the one hand, and the high levels of dislike and distrust of her on the other – is clear. As the article in *The Economist* pointed out, whenever she "sought power, including in her two Senate and first presidential campaigns ... she was in for another pounding." Moreover, by the time of her second presidential campaign, in 2016, "the pitch of loathing" had become "unprecedented." This suggests that sexism is the single most powerful explicator of "what happened" – a suggestion strongly supported by research already referenced confirming that women are more likely than men to be punished for seeking power.[23] This is not of course to imply that sexism is the only reason for Clinton's defeat. For example, we are wise now to the impact of Russian hacking in the 2016 election. Nor is it to suggest that Clinton herself was blameless. She herself has repeatedly admitted that she was a flawed candidate. But it is to say that sexism cast a significant shadow over her public life – from start to finish.

It was the more important, then, for her to muster followers who were dedicated – and in some cases more than dedicated, deeply devoted. Followers ranging from close personal friends and longtime aides to anonymous throngs. Followers who liked her personally and/or who supported her policies and/or who believed she could be, or already was, an exceptionally able political leader. This is something that Hillary Clinton was able to do – she was able to get people, sometimes legions of people, to follow where she led.

From the start of her political career, she knew that she had to build her own base of support, independent from that of her husband. Which explains why she began her campaign for senator from the state of New York with a "listening tour." The purpose of the tour was to get New Yorkers to know her – she had never lived or worked for any length of time in New York State – and to like her at least well enough. After all, they had to be sufficiently motivated to get out on Election Day and vote for a visibly smart but polarizing woman whose previous political experience was limited to being spouse of a president who recently was impeached. To these ends, Clinton restrained "her tendency toward unequivocal advocacy," and refrained from asserting "her own strongly held views." Instead, she invited voters to tell her what was important to them; she made sure not to offend; and she told her audiences "largely what they wanted to hear."[24] It worked. Though she did not have the natural gifts of a retail politician, as did her husband, Hillary Clinton was elected senator from New York in 2000 and then again in 2006.

Having won over voters, it was time to do the same with her colleagues in the Senate, many of whom initially viewed Clinton with suspicion. She was, after all, in an unusual position: juxtaposed between being a political novice and a political celebrity. Again, she did everything she could to get her colleagues on board, if not to win their affection at least to gain their respect. Ever dutiful, she arrived early to Senate meetings and committee hearings, she prioritized floor votes above the other demands on her time, and she sponsored hundreds of her own bills while cosponsoring thousands of others brought to her by Senate colleagues who "recognized her unique ability to draw attention to even the dullest regulations."[25] Veteran Washington reporter and Clinton biographer, Carl Bernstein, described her as being "deferential" to other senators, avoiding the limelight (not easy, given her star status), and hell-bent on persuading her colleagues as she had her constituents that she was deeply dedicated to the tasks at hand. "Hillary," Bernstein observed, "had always relished being a star pupil and teacher's pet, and she excelled at playing these roles in the Senate."[26] The consensus was and still is that Clinton's all-out effort to succeed as a senator paid off, within the Senate and without. She was widely admired for her work ethic. She was widely respected for her ability to enlist Republicans as well as Democrats. And she was widely appreciated for her willingness to play by Senate rules.

She was, in short, successful as a professional politician. No doubt she could have had, had she wanted it, a long, productive career as a senator from the state of New York. But for her – a woman with a lust for success – such a career was insufficient, inadequate. It was short of the top spot. So, not long after being elected to the Senate for the second time, Hillary Clinton announced that she was likely to run for president. Which she did. In 2008 she ran but lost – she lost the Democratic nomination to Barack Obama. It was a hard-fought campaign that Clinton later described as being "grueling and heated." But, though the experience had left her "disappointed and exhausted," it did not slake her lust.[27] Her lust to succeed was part and parcel of who she was and so, when President-elect Obama, for his own political reasons (to bring her and her followers into his tent), offered her the position of Secretary of State, she said yes.

In retrospect, it's easy to understand why Clinton continued to believe that she had a good shot at being the first woman president of the United States. She did. Her experience at the Department of State replicated her experiences earlier. There were haters and there were some who were indifferent. But there were also many, many, ardent supporters. In the Senate Clinton was described as having a galvanizing effect on the women who worked there. At State she had a similar impact, especially on young women who had voted for her and on older women who regarded her, rightly, as a trailblazer.[28] Moreover, during her second presidential campaign it was again apparent that millions of ordinary people "loved her intelligence, her industriousness, her grit; they feel loyal to her, they will vote for her with enthusiasm."[29]

Among the ranks of her followers were, of course, numberless men. At the same time, her most fervent followers usually were women – though her popularity among white women voters remained throughout a political problem – and women were those to whom she felt most loyal. Women poured buckets of money into her coffers; women provided diversity and political savvy; and women gave her the personal as well as political support critical to hanging in when the going got tough, which it often did. Some of the women most loyal to Clinton were political pros; others were new to the game. Together in any case her closest female aides and allies came to form a cadre, a kitchen cabinet on whom she in every way depended. They, in turn, "idolized her, believed that she was a force for moral good in American politics, and dearly wanted to see a female president."[30] As a result, after her 2008 loss to Obama, Clinton reported feeling especially bad about letting "down so many millions of people, especially the women and girls who had invested their dreams in me."[31]

But the tight tie between Clinton and women – especially women who were her closest followers – had a downside. While sexism accounted for some of the criticism, the isolation and insularity of what early on was tagged "Hillaryland" did her a disservice. Hillaryland became code for what was viewed by some as too tight a group – a group akin to a "cult," a group of aides and allies who seemed to have become acolytes exceedingly – read excessively – devoted to their matriarch.[32] Even years later, when Clinton served at State, she still was surrounded by a "small set of advisers who had most completely demonstrated that they would sacrifice themselves on the altar of her success."[33] Additionally, it could be argued that when she ran for president the second time, some of her most loyal followers contributed, however inadvertently, to her downfall. They were so totally devoted and dedicated to Clinton that they were unable to see her clearly – and unable effectively to play the role of devil's advocate, to provide dissenting opinions or objections. Huma Abedin, for instance, was Clinton's most trusted personal and political aide, beginning when she was Secretary of State. By the 2016 campaign the two women were in effect inseparable – which explains why Abedin was as deeply embroiled in the email mess as was Clinton, the email mess that probably contributed significantly to killing Hillary Clinton's chances of ever becoming American president.[34]

Hindsight

There were numberless explanations and excuses for Hillary Clinton's defeat in the 2016 presidential election – as there were numberless explanations and excuses for why Barack Obama beat her eight years earlier. Some of these were at the macro level: for example, by the second decade of the twenty-first century there was a shift in American politics, away from the centrism that Bill and Hillary Clinton long had espoused, and toward the increased extremism with which Americans have become familiar, on the right and the left. Others of these were at the micro level: for example, years later Clinton was still being lambasted for dismissing half of Trump's supporters as belonging in a "basket of deplorables."

But the specter of sexism remained – as it does still. Hillary Clinton's various virtues – say, intelligence, persistence, preparation, and dedication – were forever being touted. But what lingered – in her own mind as well as in the minds of many close observers – is the effect of her being a woman. Specifically, the effect of her being a woman with a lust for success: a lust for success that long had been palpable; a lust so great she was willing to climb over hot coals to the top; and at a time when the sight of a woman who lusted so strongly and for so long, going all the way back to her time in Arkansas and her ambitions not only for herself but for her husband, still struck many as unattractive or even unseemly.

When Clinton stepped down as Secretary of State, in early 2013, her approval rating stood at what the *Wall Street Journal* described as an "eye-popping" 69 percent. At that moment she was the most popular politician in the United States – and the second most popular Secretary of State in well over a half century. A pollster writing in the *New York Times* commented on her "remarkably high numbers for a politician in an era when many public officials are distrusted or disliked." However, just a few years later, in 2016, when she again ran for president, the tide had turned. As a headline in the *Huffington Post* put it, "The FBI and 67 percent of Americans Distrust Hillary Clinton." While during the three-year period from 2013 to 2016 her status had changed – it's one thing to step away from being Secretary of State and quite another to run for president – the drop in her approval ratings nevertheless was dramatic. A writer for *Quartz* interpreted the decline this way: "Public opinion of Clinton follows a fixed pattern throughout her career. Her public approval plummets whenever she applies for a new job. Then it soars when she gets the job . . . The predictable swings of public opinion reveal Americans' continued prejudice against women caught in the act of asking for power."[35] It was also the case that it was one thing for Clinton to be a member of a president's team, it was quite another for her to want to be president.

We cannot here do justice to the constellation of forces that enabled Donald Trump to be elected to the White House. Trump, who had had not a smidgeon of political, governmental, or military experience or expertise, and whose character was so obviously flawed that no matter what the course of American history, he would always be a national embarrassment. Still, he won, she lost.

In the several years that have passed since then, Clinton has reflected extensively on this loss, especially on how it happened that she was defeated by an opponent so obviously and variously unqualified. In her book, *What Happened*, she dedicates whole chapters to different explicators, with titles such as "Those Damned Emails" to "Trolls, Bots, Fake News, and Real Russians." But, again, sexism was a recurring theme. Clinton in a 2017 interview stated that, "With men, success and ambition are correlated with likability, so the more successful a man is, the more likable he becomes! With a woman, guess what? It's the exact opposite."[36] Similarly, Clinton writes in *What Happened*: "It's not easy being a woman in politics, but I think it's safe to say that I got a whole other level of vitriol flung my way . . . I was taken aback by the flood of hatred that seemed only to grow . . . It was flabbergasting and frightening."[37]

As Clinton herself has testified, she was aware that running for the White House a second time would be extremely difficult and frequently painful. She did not, then, make the decision lightly – but she did make it. Her lust for success remained such that it still propelled her forward. It drove her to throw her hat into the ring one final time, despite what she knew would be a knock-down drag out fight. Why does she say she did it? Why does she say she was not content to rest on her considerable laurels? True to form, she admits to being ambitious – but not to being ambitious for herself. Rather she was ambitious for another purpose: to do good in the world. Hillary Rodham Clinton writes that she decided to run for president again because "We Methodists are taught to 'do all the good you can.' I knew that if I ran and won, I could do a world of good and help an awful lot of people. Does that make me ambitious? I guess it does. But not in the sinister way the people often mean it . . . I wanted power to do what I could to help solve problems and prepare the country for the future." In the end then, while some things changed, others did not. Clinton felt no more comfortable revealing her deeply personal need to succeed in the second decade of the twenty-first century than she did in the last decade of the twentieth.

Tom Brady

Despite its violence, brutality, and high levels of injuries – especially head injuries linked to brain damage, early-onset dementia, and depression – football retains its iconic status in American sport. Or is it not "despite," but because of? Is it precisely *because* of the danger of football, the risks men take every time they play or even practice the game, especially at the professional level, that its place in American life remains still so secure?

It has been argued that "as long as football is seen as the quintessential *man's* sport and as long as masculinity is defined by the ability to be physical and domineering, injury and pain will continue to be facets of the game."[38] In other words, some Americans, many Americans, associate physicality and domination with being masculine and, so long as this association persists, so long will the fascination with football. It's an irony then that a game in which the best players – those who "dutifully ignore pain, repress emotion, embody machismo, and strive to physically dominate" – tend to end their careers on account of bashed and even broken bodies has on its roster one of greatest players ever, Tom Brady.[39] Brady remains into his forties a movie-star handsome icon with a famously gorgeous wife and near picture-perfect family; whose life as a star quarterback has almost all along seemed charmed, including as of this writing six Super Bowl wins. Specifically Brady insists on continuing to play notwithstanding his now relatively advanced age; his already having every accolade his game has to offer and every conceivable financial and material reward; and despite the threats to his health and welfare every time he steps onto a football field.

Given a few new rules of the game and improved equipment, Brady is relatively well-protected. But, while the risks of injury to him in the present might, therefore, be somewhat less than they were in the past, every time Brady plays football he's gambling on his well-being, especially given his age. Still, he plays. If that's not evidence of his lust for success, we don't know what is. But, it's also evidence of his leadership style. Brady does not lead by telling other people what to do. Rather he leads by example. Though he's made a few mistakes and missteps during the long years of his astonishing career, by and large Tom Brady has been an exemplar, a model of what it means to be a great athlete in twenty-first century America. For this he is admired if not revered by many if not most of his teammates and football fans more generally, and by countless Americans who've paid even the slightest attention.

Context

Why the National Football League (NFL) has such a central place in America's culture and consciousness is not immediately obvious. It's always been something of a "freak show," a disreputable preserve of "bruisers, hard partyers, repeat offenders."[40] But, then, to repeat, football is famously coarse, famously aggressive, famously brutal. Players are expected to play violently, and fans are expected to cheer the battering and pummeling that ordinarily we profess to detest. In fact, football rewards those players, those men, whose brutality is most evident and effective, a system of incentives not exactly at odds with the larger context within which the game is situated. For the United States is, after all, a country with a long history of violence including on its own soil.

But football obviously has other characteristics as well, some of which are admirable and all of which explain its enduring appeal, especially obviously to men. For example, the game provides players from various ethnic and economic backgrounds one of the few fields on which they can compete as equals. Football is also the quintessential team sport. It demands that every one of the eleven players coordinate on every play. Cohen provided some comparisons. Basketball, he wrote, is five guys, "a commando unit." Baseball is "a scattering," where "each player is closed in his own solitude." But football is something else altogether – eleven players acting as one, "each having to execute perfectly to win."[41] Additionally, football demands dedicated discipline and "tireless preparation." There are daily meetings, fitness trainings, and numberless practices, all part of "an incredibly detailed process that all teams go through, a painstaking progression that starts the minute one game ends and the preparation for the next one begins."[42]

The preparations though are not just physical, they are also psychological and, yes, intellectual. Football experts describe the sport, admiringly, as every bit as strategic an undertaking as a physical one. "Coaching, tactics, game plans, and playbooks structure the game from beginning to end."[43] Playbooks run to hundreds of pages, and plays can be complicated, a mix of alignments, assignments, and adjustments. Playing smart is widely considered as important as playing violent – by coaches and players, and by football fans, many of whom are rabid, if conflicted, admirers of the sport generally and of the NFL grudgingly. Finally, Americans are mesmerized by the money. Like many other professional athletes, football players earn big money. But, the *very* big money is raked in by the NFL itself. In 2017 it earned a reported $14.2 billion. It is estimated, by Roger Goodell, the NFL's commissioner, that by 2027 its annual revenues will be $25 billion.

Perhaps the most striking thing about the context within which Tom Brady has spent his professional life is how all-encompassing it is – especially how all-encompassing is the National Football League. To be sure, Brady has nearly always played on a certain team, the Patriots, and in a certain city, Boston. It's impossible, then, to separate him from the contexts of his team, which included his legendary coach, Bill Belichick, and the city that came effectively to revere him, for good reason. During the era of Belichick and Brady, both of whom joined the team in 2000, the Patriots went to the Super Bowl nine times; they won the

Super Bowl six times; they won 16 division titles; and since 2001 they have never had a losing season.[44]

But for Brady no context has been more consequential than the National Football League. It's described as a "bubble." It's a bubble within which NFL players not just work but, in effect, live. The authors of a book about the league describe it this way. "NFL players live in a distinctive world of their own ... They are immersed in a cultural, structural, psychological, and experiential world that insulates them from many mundane aspects of everyday life. The NFL may be the most totally encompassing of professional sports institutions."[45] Still, even this bubble can be burst, or at least it can be pierced by outside stimuli that sunder its hermetic seal. The NFL is not, in other words, entirely immune to what happens outside its "distinctive world." Most notably, it has not been immune to the mounting scientific evidence – and the growing public recognition – that playing football, especially but not exclusively professional football, can be dangerous. Dangerous physically, psychologically, and, or, cognitively. It took the NFL years (until 2016) publicly to acknowledge the link between playing football and developing degenerative brain disease. It was willing previously to admit that football can cause concussions, and that concussions were dangerous. But when Jeff Miller, the NFL's executive vice president for health and safety policy, said in an open forum that football posed risks to players' health not just in the short term but over the long term, the league finally admitted something it had previously, certainly publicly, denied.[46]

The question of just how dangerous football is, especially if it is played over a period of years at the college and professional levels, has not yet been fully resolved. As recently as 2018, University of North Carolina head coach, Larry Fedora, was quoted as saying, "I don't think it's been proven that the game of football causes CTE. We still don't really know that."[47] (CTE is the acronym for Chronic Traumatic Encephalopathy, a degenerative brain disease caused by repetitive hits.) Still, most Americans now accept as fact that football is not just another contact sport. "It's a dangerous game of massive bodies colliding into one another." It's a dangerous game that "can do extraordinary damage to brains and bodies." The NFL, meantime, having long downplayed and even refuted the risks of playing pro ball, especially as they relate to the connection between concussions and cognitive decline, now has no choice but to accept the obvious. But while as indicated the game is somewhat safer now than it was, so long as "human-to-human collisions are fundamental to play," anyone who plays professional football will be at risk.[48]

We know that neither Tom Brady nor his wife, Gisele Bündchen, is oblivious to the risks associated with his continuing to play, especially now that he is in his forties. It was widely reported that she wanted him to retire years ago – obviously he refused. In fact, in 2017 Brady insisted that he was by no means ready to quit. "I'm having too much fun right now. You know, I feel like I can still do it . . . So, I'm going to work hard to be ready to go, and I still plan on playing for a long time."[49] It was his way of saying that in spite of having already played for many years, and in spite of having everything that any man could possibly want, he still wanted more. His lust for success was not yet satisfied – even though the context within which he currently was playing was in one all-important way dramatically different from what it was earlier in his career. When Brady began to play pro football, there were few signs of danger. Now such signs have been posted at every turn. The authors of an article in the prestigious *Journal of the American Medical Association* summarized their findings this way. "In a convenience sample of deceased football players who donated their brains for research, a high proportion had neuropathological evidence of CTE, suggesting that CTE may be related to prior participation in football."[50]

Evidence
Tom Brady *always* strives to succeed. "The true competitors," he once said, "are the ones who always play to win." Conversely, Tom Brady *always* strives not to fail. "You never get over losses," he once said. "I've never gotten over one loss I've had in my career. They always stick with you." Brady is self-aware – he knows himself, understands what motivates him, gets that while he has other satisfactions and gratifications in life, including his wife and children, playing football, playing to win, is central. It has *always* been central. "The only thing I ever wanted to be," he has said, "was a professional football player."[51]

Brady was an excellent athlete all his life – but he was not always exceptional. Nor was he always fixated on football; in high school he also played baseball and basketball. In his senior year, though, after the regular quarterback was injured, Brady was named to replace him. His future was foretold – it was football. Success did not, however, come easily. At the University of Michigan, which he attended from 1995 to 1999, Brady first had to fight just to get some playing time. Later during his college career, he consulted a school psychologist to cope with his "frustration and anxiety." He also met regularly with a particular athletic director, to "build his confidence and maximize his performance" and to surmount "personal struggles in both athletics and life." For his fierce ambition and quiet determination Brady was eventually rewarded. By the time he graduated he ranked third in Michigan history with 710 attempts and 442 completions. Withal, as a pro ball prospect, he was no more than "lightly regarded." Ultimately, famously, he was, of course, selected by the New England Patriots, but only as a sixth-round draft choice and only as the 199th player overall.[52]

Initially, in the spring of 2001, no one on the team or in the city of Boston particularly noticed Tom Brady. To the contrary. He was "king of the shadows." He was incessantly practicing, working out, building himself up, figuring out how to compete for the position of starting quarterback, and hell-bent on playing as smart as strong. But he did it all quietly, in the background. It was not until the 2001 season opener that "the shadows that Brady operated in began to wane." Perceptions of him and what turned out to be his limitless potential began to change. Drew Bledsoe, the Patriots' starting quarterback, got injured, giving Brady the chance to prove himself. By the fifth game of the season he found his stride: Boston went on to win eleven of the fourteen games that Brady started. Still he continued to play it cool, to come across as careful and contained, concealing the real Tom Brady who "sweated behind the curtain to get himself ready for this stage."[53]

More than anything else, it is his relentless willingness, even eagerness, to "sweat behind the curtain" that testifies to Brady's lust for success. Under the leadership of their coach, Bill Belichick, the Patriots were known to practice longer and harder than any of their competitors. While players in other NFL organizations were taking it easy, the Patriots met at all hours of the day, driving themselves to the point of exhaustion. It was Belichick's way. "Adopt his vision of the football work grind, or quickly lose the opportunity to play football for work." Still, even in this all-consuming context, Brady stood out. His drive to succeed knew no bounds. One of his former teammates, Chris Eitzmann, painted the picture: "Brady and I would stay out after practice ... It was fucking horrible. Brady just wanted to keep going and going and going. I wanted some extra work too, because I was always on the bubble, but this was different ... We would just run ... until I was dead." Brady's zeal to win and willingness to do whatever it took to beat the competition was always in evidence, without exception. Even in charity games, he would scream at his teammates for slacking off. "We're fucking losing to a bunch of firefighters!" he would yell. Next thing you knew, recalled another former teammate, Damon Huard, "We're in the most competitive charity basketball game you'll ever see and Brady's banking in three-point shot after three-point shot."[54]

In Tom Brady's pro ball career there has been a single stain, one that raised questions about his basic decency and fundamental integrity. This was an incident that suggested his lust for success was not just a singular asset, but also, possibly, a serious deficit, and which implied that his zeal to succeed was so outsized it led him to cut corners. In 2015, ESPN reported that eleven of the twelve balls that were used during the first half of a game between the Boston Patriots and the Baltimore Colts had been deliberately underinflated. Underinflated balls are easier to throw, and they are easier to catch. And they are illegal. While the details of the scandal, which quickly came to be known as "Deflategate," do not concern us here, the implications do.

Early in the timeline of Deflategate, Patriots' owner Robert Kraft strenuously denied any wrongdoing. "It bothers me greatly," he said, that our team's "reputation and integrity" have been called into question. Kraft went on to insist that if the NFL's investigation was "not able to definitively determine that our organization tampered with the air pressure in the footballs," he expected the league to apologize to the "entire team and, in particular, coach Belichick and Tom Brady." Well, not only did the NFL not apologize, its own internal investigation revealed it was "more probable than not" that Patriots' personnel knowingly deflated some footballs, and that Brady was "at least generally aware" of the violations. As a result of the finding, the Patriots were in minor ways punished and Brady was handed a four-game suspension. He appealed, but the league said no – his suspension would be neither canceled nor reduced. A year and a half after the scandal broke, Brady's further appeal to a federal court was similarly denied. Finally, in July 2016, he announced that though he had considered yet another appeal, this time to the US Supreme Court, he had decided enough was enough. For whatever constellation of reasons, Brady made the seemingly sensible decision to move on.[55]

Brady had never previously experienced anything even approximating the humiliation of Deflategate. "While other players attracted public scorn … Brady's image and reputation had remained clean." What then was his response to the scandal and subsequent suspension, either one of which could have wrecked his career? He doubled down. His "preparation and wealth of football knowledge allowed him to pick up right where he'd left off."[56] He insisted moreover that he felt good, that he was ready to roll, and that the fire in his belly still burned bright. In Super Bowl XLIL, a spine-tingling game played not long after the scandal first broke – the Boston Patriots against the Seattle Seahawks – Brady turned in a "performance for the ages."[57] With minutes to go in the fourth quarter he completed thirteen of fifteen passes, a brilliant display of athletic prowess under exceedingly stressful circumstances. For the third time he was named the Super Bowl's Most Valuable Player – a goal that would have eluded him had he been unable to "overcome one of the greatest personal challenges in sports history."[58]

Several years after the scandal, answers to the question of "What is Brady's reputation now?" depend on who you ask. Football fans who lionize him (and the Patriots) wonder, "What scandal?" Football fans who despise (read envy) him (and the Patriots) obviously feel differently. Brady has, in any case, done everything humanly possible to put the crisis behind him. However insatiable his appetite for success in the past – he was always described as obsessed by just two things, football and winning at football – since Deflategate it has if anything increased.[59] His presentation of self continues to be mis-leading – he always "looks regal" and seems calm – while on the field he continues to act like a "competitive lunatic."[60]

Brady is not immune to the diminishment and decline that inevitably accompany age. Still, nearly two decades after the start of his professional football career, he continues to convey a sort of immortality. He published a book about the exercise and nutrition programs he swears account for his preternatural physical prowess.[61] He remains an astonishingly impressive player – a professor of eco-nomics found that between 2008 and 2017 (at least) Brady's averages showed no evidence of statistical decline.[62] And in 2019 he was the beating heart of a team that won a record setting (along with the Pittsburgh Steelers) sixth Super Bowl trophy. No one argued that his performance, age 41, on that day in early February was one of his best. Still, it was "Brady being Brady. Masterful reads. Pinpoint accuracy. Clutch throws."[63]

Followers

Tom Brady is a leader who gets other people to follow not on account of what he *says*, or what he tells them to do. He is a leader on account of who he *is*, how he lives his life.

Let it be said again: Tom Brady is an exemplar of singular, supreme athletic accomplishment. An exemplar of greatness in what is arguably the most quintessentially American of all sports. Still, during his entire career, even during the scandal that threatened permanently to stain his reputation, Brady maintained the measured manner, calm demeanor, and cordial interpersonal style that off the field have always been his trademarks. No one has ever claimed that Brady is warm and fuzzy. He has always been more contained than cozy, more of a quiet introvert than noisy extravert. Still, when this iconic figure meets a new teammate, he'll typically walk up to him, introduce himself, and say, "Hi, I'm Tom Brady."

Successful football teams are often extremely close; among other reasons, they spend large stretches of time together. As one former player states it, "You are with your teammates more than you are with your family."[64] Moreover, team members rely on each other for their livelihoods, and they experience similar or even identical mental and physical stresses and strains. This explains at least in part why, notwithstanding his advanced age (about a third of his teammates are now closer in age to his early adolescent son than to Brady himself), and notwithstanding his exalted status, Brady still tries to fit in, to in some ways be one of the guys. "I just feel like I'm doing what I've always done. I really enjoy it, having a great time practicing, playing. It's great being part of a team."[65]

It seemed the older Tom Brady got, the more his teammates came to value, even cherish him. Patriots player Stephon Gilmore described him "as a great teammate" – and as a leader. "He's one of the hardest workers I've ever played with. He's smart. He comes to work every day . . . He hates losing . . . He pushes players." One of the Patriots' coaches, Josh McDaniels, also described Brady as a leader, saying he pours "himself into his teammates so they know that they can communicate with him and talk to him about anything, whether it's football or not. So it makes him such a special leader."[66]

This mix – Brady is deeply admired professionally and greatly liked personally – is what shines through. Teammates regularly cited his civility and decency, even long after he was a big star and they were just rookies. They spoke of his character in glowing terms. "He's such a great person," said Brian Hoyer. "You all get to see how great of a player he is and ... he's a great friend, a great father, and a great husband."[67] Said another teammate, Trent Brown, "I don't think I can say enough about how good or cool of a guy he is ... He doesn't even think of himself as a superstar, which may be why he treats everyone the way he does."[68] Seek and you shall find? Not in this case. If you're looking for a fly in this ointment, you're looking in vain. To a man, Brady's teammates genuinely seemed to think of him as being thoroughly decent, as well as being, obviously, among the greatest athletes and fiercest competitors of all time. It's why the Boston Patriots took "their cue from him."[69]

Of course, as earlier implied not everyone was in love, either with the team or with its supernatural superstar. Some people hated the Patriots and some people hated Tom Brady. Why exactly? One close observer put it this way: I "think that criticisms of the team are ... probably ... born of jealousy."[70] Similarly of Brady, who can be annoying precisely because he is amazing: "He has lived a charmed life," who, however, "never lets us forget he was the 199th player selected in the 2000 NLF draft, wearing that chip like a badge of honor ... But it's his narcotic and he's addicted." What exactly is he addicted to? He "loves competing." He "loves playing football." He loves "trying to improve and be the best [he] can be."[71]

The fact that football fans everywhere, including in China (yes, in China), are caught up in Brady's mystique is also attributable to his willingness to play to the stands. He has taken care, for example, to curate his online presence, which includes everything from family photos to inspirational messages. And on the Mondays after the Sundays on which he played, he regularly went on the radio and gave extended interviews. Brady's charisma has been attributed as well to his storied relationship with his coach, Belichick, with whom he was paired since both joined the Patriots virtually simultaneously. During the nearly two decades that they worked together, there were, unsurprisingly, rumors of some tensions. But both always sought promptly to dispel them – in 2019 Belichick described his relationship to Brady as "thriving" – and their singularly successful tandem record spoke for itself.[72]

Interestingly, in his relationship to Belichick, Brady thought of himself not as a good leader, but as a good *follower*. Belichick is known as a tough guy, a longtime coach of professional football who minces no words; who would never pamper even the most prominent of his players; and who, when need be, was ready and willing to chew out his star quarterback. Tom Brady, Sr. reported that his son, "Tommy," said to him on more than one occasion that "Belichick has the perfect soldier with me" – that is, that Belichick had in him, in "Tommy" Brady, the perfect follower.[73] Of course, when other Boston players saw the great Brady do what Belichick told him to do, they were similarly inclined to fall into line.

Hindsight

Tom Brady is a certain type of leader, perhaps best described as a role model. He leads primarily by example. It's clear he wants to motivate his teammates – actually, it's clear he *must* motivate his teammates lest he himself fail. Therefore, he leads less because of what he wants to get others to do and more because of what *he* wants to do. To stand out. To excel. To supersede in excellence everyone else. Brady is, moreover, single tracked, focused laser-like on playing the game, and not on what to him are tangential issues, such as the impact of repeated blows to the head on people who play professional football. It might even be said of Brady that though he has been described as the ultimate teammate, he is singularly self-focused. His lust for success, *his* success, unbridled through a professional lifetime of playing football, is so great that he himself, his mind and his body, is the temple at which he worships.

Those closest to Brady, particularly his family, are part of the picture of perfection that he chooses deliberately to put forth. His wife, the aforementioned world-famous model Gisele Bündchen, presents herself as a "force of nature," a "sunbeam," a woman who draws from, for example, astrology, Buddhism, Taoism, and Mexican spiritual guru Don Miguel Ruiz to find "the goodwill in all of us."[74] Moreover, though she is said to worry that her husband will end hurt, she has what we are supposed to think is the decency and good sense to leave him alone. "I want him to do whatever makes him happy," Bündchen told TV host Ellen DeGeneres.[75] Similarly Brady's parents. On their fiftieth wedding anniversary, Brady posted their pictures along with a congratulatory message on Instagram and Facebook. "The strength of their marriage," he wrote in his post, "has always been an inspiration and the best example to me and my sisters of what true love, respect, and commitment means."[76]

The supreme celebrity status achieved by Brady and those closest to him is reminiscent of that of another storied family from the state of Massachusetts – John F. Kennedy's, in its collective heyday, the early 1960s. As was the case then, is the case now. We cannot get enough of the man and his clan, especially his beautiful wife and their adorable children. Here's a glimpse of what it's like to be Tom Brady. "At some point during his career, likely around the time he married a woman whose fame and income dwarfed even his own, he ascended to a level of celebrity that is almost impossible for mortals to comprehend … Every Instagram post, every scarf choice, every scooter ride in the park with his kids sparks minor hysteria … Even the smallest things in Brady's life … set off a frenzy of gawking, sharing, and arguing."[77]

Notwithstanding the foolishness, as Brady nears the end of his career two of his many attributes stand out. And they make clear why with every passing year he has been more lionized and idolized even than before. First his performance on the football field, which has continued to astonish even into his forties. Second, his lust, his lust for success that won't quit, which explains why at his advanced age he still plays, assuming considerable risk just to rack up yet another record-breaking or, at least, winning season. At this point even seasoned observers are struck by Tom Brady's longevity, watching for signs of his decline which, in truth, were easier to detect in 2019 than they were before.[78] Still, Brady insisted shortly before and after Super Bowl 2019 that he had every intention of keeping on playing. Nothing, he claimed, would stop him getting back onto the field till the ancient age of 45. It's a theme he continued to repeat – a destination he continued to confirm – well into the next year, well into the next football season. No great surprise then that before his career was over Tom Brady chose, after two decades, to quit the Boston Patriots to become the quarterback of the Tampa Bay Buccaneers. Brady seemed to think that maybe, just maybe, he could lead this Florida franchise to the Super Bowl.

Brady's stellar performance and extraordinary longevity in so difficult and demanding a sport as professional football is partially attributable to luck. Obviously not every pro athlete is endowed with his natural physical attributes and abilities – or blessed with his enduring good health. But, of course, his singular, stellar career must also be attributed to his work ethic, which from the start was exceptional, even extreme. Brady's work ethic has been the external manifestation of his internal drive to succeed. His need to succeed *explains* his work ethic. It explains why he has been willing for so many years, eager for so many years, to push himself far beyond what the rest of us mere mortals can even begin to contemplate.

Brady is a marvel even to those who know him – and the game of football – best. Grant Williams, an offensive tackler on Brady's first two Patriot teams, remarked, "It's just hard to believe ... There's so many good books out there with sports psychology. I don't know how you can not have a chapter on [Brady] in every one of them. He's just the epitome of what drives wining and focus." Similarly, wide receiver Troy Brown, who played all fifteen of his NFL seasons with the Patriots: "I love football. And I've been around a lot of guys that have played football, and I've seen guys just lose the passion for it ... willing to walk away from it ... [Brady's] ability to hold on to that passion for the game ... for this long, 19 years, man, and still have the same fire. It's amazing."[79]

It has been Brady, though, who has been most revealing – about Brady himself. In 2018, he was interviewed by Oprah Winfrey. She asked if he thought he had "insatiable drive." To which he replied, "Yeah, I do. To be the best I can be. Not to be the best what anyone else thinks. Just to be the best I can be. Why am I still playing now? Because I feel like I can still do it ... It's just, I love it."[80]

Coda

In the prelude to this chapter we indicated the lust for success suggests a relentless quest for one of, some of, or all of the following: (1) achievement; (2) attainment; (3) accomplishment; (4) acquirement; and/or (5) acknowledgment, sometimes to the point of adulation. As we have seen in the cases of both Hillary Clinton and Tom Brady, the lust for success is pure in that it is independent of financial rewards or material goods. This is not to imply that either Clinton or Brady has been immune to the temptations of money, or for that matter to the temptations of anything else. But all along both have been driven by the need to stand out – to excel without surcease in whatever the enterprise into which they chose, heart and soul, to pour themselves. They have been insatiable, willing in both cases to put themselves through what most of us would consider the wringer – intolerably punishing schedules, supremely arduous workloads, and severe psychological stresses – in order to reach their chosen goal. Their chosen goal – their *shared* goal? The pinnacle of success. No less would suffice.

There is, though, a single all-important difference between them. Tom Brady is a man and Hillary Clinton is a woman. Moreover, Clinton is a woman who wanted desperately to succeed in what had been nearly entirely a man's game – American politics, and ultimately the American presidency. This difference always did have and likely will continue indefinitely to have consequences. Brady is a hero and, in so far as we can foretell, will remain one to the end of his days. In other words, he has been and will continue to be rewarded in every possible way for his success. Clinton's case is murkier, as will be her legacy. She too has benefited handsomely from her success. And she too will be remembered in American history for being as excellent as she was exceptional. But in the wake of her unexpected and embarrassing defeat in 2016 – in a campaign in which she outspent her opponent by nearly two to one – her presence on the national stage receded. She was no longer considered, even by Democrats, reliably a political asset, and so she stepped back.

Her lust for success was, then, finally frustrated because she failed to get what she most wanted. But it was frustrated not because she had had enough, but because the American people had had enough. As with Tom Brady, all Hillary Clinton's life was a connection between lust and leadership. But in the twilight of their careers his leadership was sought, valued, and appreciated, and hers was not or, at least, not so much. Put differently, with a single exception Brady's lust for success and his leadership were always considered admirable – never offensive. However, Clinton's lust for success and her leadership were sometimes considered admirable – and sometimes offensive. Similarly, with a single exception his lust for success and his leadership were always rewarded – never censured. But her lust for success and her leadership were sometimes rewarded – and sometimes censured.

5   LUST FOR LEGITIMACY

Prelude

"Leaders who lust for *legitimacy* tirelessly claim identity and demand equity."

The lust for legitimacy is about acceptance above all. About leaders who have an intense desire for, a ceaseless drive for, and a ferocious commitment to gaining acceptance for a group – typically though not necessarily the group to which they belong. This group can be identified in different ways, by, for example, gender, race, religion, sexual orientation, or ideology. The key is that it is, relatively, a weaker group that has been stigmatized and ostracized by the stronger group of which it is, nevertheless, a part. By legitimacy, we mean that the latter, the stronger though not necessarily the larger group, has finally come to agree, to accept, that the former, the weaker though not necessarily the smaller group, should be integrated into the whole. That it should be fully a part of the society to which it belongs.

Leaders who lust for legitimacy are, then, driven by their mission. Their mission is to legitimize a previously marginalized group, again, typically a group of which they are a member. Shakespeare's Shylock comes to mind, a character in *The Merchant of Venice* who, as a Jew, was invariably excluded, occasionally persecuted. Why, he asks, rhetorically, bitterly, "I am a Jew. Hath not a Jew eyes? Hath not a Jew hands, organs, dimensions, senses, affections, passions ... If you prick us," he continues, "do we not bleed? If you tickle us, do we not laugh? If you poison us, do we not die?" Shylock's rage at being perpetually relegated, perpetually marginalized, is palpable.

Of course, some leaders seek to legitimize their group while, simultaneously, they seek to further their own interests, such as increasing their power and wealth. Here though the focus is narrow. It is on leaders whose overriding passion, whose insatiable desire, whose unquenchable thirst is to bring into the fold a group that previously deliberately was left out. That previously deliberately was relegated to second class status, or even excluded altogether.

Social movements have been studied for years by, among others, historians, political scientists, and sociologists. The same cannot though be claimed for *leaders* of social movements. As sociologist Aldon Morris put it, their "leadership" cadres have "yet to be adequately theorized."[1] While the reasons for this are not immediately obvious, the collective nature of social movements has likely discouraged researchers from looking at individual leaders as agents of change. Similarly, conversely actually, researchers seem to have been reluctant to assign those who constitute social movements, ordinary people, to what might be perceived as bit parts, to being "merely" followers.[2] Of course, as will be evident by now, our own approach to leaders hell-bent on legitimizing groups that previously were stigmatized and ostracized, is inclusive. Such massive undertakings must be understood by taking account of the leaders themselves, and of their followers; and of the contexts within which their stories unfolded.[3]

Leaders who lust to legitimize a marginalized group knowingly, purposefully, take on a task that is almost overwhelming. Generally, this task is in two stages. First, these leaders must to at least an extent mobilize the weaker group. Second, these leaders must also to at least an extent mobilize the stronger group – people in positions of power as well as the broader public. Therefore, for leaders who lust for legitimacy to realize what they set out to achieve, they must be able to lead both the oppressed *and* the oppressors. As one expert put it, leaders like these must be able to function effectively within the weaker group as "mobilizers," capable of enlisting and inspiring followers. And they must also be able to function effectively within the stronger group as "articulators," capable of communicating to it the urgency, the legitimacy, of their demands.[4] To repeat, this is no mean feat. For it is all too easy for leaders to make enemies within the weaker group that they are seeking to legitimize, and to make enemies within the stronger group that they are seeking to influence.

Leaders such as the two discussed in this chapter face another major challenge. On the one hand, they are trying to create change, to transform society. On the other hand, they are trying to legitimize their groups from the inside – from within the stigmatized, ostracized group of which they are members. This means they have to fight the perception, certainly within the larger society, that they are not, really, leaders, or even suited to be leaders.[5] For example, Americans' traditional mental model of a leader – social scientists call this a "prototypical leader" – has been a straight, white male. Thus, historically, gay leaders, and African American leaders, and women leaders, have been, in effect, excluded from the preferred category, the category of the prototypical leader. No wonder leaders who seek legitimacy must be lusty – must be fiercely determined and tirelessly driven. For the odds against them – against leaders driven to legitimize, from within, a group that society has delegitimized – are dauntingly high.

What are leaders who lust for legitimacy to do? Given the deck stacked against them, how can they increase the probability that their goal – to change society in some significant way – will be reached? Research suggests several steps: first, defining the problem; second, proposing a solution; third, modeling the action; and fourth getting others to sign on, to join in, to follow.[6] Some of these tasks are strategic. For example, leaders who seek to define the problem must be able clearly to articulate the group's – the weaker group's – grievances.[7] Generally, these grievances are best based on moral imperatives – for example, injustice and unfairness – that make clear the deficits of the existing social order – the social order in which the stronger group excludes and indeed squelches the weaker group.

Others of these tasks are tactical – leaders who lust for legitimacy must be prepared to propose tactics that seem at least as if they might create change.[8] Such leaders must, in other words, be prepared with some answers to this question: What, specifically, concretely, can be done, can be done *now*, that might right what's wrong, that might fix what's broken? One of the challenges is to get people in both groups – the weaker and the stronger one – to picture a future that looks dramatically different from the present and the past.[9] The Reverend Dr. Martin Luther King's "I Have a Dream" speech is an example, a towering example, of what we mean when we say that one of the tasks of leaders who lust for legitimacy is to picture a future that is unfamiliar – but that seems nevertheless to be within reach:

> I have a dream that one day this nation will rise up and live out the true meaning of its creed: "We hold these truths to be self-evident that all men are created equal" . . . I have a dream that one day even the state of Mississippi, a state sweltering with the heat of injustice, sweltering with the heat of oppression, will be transformed into an oasis of freedom and justice. I have a dream that my four little children will one day live in a nation where they will not be judged by the color of their skin but by the content of their character.[10]

Among the numberless strengths of King's speech is its extreme simplicity. It caught the nation's attention on the spot, then and there, in 1963, at the Lincoln Memorial. Then, in time, it was recognized as a rhetorical masterpiece – simple but not in the least simplistic. Pricking the conscience and, in consequence, securing support from the oppressor as well as the oppressed is an achievement exceedingly infrequent.[11]

Leaders who lust for legitimacy in their fight for a "just society" draw on seeming endless reservoirs of effort – mental, physical, even spiritual.[12] Such sacrifices incur costs that can and often do include good health, stable relationships, and general well-being. To wit King who, among his other tribulations, was beaten and jailed and finally assassinated. It's why at least some of today's activists and organizers speak to the need for "self-care." It is important, we are now told, that leaders who lust for legitimacy avoid getting burned out, too tired and spent to go on. For example, Alexandria Ocasio-Cortez, the star Congresswoman from New York's 14th Congressional District, announced after months of hard campaigning to become the youngest woman ever elected to Congress that she was taking a week off. "Self-care is important for activists," she said, "because without it we will burn out and walk away."[13]

We render no judgment. We do, however, note for the record that leaders who legitimately lust for legitimacy – "social justice warriors" they are sometimes called – seem not only willing but compelled to burn the candle at both ends. Certainly, the two leaders profiled in this chapter, Nelson Mandela and Larry Kramer, did just that. Neither took a tempered approach, or tempered even for one moment their rage, their outrage at the burdens their constituents, the oppressed, were being obliged by their oppressors to bear. To the contrary. Mandela especially, extremely, and to a lesser extent Kramer, suffered for their causes because it seemed to them that without their suffering they would fail. They would fail to get to where they were hell-bent on going. It was precisely this – their ceaseless ferocity, their relentless tenaciousness, and their willingness to sacrifice – that made them so effective. And so attractive – attractive to the legions who followed where they led.

Finally, there is this. For a leader to lust for legitimacy is not, by definition, for a leader to be good. Such leaders are not necessarily effective, nor are they necessarily ethical. Different groups can and do have different conceptions of what is right and good and true. Here, however, we chose to accentuate the positive. In particular, we ignore leaders of, say, neo-Nazi groups in favor of leaders who lusted against all odds to legitimize, in the first case, black men, women, and children in South Africa; and, in the second case, gay men and, by extension, gay women, in the United States. Of both Mandela and Kramer, it must be said that they were both effective and ethical.

Nelson Mandela

Nelson Mandela was born in 1918 into the royal Thembu family of the Xhosa tribe in what was then British South Africa. Mandela studied law and it was as a lawyer that he first worked in Johannesburg, then as now South Africa's largest city. Early on he became involved in African nationalist politics: he joined the African National Congress (ANC) in 1943 and, not long after, he co-founded the ANC's Youth League. In 1948, the white-only government instituted apartheid, a system of racial segregation and discrimination that codified privileging the white minority over the black majority and other non-white minorities. In virtually immediate response, Mandela and the ANC committed themselves to abolishing apartheid, a system that allowed, indeed institutionalized one group's claim to supremacy while simultaneously denying every other group even a semblance of fairness.

Effectively lifelong Mandela sought to right what was wrong and to to legitimize the majority group – black South Africans – of which he was a member. First his tactics were peaceful. When these failed, he turned militant. In consequence of his armed resistance, he was sentenced to prison, where during the longest of his sentences he remained for over twenty-seven years. Being behind bars did not, however, stop or even slow him. It was during his time behind bars that he developed into a leader, into the great leader who spearheaded the movement against apartheid not only at home, within South Africa, but abroad.

In February 1990, Mandela was finally released from prison. Several years later, in 1994, aged 75, he was elected South Africa's first post-apartheid president. Nelson Mandela – lawyer, anti-apartheid activist, and longtime political prisoner – would serve in this capacity until June 1999. As South Africa's first non-white head of state, he viewed his task primarily as the "reconciliation and unity of a society divided by racial hatred," though he began also to address some of the near overwhelming problems facing his country, such as extreme poverty and radical inequality.[14] In 1999 Mandela officially retired from politics, but his lust for legitimacy did not cease. Until his death at the age of 95, he continued to be a tireless, tenacious leader for Black South Africans, and an advocate for human rights the world over.

Context

Mandela himself testified to the importance of context. "I have done whatever I did, both as an individual and as a leader of my people, because of my experience in South Africa and my own proudly felt African background, and not because of what any outsider might have said."[15] His family and the tribal community within which he was raised are key to understanding the genesis of his lust for legitimacy, and what drove him to try to satisfy his lust even at enormous risk. Mandela's father was chief of his tribe, and he was a principal counselor to the acting king of the Thembu people. Mandela, then, was raised in a strong, powerful family group, which makes it easy to understand why he especially was infuriated and affronted by apartheid, which was institutionalized when he was 30 years old.

After the death of his father, Mandela, still a boy, was adopted by a high-ranking Thembu regent who began grooming him for a position of tribal leadership. Mandela has described the impact of being singled out early in life: "As a leader, I have always followed the principles I first saw demonstrated by the regent at the Great Palace. I have always endeavored to listen to what each and every person in a discussion had to say before venturing my own opinion. Oftentimes, my own opinion will simply represent a consensus."[16] Mandela's emphasis on consensus sheds additional light on why apartheid – which, by definition, devalued and denigrated the other – was so enduringly enraging to him especially.

The key context for leaders who lust for legitimacy is the societies – *their* societies – that deny it. Between 1948 and 1994, when apartheid was finally abolished, South Africa was obviously an extreme case in point, an extreme case of a context of denial and deprivation. It was also a complicated one. In 1652, Dutch settlers arrived in South Africa. Many of their descendants stayed and then settled there, permanently, in time developing their own language, Afrikaans, and becoming known as "Boers," farmers. At the end of the eighteenth century newcomers arrived: British settlers (and the powerful British Navy) came and they also stayed, setting off almost a century of wars that pitted the Boers against the British, while also ensnaring Africans in their conflicts. In the end, after the Anglo-Boer War which the British won, South Africa came under the control of the British Empire.

To solidify their rule, the British empowered the white minority at the expense of the black majority. These efforts met almost immediately with resistance, notably among black South African activists who in 1912 formed the African National Congress. When Mandela joined the group, some thirty years later, he was 25 years old. Within a year he helped to establish the previously mentioned ANC Youth League, which, notably, was more ambitious and aggressive than the ANC itself. After the Second World War, as the British started to scale back their global empire, South African whites pushed for, and gradually won, complete independence from Britain. (South Africa became a Republic in 1960.) But they also expanded the system of racial dominance and, in time, they institutionalized it.

Apartheid – and the lack of legitimacy to which it subjected the black South African majority – was the context within which Mandela as a leader came to maturity. Apartheid was the law: it determined where people were permitted to live, who they were permitted to marry, and what types of jobs they were permitted to have. While all non-white groups were discriminated against, blacks were the most egregiously excluded. Not only were they barred from voting, and from holding office, they were denied citizenship. Further they were forced to live physically apart – in "homelands" and "townships" – a handful of which resembled remote suburbs, but most of which were vast camps, or shantytowns.

Black opposition to the white regime naturally grew, and it intensified. The government, in turn, continued to resist the resisters. In fact, the regime dug in. Throughout the 1960s, 1970s, and 1980s, the fight over apartheid became increasingly rancorous, then violent, then, from time to time, lethal. One infamous event was in 1960, the "Sharpeville Massacre," named for the town in which it took place. After a day of protests, the crowd, estimated at between five and seven thousand, descended on the local police station. The police responded by opening fire. According to a BBC account, men, women, and children fled "like rabbits" as up to 300 officers began randomly shooting at the assembled crowd.[17] When it was over 69 people had been killed and 180 injured.[18]

Was the crowd peaceful? Did some people hurl stones? The accounts varied, of course, but the impact of the Sharpeville Massacre was in any case enormous. The authorities, now scared, redoubled their effort once and for all to silence the opposition. Instead of trying to curb anti-apartheid protesters they attempted to shut them down altogether – by whatever means necessary. Measures that ensued included: outlawing the African National Congress and a second anti-apartheid group, the Pan Africanist Congress; expanding restrictions on press freedoms; revoking black workers' rights, including their right to organize and to strike; and forcibly removing three-and-a-half million black South Africans from their homes in what became designated "white areas" and obliging them to resettle in the Bantustans, territories set aside for blacks. When the ANC responded, arguably predictably, by switching from non-violent resistance to violent resistance, so far as the government was concerned Nelson Mandela was transformed from political opponent into implacable terrorist.

Mandela had, however, been in trouble, sometimes in dangerous trouble, with the law for years. Charges against him included leaving the country without a passport; incitement; sabotage; conspiring to overthrow the government; and high treason. In 1962, he was sentenced to five years' imprisonment. In 1964, he received the life sentence of which he ultimately served more than twenty-seven years. Inevitably, then, prison was a context of consequence. His nearly three decades behind bars – the extraordinarily high price he paid for his lust to legitimize black South Africans – did many things, including making him a man of major stature and a leader forever to be reckoned with. This small story, told by a fellow prisoner, suggests Mandela's leadership role, even in jail. On the way to the quarry where they were forced to work, "the prison authorities would rush us ... 'Hardloop!' That meant run ... It was Nelson who said: 'Comrades let's be slower than ever.' It was clear therefore that the steps we were taking would make it impossible ever to reach the quarry where we were going to. They were compelled to negotiate with Nelson."[19]

Over time, and depending on who was running the prison, certain privileges were granted to Mandela, including permission to study. ANC member and Communist Party stalwart Mac Maharaj, similarly incarcerated, remembers this as occasioning an argument with Mandela while simultaneously it signaled his maturation as a leader: "He was urging us to study Afrikaans and I was saying no way – this is the language of the damn oppressor. Mandela [replied], 'Mac, we are in for a protracted war. You can't dream of ambushing the enemy if you can't understand the general commanding the forces. You have to read their literature and poetry; you have to understand their culture so that you get into the mind of the general.'"[20]

Mandela was behind bars from approximately the age of 44 to 71. His legendary leadership cannot be understood independent of this circumstance.

Evidence

Mandela's lust to leave a legacy was in evidence until the day he died. "There is no passion to be found playing small – in settling for a life that is less than the one you are capable of living," he once said.[21] More dramatically, after he and several others were convicted and sentenced to life imprisonment in Rivonia in 1964, he testified in an open courtroom to his willingness, his readiness, to pay the ultimate price for the cause in which he believed. "I have cherished the ideal of a democratic and free society in which all persons live together in harmony and with equal opportunities. It is an ideal which I hope to live for and to achieve. But if needs be, it is an ideal for which I am prepared to die."[22]

There is no more powerful and persuasive evidence of Nelson Mandela's lust for legitimacy than his transformation from believer in non-violent resistance to believer in *violent* resistance. An early apostle of Mahatma Gandhi and his tactics of civil disobedience, of non-violent resistance, it was precisely the failure of such tactics that convinced Mandela that he no longer had a choice. That in order to force an end to apartheid, and to finish it off once and for all, the only recourse was resistance that resorted to violence.

In consequence of his change of heart, and of mind, in 1961 Mandela co-founded Umkhonto we Sizwe (MK) – "Spear of the Nation." He became the first leader of MK, which, as its name, Spear of the Nation, suggests, was a new, armed wing of the ANC. At his trial in 1964 he described the reason for his radical departure from the ANC's original and long-held adherence to non-violence. "[It] would be wrong and unrealistic for African leaders to continue preaching peace and nonviolence at a time when the government met our peaceful demands with force. It was only when all else had failed, when all channels of peaceful protest had been barred to us, that the decision was made to embark on violent forms of political struggle."[23] So when we say that Mandela *fought* for legitimacy, we mean it literally. His lust to legitimize black South Africans, to secure for them complete acceptance, took him to a place that neither Gandhi nor another one of his disciples, Martin Luther King, Jr., ever chose to go. Possibly if not probably because, as they perceived it, they were never forced by their circumstances into doing so.

Actions speak louder than words. But Mandela's words also provide strong evidence of his lust for legitimacy. During that same trial in Rivonia, Mandela spoke eloquently about the injustices ordinary black South Africans were every day obliged to endure. He described their dehumanization and their delegitimization as they aspired to do no more than to lead ordinary, normal lives. He described the effects of enforced poverty, including the breakdown of family life. Children wandered the streets of townships, Mandela explained, because they had no money for school – or no school to go to. In other words, he painted a profoundly disturbing picture of the everyday degradations of black South Africans and of their desire, their demand, for the entry and equity that they were still being denied.

Mandela's lust to legitimize his people is also in evidence in his unusual refusal to accept the government's bid to release him from prison in exchange for his willingness in some way to compromise. For instance, in 1985, Mandela was offered his freedom by South African President, P. W. Botha. However, there was a catch, a string attached. In return for his release he had publicly to reject violence as a political tactic. Mandela turned down the offer. "What freedom am I being offered," he asked, "while the organization of the people remains banned? Only free men can negotiate. A prisoner cannot enter into contracts."[24] Similarly he wrote to his daughter from jail, "I cannot and will not give any undertaking at a time when I and you, the people, are not free."[25]

As the years dragged on, the government of South Africa attempted a measure of conciliation: it tried to persuade black South Africans to work within the existing system. But, Mandela's repeated refusals to be co-opted paved the way for others also to insist on more than incremental reform, and to insist that apartheid be abolished entirely and forever. "Many more people might have succumbed to this false promise of gradual change were it not for [Mandela's] example," said Patrick Lakota, a leader of the United Democratic Front, a coalition formed in the early 1980s to combat apartheid.[26] As Mandela himself put it, "If white leaders do not act in good faith toward us, if they will not meet with us to discuss political equality and if, in effect, they tell us we must remain subjugated by whites, then there is really no alternative other than violence."[27]

Mandela's increasingly militant stance led to his final arrest, when he was imprisoned for sabotage and conspiring to overthrow the state. At the end of his trial, as his sentence of life in prison was read aloud, his face broke into a wide smile. And just before he was put on the truck that took him to jail, presumably for life, amid cheers from the crowd that had assembled he raised his thumbs in a gesture of *victory*. Mandela was by no means a masochist – he most certainly did not seek punishment and suffering. But because effectively lifelong he had lusted for legitimacy, he was, apparently, at peace despite his sentence, knowing full well that his claim to acceptance had become an ineluctable, unstoppable, integral part of South Africa's political life.

What Mandela endured during his nearly three decades in prison is impossible fully to imagine. The deprivations took almost every conceivable form, all for the cause that had become in effect his life. Still Mandela refused in any way to compromise or be co-opted. Anything short of a full retreat from apartheid was rejected as unacceptable. On February 11, 1990, he was finally released from prison, unconditionally, a hero in South Africa, and a hero in much of the rest of the world as well. Thus began four years of negotiations with the South African government, with Mandela, now president of the African National Congress, straddling an extremely fine line between continuing to demand an end to apartheid on the one hand, and striving to reach a reasonable agreement with the South African government on the other hand.

It was an almost impossible task, the extremes at both ends of the political spectrum making the discussions inordinately complex and difficult not only for Mandela, but for his white South African counterpart, President F. W. de Klerk. It took four hard years for the two men finally to hammer out an agreement. For their efforts on behalf of all South Africans, in 1993 they were awarded the Nobel Peace Prize, jointly. It cited "their work for the peaceful termination of the apartheid regime, and for laying the foundations for a new democratic South Africa." In April 1994, South Africa held its first national, open, all-race democratic elections. Mandela's African National Congress won a sweeping victory and shortly thereafter he, as the president of his party, was formally elected South Africa's first black chief executive. By this time Nelson Mandela's fame was so great that his presidential inaugural speech in May 1994 was televised; some one *billion* people watched worldwide. But, from the outset, the newly elected chief executive made clear that he would serve as president for only one term.

Nelson Mandela's retirement from the day-to-day combat of politics did not signal his retirement from fighting for the causes in which he believed. Almost immediately after leaving office, in 1999, he founded the Nelson Mandela Foundation. Its mission was to "provide people and politics with the relevant tools [so that] there can be informed discussions that lead to justice and freedom for all."[28] Justice and freedom not just for *some* people, or for *most* people, but justice and freedom for *all* people. Toward the end of Mandela's long life he sought to include yet another stigmatized and ostracized group, those living with HIV/AIDS. In 2000 one quarter of South Africans between the ages of 15 and 45 tested positive for the virus.[29] So, Mandela – who had come to regret that as president he had not done more for victims of the disease – decided to act. With a groundbreaking speech at an International AIDS conference in Durban, he "single-handedly set a new agenda for the future fight against HIV/AIDS." It was a fight in which he remained engaged until his death in 2013.[30]

Followers

In the mid-1980s the world slowly woke to the plight of black South Africans living under apartheid. Although Mandela was still behind bars, he managed to speak so people could hear, not only at home but abroad. How did he do it? How was he able to persuade South Africans, and Americans, and Europeans, and people from all parts of the world to follow where he led? After all, Mandela spent the first eighteen of his twenty-seven years locked away in a prison on Robben Island, a remote place notorious for its brutal regime. He was, moreover, confined to a small cell without a bed or plumbing and forced to do hard labor in a quarry.[31] So, again, under these conditions how was he able to lead?

Essentially the answer is this: Nelson Mandela managed to be heard, to continue to protest, from behind bars through any and all contacts with humans, however brief and infrequent. In the beginning, he was permitted to meet with a single visitor, once a year, for 30 minutes. Additionally, he was able once every six months to write a letter, and once every six months to receive a letter. Over time and depending on the ways and whims of prison officials, the number of visits he was permitted began gradually to increase. As did the number of letters and messages he was permitted to send and receive. Mandela's missives were written not just for the benefit of family members, who typically were the ostensible recipients. Rather they were penned specifically to be shared widely. Mandela also relied on the assistance of his fellow prisoners, especially the visitors they were allowed to have, some of whom smuggled out letters and other documents all intended further to fuel what in time became the accelerating anti-apartheid movement. By 1976, Mandela had managed even to write an autobiography, which he also arranged to have smuggled out, in this case by a prisoner who was being released.

Mandela was able to inspire, to enlist on his behalf, even a few of his jailers, of whom Christo Brand is an example. Brand was an Afrikaner who, despite his race and ethnicity, and in spite of being one of Nelson Mandela's guards for over a decade, became a confidant and, later, an accomplice who helped him to keep in contact with other activists and others who were politically like-minded. Mandela was Brand's captive, but this captive treated his captor as his friend. Mandela encouraged Brand to continue his studies, he congratulated him on his marriage, and he expressed pleasure and excitement at the birth of Brand's children. Over time, then, Christo Brand became Nelson Mandela's friend – and Nelson Mandela's follower.

Most important of all though was Winnie Mandela, not exactly a follower perhaps, but certainly a fellow traveler, a like-minded woman, deeply committed also to the anti-apartheid movement, who, since 1958 had been Nelson Mandela's second wife. Winnie Mandela followed her husband's lead: she too was an activist fiercely opposed to apartheid; she too rose to prominence within the anti-apartheid movement; and she too was willing to take enormous risks and make enormous sacrifices for the cause in which she believed. (Winnie Mandela herself was tortured and she spent several months in solitary confinement.) In fact, during most of the twenty-seven years that Nelson Mandela was in jail, it was his wife who was his public face. This meant, in effect, that she along with her husband became by far the most public and prominent faces of the anti-apartheid movement. Winnie Mandela's legacy turned out to be complicated and mixed at best; moreover, she and Nelson Mandela divorced not long after he was released from prison. Still, during the many years of his incarceration she was his tireless constituent and advocate.

As Mandela's fame grew along with the anti-apartheid movement, he and his cause became a phenomenon not only at home but abroad. He understood that the media had "shrunk the world and [has] in the process become a great weapon for eradicating ignorance and promoting democracy."[32] And he understood that he and the messages he sent were grist for the media mill. So he played into what had become "a relentless explosion of media attention that grew until the day Mandela was finally released."[33] Mandela had become an international star whose mission it was to urge his followers forward by calling on "democrats of all races" to unite, to mobilize, and to fight on. "Between the anvil of united mass action and the hammer of the armed struggle, we shall crush apartheid and white minority racist rule. . . . The whole world is on our side."[34]

Given the moral basis on which he made his claim, the ethical foundation on which he stood his ground, political and religious leaders from all over the world fell into line – they called for Mandela's release. The United Nations created a Special Commission

Against Apartheid. Members of the United States Congress formally requested permission to travel to South Africa not to visit with the head of state, but to see Nelson Mandela. Universities everywhere bestowed on him honorary degrees while he was still in prison. In short, even from behind bars Mandela had managed to become a global symbol for the "struggle for freedom, human dignity, and resistance to apartheid."[35]

By this time there was no going back. The calls for his release and the end of apartheid became increasingly, relentlessly, more rancorous and clamorous. In his celebrated, if controversial Graceland tour (1987), singer Paul Simon sang, "Bring Him Back Home," explicitly requesting that Mandela be freed. Similarly, in what was an unprecedentedly large and star-studded media event, anti-apartheid activists produced a ten-hour concert at Wembley Stadium in London (1988): the Free Nelson Mandela Concert. Luminaries such as Whitney Houston, George Michael, and Phil Collins were among those who shone their light on the case of Nelson Mandela – and his cause. The concert filled the enormous stadium; the performances were televised worldwide.[36] Almost miraculously – well before the advent of social media – Mandela led large swaths of people and the rest of the world followed. It goes almost without saying that the more followers he had, the more clout he had. And the more constrained were the South African authorities in dealing with the man who had become a world-famous political prisoner. South African archbishop and fellow freedom fighter Desmond Tutu explained the phenomenon this way: "[Mandela's] imprisonment represents our oppression. His self-sacrifice is what we would all like to be in resisting that oppression."[37]

Of course, nowhere was Mandela more revered than in South Africa itself. Graffiti reading, "Mandela is with us!" were painted on the walls of black urban ghettos. His picture appeared in clandestinely printed anti-apartheid pamphlets, posters, and banners. Songs about him and poems about him were performed in townships across the country. Children were named after him even in the most remote villages. So successful was Nelson Mandela at securing followers, that when he was released from prison in 1990, hundreds of journalists and television crews from all over the world descended on South Africa to make their way to the dusty street outside his home in Soweto, to meet him, to greet him, to see him in the flesh and to hear him speak.

When Mandela got out of jail, he appeared astonishingly free of rancor. There was no evident trace of bitterness toward anyone – not toward government officials, not toward his jailors, not toward his political opponents. Instead, to avoid what he most feared, civil war, he used his moral authority to champion South African reconciliation, along with cooperation, collaboration, and nation-building. For example, he strongly supported South Africa's "Committee for Truth and Reconciliation," a court-like restorative justice body that was charged with investigating crimes committed under apartheid from 1960 to 1994. What made the committee unique was that its goal was not to prosecute or punish, but rather to encourage mutual acknowledgment of what both sides had inflicted, all sides had inflicted, on the other. It was another way of conferring legitimacy on black South Africans without depriving white South Africans of their claim to the same.

Mandela's commitment to inclusion had its genesis in his lust for legitimacy. Not supremacy, just legitimacy. Mandela understood that to secure the legitimacy he sought and had fought for all his life, bringing together the antagonists, in some semblance of comity, was critical. His lust was for acceptance and respect, not for obedience or even deference. Not for nothing did Barack Obama compare South Africa's Nelson Mandela to America's George Washington.

Hindsight

Nelson Mandela never gave up. In fact, he remarked, "A winner is a dreamer who never gives up."[38] He was tireless even in his retirement years, continuing to serve as a "globally recognized ambassador for a multiracial South Africa, the conscience of his continent and an inspiration for strugglers against oppression everywhere."[39] He was never going to fade quietly into the history books, and so his work continued as he continued to lend his "tireless support to the fight against social injustice and poverty in South Africa and beyond." Not at this point in his life, through sustained political protests, whether non-violent or violent, but rather though sustained fundraising, most notably on behalf of the Nelson Mandela Foundation and the Nelson Mandela Children's Fund.[40]

He was not yet done fighting. In his new role as an advocate for sufferers of AIDS, Mandela went so far as publicly to criticize Thabo Mbeki, his successor as president as well as his close colleague and personal friend, for his prevarication in combating the disease. Mandela set up the HIV/AIDS charity 46664 – named after his prison number on Robben Island – and in 2003 he recruited stars such as Bono and Beyoncé to perform at a fundraising concert in Cape Town.

Mandela's single regret? Not spending "more time with his loved ones."[41] By his own testimony he gave himself fully, wholly, to the fight first for the end of apartheid in South Africa, then for reconciliation in South Africa, and finally for freedom and justice everywhere. He "never stopped pursuing the justice and equality that he knew all people deserved."[42] Toward the end of his life, in 2007, he co-founded "The Elders," a group of widely respected former statesmen and world leaders dedicated to bringing their expertise, experience, and moral authority to bear on the world's most pressing political and social issues. Members included Archbishop Desmond Tutu, former UN Secretary-General Kofi Annan, and former US President Jimmy Carter.

But while his stamina was seemingly never ending, the magnitude of the tasks he took on was almost overwhelming. Mandela's accomplishments were – to state the obvious – historic. But even he could not as if by magic transform South Africa into a land of milk and honey for everyone. The truth is that twenty-five years after its first post-apartheid election, South Africa remains a place of enormous disparities and inequities – political, economic, and social. The gap between rich and poor in South Africa is wider than in any other country where comparable data exist.[43] Further, "both racial identity and racism remain fixtures of South African life."[44] The average lifespan for black South Africans is about 50 years, while for white South Africans it is about 70 years.[45] Additionally, a series of brazen corruption scandals involving a series of South African leaders has badly tarnished the reputation of Mandela's beloved African National Congress. The data are disheartening if not downright depressing. "They suggest that South Africa has done *worse* over the last five years than any other country in the world except for those in a state of war."[46]

Nelson Mandela was a singular leader – and the change he created was of singular consequence. But an enormous amount of work remains to be done. Mandela made it possible for black South Africans to claim legitimacy. But he did not, he could not, make it possible for them to claim equity.

Larry Kramer

Larry Kramer was a writer and activist who is considered one of the most important leaders of the gay rights movement – if not *the* most important. He was critical to drawing attention to the cause. And he was instrumental in establishing both the Gay Men's Health Crisis (GMHC) organization and the protest group, ACT UP. Through his writing, speaking, and his, no two ways about it, over-the-top acting up and acting out, he stirred controversy in the gay community and beyond, including the political, medical, and pharmaceutical establishments.

For over four decades, Kramer was an angry, furious in fact, advocate for the legitimacy of gay men. To straight America, in 2007 he had this to say: "Our own country's democratic process declares us to be unequal, which means, in a democracy, that our enemy is you ... You treat us like crumbs. You hate us. And sadly, we let you."[47] Speaking at a leadership forum, he remarked: "If I were to teach anything here it would be how to confront the system, not work within it. Hit it over the head with a bat and take no prisoners."[48] Kramer was a leader who lusted for legitimacy because, as his words make clear, he fervently believed that for far too long the dominant heterosexual culture, notably in the United States, either ignored or flat out hated gay men and gay life. He was convinced that the dominant heterosexual culture denied gay men their legitimacy.

Kramer became intensely involved in the gay rights movement during the AIDS crisis of the 1980s and 1990s. All along though, his overarching concern was with how the gay male community generally was faring in a world that remained, as he perceived it, implacably hostile. Kramer always wore his own gay identity loudly and proudly. Hence his activism, though it was triggered by the AIDS crisis, was not only about AIDS. What it really was about was gaining legitimacy for gays – acceptance in every sense of this word and in every aspect of American life.

Kramer's lust for legitimacy was always focused on gay men. It is impossible, however, to separate his fight for the rights of gay men from the larger war within which Kramer played such a critical part. Kramer was a path breaker in the quest for LGBTQ rights more generally – for the rights of those who identify as lesbian, or gay, or bisexual, or transgender, or, more recently, queer. Kramer was one of the leading "social warriors" of the rights revolutions of the last decades of the twentieth century. Though for reasons that remain not fully clear, Kramer's name is still not well known, but there is no doubt that his work was transformative. It is work for which he will forever be remembered.

Context

Larry Kramer's life was strongly affected by his relationship with his father, which was contentious. His father was disappointed – some have said disgusted – by what he perceived to be his son's insufficiently sturdy, read manly, behavior. Kramer's own accounts were unflinching: "I could never do anything right," he recalled. "He [his father] always picked on me and yelled at me and occasionally hit me. I was a creative person whose creativity was always looked on as suspect by my parents."[49] However, Kramer also remembered that he would fight back, that even though he was shy as a boy, he would give almost as good as he got, not physically, but verbally, refusing for the most part meekly to tolerate his father's taunts. Kramer's memory of standing up even as a child to his father's diminishment and disapproval seems to have been the platform on which he stood as a man. Society generally outright rejected or at least repudiated Kramer's homosexuality – which, in turn, triggered in his adulthood that which it had triggered in his childhood. Anger. And, then, almost immediately thereafter, a fierce impulse to fight back. To fight back hard. To use words as weapons with which to hit back at those who dared to target him and his kind.

However, if Kramer's family taught him how to hate, it also taught him how to love. Arthur Kramer, his older brother by eight years, was the athletic, and heterosexual, son that was their father's imagined ideal. By all accounts, if Arthur Kramer was his father's ideal son, he was also Larry Kramer's ideal brother, a brother whose love for Larry rivaled his father's disdain. Arthur pulled his brother "out of trouble all the time." Larry himself recalled that, "When I went to Yale and tried to commit suicide by taking 200 aspirins, Arthur came and took care of me. At 30, when I came out of the closet, Arthur understood. And although he does not support gay causes openly, he supports me."[50] According to Kramer's good friend, writer Calvin Trillin, Arthur Kramer "was the single best big brother in the world, and the most tested. If there was a way to find out whether he could push Arthur away, Larry explored it . . . And no, there wasn't a way."[51]

The context within which Kramer – he was born in 1935 – experienced his early adulthood was notable for, among other things, the various rights revolutions, including the sexual revolution. During the 1960s and 1970s, traditional codes of behavior relating to relationships and, especially, to sexuality, were initially challenged and then, often as not, tossed into the dustbin of history. One of the many changes that characterized this period was the increased visibility of – though not yet the widespread acceptance of – homosexuality. During this period, Kramer was living in New York, one of the several epicenters of the sexual revolution. Though later he would come to criticize it, particularly in his 1978 novel, *Faggots*, contemporaneously Kramer took part in the urban gay culture of cruising and promiscuous sex typical of that time and place.

It was also during the 1970s that Larry Kramer first met and fell in love with David Webster. Kramer was deeply serious, but Webster had no interest, at least not then, in settling down which, predictably, infuriated Kramer who, in turn, got back at Webster by viciously satirizing him in *Faggots*. The rift between the two men was so great that for more than decade they did not speak.[52] Then, in 1992, Kramer asked Webster, who had gone on to become an architect of note, to design a house for him. Their relationship was rekindled and this time it blossomed – the two men married in 2013 – just as Kramer had always wanted.[53] This matters to the chronicle of Kramer because his feelings for Webster, his enduring love for the man who became his husband, are ones that Kramer had long wanted, desperately, to be able to claim – publicly. But because gay men were stigmatized and ostracized, most had to think carefully about "coming out." In fact, most chose carefully to conceal their sexual identity – many if not most still do – and to hide it indefinitely from public view.

In Kramer's long, complicated life the most significant of the many circumstances within which he was embedded was the AIDS epidemic of the 1980s. Of course, LGBTQ people had been delegitimized in, and by, American society long before AIDS. However, the disease, the fearful plague that was AIDS in the early days, electrified Kramer the writer and, simultaneously, Kramer the activist. It provided the context, the frame, within which he could see with complete clarity the degree to which gay men, who at the time were much the most threatened by the disease, had been marginalized and relegated. Gay men were so far from being *legitimate* members of American society that they could "die like flies" and no one – including the government and the medical establishment – would lift a finger to help. "AIDS changed everything," Kramer later recalled. "In [Greenwich] Village, you couldn't walk down the street without running into somebody who said: 'Have you heard about so-and-so? He just died.' Sometimes you could learn about three or four people just walking the dog. I started making a list of how many people I knew, and it was hundreds."[54]

The AIDS crisis was the trigger for the most intense of Kramer's enduring angers. He lashed out at health care workers who refused to treat people with AIDS. He lashed out at the medical and pharmaceutical establishments which, as he saw it, were responsible for finding a cure but chose not to do so because they did not care or, at least, they did not care enough. He lashed out at gay men themselves, for refusing to curb their sexual appetites, for refusing to restrain their inclinations and proclivities, even if doing so would save their lives and those of their sexual partners. And he lashed out at the political system for failing to provide the necessary supports for victims of AIDS which is why, in 1981, he convened the first meeting, in his Greenwich Village apartment, of what later became the Gay Men's Health Crisis – one of the earliest and most ambitious of what eventually became many different AIDS service organizations. And again, years later, when Kramer had a bitter falling out with the people at GMHC, he went right ahead and founded (with others) an even more confrontational organization, AIDS Coalition to Unleash Power – or, simply, "ACT UP."

It is impossible to understand Larry Kramer's lust for legitimacy – the levels of his ambition, determination, and driving rage – without understanding just how horrifying was the AIDS epidemic before anyone had figured out what the hell was going on. In 1982 and 1983, almost nothing was known about the disease. At first it was called "the gay cancer," because no one knew what it was. The only thing that was known, indeed crystal clear, was that people, mainly gay men, were dying from AIDS in awful ways and at frightening rates. In 1982 (the first year of the Center for Disease Control's surveillance of AIDS in the United States), 451 people died of AIDS; by 1985 that number had climbed to 7,000.[55]

Kramer recognized the importance of the AIDS crisis to him personally and politically, and in motivating him to play a major leadership role. "I was able to support myself as a [successful] writer and I didn't feel particularly ostracized. It wasn't until AIDS came along that I was faced with the very stark reality that it didn't make any difference if I had money in the bank or had gone to Yale. My success wasn't going to make anybody pay attention to what was happening."[56] The more aware he became of what was happening, the more angry and more active he grew. Ultimately, the more active he became, the more driven he became in his lust for legitimacy on behalf of gay men. (Kramer was himself diagnosed with AIDS, though not until 1987.)

Another context of consequence was the Holocaust – the Nazis' persecutions and eventual mass murders of Jews and homosexuals. On a trip to Germany in 1984, Kramer visited Dachau, the site of a concentration camp just outside Munich. He was surprised to learn that it was set up not long after Hitler came to power, in 1933, and that neither the German people nor anyone else did anything at any point to shut it down. Kramer concluded there was a parallel between Germany in the 1930s and the United States in the 1980s. In both cases outcomes were being determined not only by perpetrators, but also by bystanders. By people who were aware of what was happening but who chose, deliberately, for their own reasons, to say nothing and do nothing while other people, people who had been delegitimized, were being hounded to death.

After that trip to Germany, Larry Kramer referred to the AIDS epidemic as a "Holocaust" because just as Europe had failed to respond when the Nazis did their dirty work, so did the United States fail to respond when AIDS began to kill gay men. "We are being exterminated just like the Jews were in the Holocaust," he declared, "only we have the chance now to fight back ... I don't understand why every gay person in America isn't as angry as I am."[57] While one can debate whether the two "Holocausts" are comparable, to Larry Kramer they were. When he published a collection of his observations on the epidemic, in 1989, he titled it, *Reports from the Holocaust: The Making of an AIDS Activist.*

Evidence

Larry Kramer, the author, and Larry Kramer, the activist, were both driven by the same impulse: his lust for legitimacy. After the AIDS crisis erupted, Kramer determined to use his pen as a weapon. To use his essays and articles, novels and plays, to skewer whoever needed to be skewered to ensure the disease would not be ignored. In 1981, he led by addressing his primary constituency: gay American men who had to be made to understand the growing threat posed by what then was still a little-known illness. The opening lines of one of his most famous essays, titled, "1,112 and Counting," read, "If this article doesn't scare the shit out of you, we're in real trouble. If this article doesn't rouse you to anger, fury, rage, and action, gay men may have no future on this earth. Our continued existence depends on just how angry you can get."[58] He goes on to rage against the National Institutes of Health, the Centers for Disease Control, Memorial Sloan-Kettering Cancer Center, New York City Mayor Ed Koch, and insurance companies, all for their collective failure to value the lives of gay men. Then he goes on to vent every bit as virulently against promiscuous gay men for failing to value their own lives and those of their sexual partners. Interestingly, even his novel, *Faggots*, written before the appearance of AIDS, struck a blow on behalf of the dignity of gay men. "*Faggots* struck a chord," wrote Andrew Sullivan, an openly gay political commentator. "It exuded a sense that gay men could do better if they understood themselves as fully human, if they could shed their self-loathing and self-deception."[59]

Kramer also reacted to the AIDS crisis by transforming into something he had never been before – an activist. He intended now to lead – to change hearts and minds – not only through the power of his pen but through the power of political action. As he saw it, the epidemic required an immediate, massive response designed to get the attention of at least three constituencies: first, those most affected, gay men themselves; second, those in the medical and pharmaceutical establishments with the expertise effectively to tackle the disease; and third, everyone else, from powerful politicians to ordinary people. Kramer subsequently said that he did not consider himself a writer first and foremost; rather he thought of himself as "a very opinionated man who uses words as fighting tools."[60] This seems accurate: he used words as "fighting tools" both on the printed page and on the streets, effectively yelling and screaming to get the nation's attention. Gay men, he reasoned, must not only be medically treated – though that was their most immediate need. They must, additionally, once and for all, stake their claim to acceptance, to total political and social acceptance.

Initially Kramer founded GMHC to provide HIV-positive people in the greater New York City area with medical guidance, social services, and emotional support. (Eventually GMHC became the largest organization of its kind in the world.) The idea behind it was to empower gay men themselves, to wean them off their dependency on, for example, local health authorities, the federally funded Center for Disease Control, and private foundations. Kramer insisted that gay men had to fight for themselves – fight to legitimatize themselves. But before long, he lost patience. He began to think the GMHC too careful, too conservative, too non-confrontational. He on the other hand was anything but careful, conservative, and non-confrontational. He was just the opposite. He was loud, aggressive, angry, rude, impatient, insulting, and impossible to deal with – which explains why the powers that be at GMHC lost patience. They threw Kramer out – founder or no founder.

What did he do? He went on to organize a new and different sort of protest group, this one far more insistent and demanding, more clamorous or onerous, depending on your point of view. This group was the previously mentioned AIDS Coalition to Unleash Power – better known as ACT UP. The organization was true to its name. It took on the establishment by specializing in street theater. It staged outrageous, offensive, disruptive, and dramatic confrontations intended to force – not to ask, not to encourage, but to *force* – various medical, business, and political authorities to pay attention and deliver the goods. What were these goods? Primarily the mission of ACT UP was to get the various establishments – including the political, medical, and pharmaceutical establishments – to mount a crash campaign to develop a cure for AIDS. Members of ACT UP were prepared to do whatever it took to get the nation's attention – which meant nothing so much as being disruptive. ACT UP managed to stop trading on the New York Stock Exchange floor. Its tactics included staging mass "die-ins" in front of the White House; interrupting CBS anchor Dan Rather's *Evening News* mid-broadcast; and shutting down for a time the Food and Drug Administration (FDA). The tactics worked. They had their intended effects. The largest single demonstration in Washington since the Vietnam War helped to push and prod the FDA to fast-track several experimental medications.

In a similar protest, under Kramer's direction activists planned and executed a blockade of Wall Street. After the HIV/AIDS drug azidothymidine (AZT) was approved by the FDA, it was patented by the drug company Burroughs Welcome. The patient, however, would be obliged to pay for the drug, to the tune of approximately $10,000 annually. This effectively established Burroughs Welcome as a lucrative monopoly, while other promising drugs were left to languish. To protest what they thought outrageous, in September 1989 a small group of activists snuck into the New York Stock Exchange. They hung a banner supporting the sale of Burroughs Welcome shares – and then they chained themselves to a railing. Simultaneously, more than 1,000 activists outside the building chanted and distributed flyers similarly encouraging the sale of Burroughs Welcome stock. The result of Kramer's, of ACT UP's, activities? The price of AZT was lowered from about $10,000 a year to about $4,000 a year.

In another such stunt, Larry Kramer and his merry band of ACT UP activists occupied New York City's St. Patrick's Cathedral. Their purpose was to protest the Catholic Church's positions on prophylactics particularly, and on homosexuality generally. For many parishioners, such an "invasion" of their cathedral by dozens of angry protesters was "an act of desecration." The *New York Times* described members of ACT UP as being "virtually impossible to please," and the attack on the house of worship as "rude" and "rash" – but, ultimately, tellingly, "effective."[61]

Kramer himself took special aim at Dr. Anthony S. Fauci, a leading AIDS researcher who was also head of the National Institute of Allergy and Infectious Diseases. (This Dr. Fauci is, of course, the same Dr. Fauci whose name became virtually a household word during the coronavirus crisis.) Outrageously, Kramer compared Fauci to Adolf Eichmann, the notorious Nazi war criminal. In 1998, Kramer wrote an open letter to Fauci: "I have been screaming at the National Institutes of Health since I first visited your Animal House of Horrors in 1984. I called you monsters then ... and now I call you murderers. You are responsible for supervising all government-funded AIDS treatment research programs. .... You make decisions that cost the lives of others. I call the decisions you are making acts of murder." Kramer, who spoke years later about his peak period of AIDS activism, when he was "operating on all cylinders," remembered "it was a euphoric feeling: to be useful, to not have enough hours in the day." This is what we mean when we reference a leader who lusts – someone like Kramer near desperate to bring in from the cold, to bring into the fold, gay men.

Further evidence of Kramer's indefatigable zeal is the multiplicity and variability of his labors on behalf of gay men and, later, women. For example, in 1996 he tried to fund a gay studies program at Yale University, his alma mater and as prestigious an institution of higher education as there is in the United States. Kramer offered Yale $250,000 if the university would agree to fund a gay studies program. Yale turned him down which led, predictably, to Kramer's lashing out – he charged it with being "homophobic."[62] Yale responded by insisting that financial considerations made Kramer's proposal unfeasible, adding that it would take at least $2 million to fund a Yale gay studies initiative. A year later Kramer came back to Yale, and this time he offered the university several million dollars "to endow a permanent, tenured professorship in gay studies and possibly to build a gay and lesbian student center."[63] Yale's provost, Alison Richard, again responded negatively, insisting that gay and lesbian studies was too narrow a specialty for a program in perpetuity. In 2001, both sides agreed to a short-term (five-year) trial, funded with seed money from Kramer of $1 million. At the conclusion of the initial five years, the program was terminated.[64]

Perhaps the least effective but most perfectly prototypical evidence of Kramer's lust for legitimacy was his self-proclaimed magnum opus, a mammoth novel spanning the entirety of American history, titled *The American People*. As Calvin Trillin put it, gently joshing his old friend, Kramer's "idea of history is that everyone was gay: Joe Louis, De Gaulle, anybody." Indeed, the book joyfully outed as homosexual everyone from George Washington and Abraham Lincoln to Mark Twain and Richard Nixon, not forgetting Benjamin Franklin, Alexander Hamilton, the Marquis de Lafayette, Andrew Jackson, Meriwether Lewis, Franklin Pierce, James Buchanan, and Herman Melville. For Kramer, this was his final and most comprehensive assertion of the fundamental centrality of gayness to American life. He insisted his claims were true, while explaining that his book's title had its origins in Ronald Reagan's always "making speeches about 'the American people' and it totally pissed me off because his American people didn't include me or us. So that's the name of the book, but it's the gay American people."[65]

According to Larry Kramer, the greatest obstacle to securing legitimacy, especially for gay men, is "we're all anxious to have everyone love us."[66] But because his own lust for legitimacy was, by definition, insatiable, he claimed never to have worried that people would dislike or even detest his own public persona. He was, in any case, or at least he appeared to be, wholly unafraid. In 1990 he insisted that the time had come for terrorism. The "new phase is terrorism," he claimed. "I don't know whether it means burning buildings or killing people or setting fire to yourselves."[67]

Followers

Larry Kramer sought to persuade people – to enroll followers – both as a writer and as an activist. For example, Randy Klose, a gay Beverly Hills developer who went on to become a gay rights activist and early leading fundraiser in the fight against AIDS (later he died of AIDS), credited Kramer with having sparked his full-time involvement in national AIDS fundraising. An independently wealthy man, Klose ultimately contributed substantial sums of money to the cause, saying that it was Kramer's essay, "1,112 and Counting," that had persuaded him to become political. Specifically, to fight for a prompt public and private sector response to the AIDS crisis, as well as for the rights of gay people in America more broadly.

Kramer recognized early on that the fights against AIDS, and for the legitimization of gays in America, would have to be political. In turn, he understood that if he personally was going to take a leadership role, not to mention a prominent one, he would have to find followers. Find followers from within, from within his stigmatized, ostracized group of gay men; and find followers from without, from the dominant group, including the various establishments (medical, pharmaceutical, political), to which we earlier referred.

Kramer once complained he did not understand why "every gay person doesn't agree with everything I say – and I'm serious."[68] One way to get "every gay person" on board is to be founder of an organization intended to attract gay members, gay followers, which, as we saw, Kramer did not once but twice, with the Gay Men's Health Crisis and ACT UP. At its peak, ACT UP boasted more than 130 national chapters and a budget of over a million dollars – all, remarkably, without a single paid staffer.[69] As the leader of ACT UP, Kramer was seen, certainly by some, as "the most iconic figure of the AIDS movement."[70]

ACT UP members were willing not just to follow Kramer's lead in some vague way, but, as we have seen, to undertake, along with him, some highly unconventional and, to many sensibilities, crazy, risky activities. On the day that ACT UP activists went after the FDA, they sought to seize control of the building in which the agency was housed. When the FDA refused even to discuss their demands, hundreds of Kramer's followers converged on its headquarters. "One group were wearing lab coats that were stained with bloody hands," recalls David Barr, then a young lawyer and burgeoning activist.[71] Kramer's minions brought homemade tombstones to the site, then proceeded to lay down beside them in front of the FDA building. The signs alongside read, "Dead from FDA red tape." The activists advanced in rows, blocking the entrances to the building, making the national news. Within days the FDA caved in. They agreed to meet with Kramer and his group, and within short order there was palpable progress. FDA officials liberalized its policies on providing AIDS sufferers with access to experimental drugs, which, for thousands of gay men confronting near-certain death, was a potentially lifesaving change of bureaucratic heart.

Part of the reason ACT UP succeeded in having a significant impact is that it enlisted allies. The early AIDS groups were small, limited primarily to AIDS sufferers able to provide mutual assistance and support.[72] But as time went on, organizations such as ACT UP learned to use their *moral authority* to establish their *political credibility*. Kramer's playbook was to try to solicit followers not just to care about AIDS sufferers generally, but, specifically, to enlist them as political allies, medical experts, and financial supports.

For example, a geneticist and virologist by the name of Dr. Mathilde Krim came to be an important soldier in what, broadly speaking, was Kramer's war. She was an experienced cancer researcher with a passion for social justice. Inspired in part by Kramer, she drew on her expertise to encourage research on the virus but, as importantly, she was a "warrior in the battle against superstitions, fears and prejudices that ... stigmatized many people with AIDS, subjecting them to rejection and discrimination."[73] She helped to raise money and to educate the public. And she "mobilized a galaxy of friends from the worlds of politics, the arts, entertainment, society and Wall Street" to fight the good fight.[74] Well-heeled and fabulously well connected, Krim had been affiliated with several preeminent scientific institutions such as the Weizmann Institute of Science in Israel, and the Sloan Kettering Cancer Center in New York. All of which gave her the credibility she needed to create, along with others, the AIDS Medical Foundation to raise money specifically to support AIDS research. Later it merged with another organization to form the American Foundation for AIDS Research, or amfAR, which became the nation's pre-eminent private supporter of AIDS research, prevention, treatment, and advocacy.[75]

For all her contributions to the cause, Krim was not, of course, spared Larry Kramer's wrath. At one point, Krim recommended that Dr. Woodrow A. Myers Jr. become New York City's health commissioner – a recommendation with which Kramer strongly disagreed. "I think she's exceptionally naïve politically," said Kramer at the time. "We are all very angry with her." But, then, being no fool, Kramer went on to say, "so far as one can ever get angry with Mathilde, because we love her so."[76] For her part, Krim, who died in 2018, was clear about her opinion of Kramer. She deeply admired him. "In some ways, [Kramer] has been like a prophet in the wilderness," Krim said. "A lot of people do not like his methods, and he says things that are extreme, that I do not agree with. But Kramer was a catalyst in rallying public awareness on this disease, especially at a time when a lot of people were not willing to focus on it."[77]

As Kramer and his allies continued over the years to sound the alarm, his followers came to include bands of ordinary people and, increasingly, celebrities who themselves attracted attention to his cause. Barbra Streisand, Woody Allen, Warren Beatty, and Elizabeth Taylor ultimately were sympathizers and fellow travelers. Taylor became a formidable AIDS activist in own right, which did not, again, predictably, spare her from one of Kramer's tongue-lashings: "Let's talk about Elizabeth Taylor. She was buddies with Reagan. She never once went to him about this. She lent her name, but she didn't use her power to confront the powers that be."[78] In addition to enlisting followers who were relatively amenable to coming on board, Kramer excelled at winning converts. At converting people who originally were enemies into allies, followers, and sometimes even into friends.

The best known of these was probably the previously mentioned Dr. Fauci. Early in their relationship Kramer relentlessly attacked Fauci, calling him an "incompetent" and even a "criminal." This went on for years – Fauci serving as Kramer's punch bag. But, eventually, Fauci came around. Eventually he recognized the role that Kramer was playing in securing for victims of AIDS the help, specifically the drugs, they required. This is why he morphed from being a Kramer detractor to being one of his staunchest supporters. "What Larry did, by his provocative approach," Fauci later acknowledged, "is change the medical landscape in this country for the better. How patients talked to their doctors. How constituencies interacted with researchers at the NIH and regulators at the FDA. I have a phenomenal amount of respect for Larry, a tremendous amount of admiration."[79] Fauci eventually invited AIDS activists to participate in NIH proceedings, crediting Kramer and his fellow activists with "forcing government agencies to change the way they test drugs."[80] Finally, Fauci concluded that medical research on AIDS could be divided into two distinct periods: "before Larry" and "after Larry." "He was fearless," Fauci recalled. "He scared people. He angered a lot of people. But his heart was always in the right place, and he always wanted to do things for the good of his people."[81]

Withal, any honest account of Kramer's relationships must mention those who were driven away by the extremities of his personal furies and political strategies. One activist held that, "the mere mention of Kramer's name produces laughter and disgust in some circles because many activists say privately that they are tired of Kramer's 10-year temper tantrum and nearly hysterical tone of outrage." Said another, "I think everybody living with HIV can understand his anger and rage ... But he's not our spokesperson."[82] Kramer himself always believed that his followers were far fewer in number than they should have been. "I am so very, very tired of fighting with so few troops," he complained in 2005, in *The Tragedy of Today's Gays*. One observer noted that he was like the "general who fails to notice that the war has long since moved on," and who, therefore, "keeps beating the drums and waiting for people to show up."[83]

While Kramer long railed against the various establishments, and the political system, he also, all along, railed against his own kind. In his view, however much society betrayed gay men, which it did, they also, all along, betrayed themselves. Betrayed themselves through their own irresponsible promiscuity and their own irresponsible passivity. Put directly, even during the years that AIDS victims tended to be depicted as saintly sufferers, Kramer never wanted any of it. He wanted gay men to be held to account for what they did do, and for what they did not do. "We have a responsibility to our bodies and to the people we care about. I am not against sex. I am just begging for responsibility."[84]

Hindsight
In Larry Kramer's play, *The Normal Heart*, a character based on Kramer himself tells his friends, "That's how I want to be remembered: as one of the men who won the war."[85] Which he will be. He will forever be remembered as *the* leader in the fight against AIDS, a struggle that finally succeeded in bringing to market drugs that

make it possible for HIV-positive people to live reasonably normal lives.

Not that Kramer was ever satisfied – how could he have been? He was a leader who lusted, so enough was never enough. "I still don't understand why every gay person is not an activist," Kramer complained in 2017. "I worry we have to fight this all again. I hope we have the strength to say, 'I am entitled to the same rights as everyone else, and I am going to fight for them.'"[86] In an opinion piece he wrote in 2018 for the *New York Times*, titled "The Worst Is Yet to Come," Kramer warned the LGBTQ community: "I still can't see enough of us, in all our numbers and our splendor and our magnificence. Our activist organizations are a diminished presence. We still have no respected and accepted leaders who can speak for us as a people. And what little power we do have, lobbying or otherwise, in Washington or anywhere else, is woefully inadequate."[87] Referencing the massive turnout for the 2018 Women's March on Washington, Kramer asked, rhetorically obviously, "Where are the millions of gay people being angry and vocal and visibly fighting back?"[88]

LGBTQ rights have, of course, made great strides in recent years, specifically in the United States in consequence of several landmark Supreme Court rulings. For example, in 2003, the nation's highest court ruled that sodomy laws were illegal, which meant that whatever and wherever the existing sodomy laws nationwide, they were struck from the books. Ten years later the Supreme Court went further. It ruled that the federal ban on same-sex marriage was unconstitutional. (In 2015 the Court took another step, requiring all states to grant same-sex marriages and recognize those granted in other states.) When he was asked if he thought he would live to see marriages like his own protected by the high court, Kramer replied, "I honestly never expected this would happen while I was still alive. Honestly, the whole thing is a bit surreal."[89]

Some have argued that the struggle for LGBTQ rights is over – which is not, of course, what Larry Kramer believed, not by a long shot. He was correct to be cautious. For example, it is not yet clear if the Supreme Court will decide, during its term beginning in October 2019, that Title VII protections from workplace discriminations should extend to gay and transgender people in each of the fifty states. Even now, there are some states in which it is legal to deny sexual minorities various opportunities and to refuse them certain services. Moreover, it appears the level of social acceptance has stopped increasing and is, instead, decreasing. A survey conducted in 2019 found that the number of Americans aged eighteen to thirty-four who "are comfortable interacting with LGBTQ people" dropped from 63 percent in 2016 to 53 percent in 2017, and in 2018 it slipped still further, to 45 percent.[90] Surprisingly, ominously, this is precisely the age group, the younger demographic, that had been assumed the most LGBTQ-tolerant.

Around the world the picture usually is bleaker, in some places much bleaker. In seventy-three countries – most in the Middle East, Africa, and Asia – homosexual activity between consenting adults remains illegal. And in eight countries homosexuality is by law punishable by death. This explains at least in part why Kramer never missed an opportunity to point to the work that remains to be done – and why so far as he was concerned the future is, at best, uncertain. His level of comfort with the presidency of Donald Trump was, for example, low. "There is not one cabinet member who has supportive or welcoming words for us. Every week, it seems, Mr. Trump appoints another judge who is on record as hating us. They will serve for many years. A new Supreme Court will further echo this disdain."[91] Small wonder that Larry Kramer died in 2020 still so angry, still so hungry for the acceptance he had sought all his life.

Coda

In 539 BC, the armies of Cyrus the Great, founder of the Achaemenid Empire, conquered the city of Babylon. But Cyrus chose not to act like a conqueror, not to pillage the city or to subject its people to punishments. Instead, he freed slaves and promoted greater equality, autonomy, and legitimacy. Notwithstanding his historical example, humankind continues to oppress and suppress; to inhibit and exploit; to degrade, dehumanize, and, yes, delegitimize. The reasons for these persecutions and exclusions vary, of course. But, typically, they are now as they always have been: second-class status or worse assigned on grounds of, to list obvious examples, race, religion, region, gender, class, and sexual orientation. The result in any case is the same. The weaker group is consigned by the stronger group to suffer the indignity of illegitimacy.

Some of us feel a vague moral imperative to address such a wrong. Fewer of us make any attempt to right such a wrong. And fewer of us still, far fewer, are driven by such wrongs completely to commit ourselves to crushing them once and for all. In this last, small, select group are leaders who lust for legitimacy. Leaders who cannot rest so long as relegation to second-class status or worse persists. Both Nelson Mandela and Larry Kramer fall into this last category. The level of their moral outrage was such that they could not cease and desist, would not cease and desist, until they created transformative change.

Mandela came to believe that violence against the apartheid regime was necessary, though he never preferred it. In fact, he originally thought that the government "would crumble more quickly and fully when faced with revolutionary love and compassion than when faced with anger and violence."[92] Like Mandela, Kramer's lust for legitimacy was with every fiber of his being, with as much fervor and fever. But unlike Mandela, Kramer was ceaselessly combative. If there is any evidence of his extending to the straight majority even a smidgeon of "revolutionary love and compassion," we do not find it. Kramer's modus operandi was to be combative, to tap into his rage and outrage, relentlessly to rail.

It is no surprise then that Nelson Mandela is regarded virtually as a secular saint – while for Larry Kramer there is no such veneration. In fact, unlike Mandela, and despite his having had a critical impact at a critical moment in American history, Kramer's name is not widely known – it is widely even unknown. Is this because of the differences between them in tactics and strategies? Or because of the differences between them in personas and personalities? Or is it, perhaps, because black South Africans were, are, an easier cause to support, worldwide, than gay Americans?

While definitive answers to questions such as these are impossible to provide, what we can say with certainty is that in considerable part both Mandela and Kramer achieved what they set out to achieve, despite the astronomically long odds against them. Both were able to mobilize their own, weaker group; and both were able also to motivate the other, stronger, group, the group from which they were excluded. They were also able to do the work that had to be done: to define the problem, to propose a solution, to model the action, and to get others to sign on, that is, to follow their lead. Though they are significant, whatever lacunae persist do not detract one whit from the great accomplishments of these great men. In the end, they are of a piece – leaders whose lust for legitimacy changed the ways of the world.

6   LUST FOR LEGACY

Prelude

"Leaders who lust for *legacy* long, effectively lifelong, to leave an imprint that is permanent."

Legacies are what we leave behind after we leave the scene, usually though not necessarily after we die. Some legacies are intangible, such as how we are remembered. Others are tangible, palpable, observable, material. Some legacies are evident while we're still alive, for example, those of Henry Ford, Jonas Salk, and Margaret Thatcher. Others are not apparent, or at least not appreciated, until long after we've passed. During his lifetime the American writer and philosopher Henry David Thoreau was almost unknown, obliged to self-publish most of his essays and poems. But in time his ideas on civil disobedience had a major impact, including on lionized leaders such as Mahatma Gandhi and Martin Luther King, Jr. Further, in time, his reflections on living in natural surroundings, *Walden*, came to figure "on every list of essential American books."[1]

Some leaders try to leave a legacy but never do. Other leaders do leave a legacy, but one they neither wanted nor intended. And still others leave a legacy that is malignant. This chapter though is narrow in its conception. It looks at leaders who lust to leave legacies that are large, that last long after they are gone, and that are intended to improve the lives of others. Like each of the lusts discussed in this book, the lust to leave a legacy is an irresistible force. It does not stop or slow even after a significant legacy has already been left. Moreover, it is so strong, so powerful, that those who evidence it are willing, even eager, to make extraordinary efforts and considerable sacrifices to try to satisfy it.

The two men and one woman we discuss in this chapter are all fantastically well endowed: they have enormous resources, not least financial resources, to invest in satisfying, or trying to, their ceaseless, restless lust. But we want to be clear. Though the capacity to leave a legacy is often associated with having great wealth, other resources equally pertain. Salk's polio vaccine came to market for the first time in 1955. But he had already invested many years and his own great store of personal and professional resources in the development of the vaccine. His was an arduous effort that could, incidentally, have paid off handsomely. Had he patented his prize, he could have made many millions of dollars.[2] Instead Salk chose to ensure that his vaccine would be widely available and easily affordable – which explains how it came to pass that, in considerable part in consequence of his work, cases of polio were reduced by more than 99 percent.[3]

Humankind is forever grappling with problems of seismic magnitude – such as poverty, disease, war, migration, addiction, oppression, suppression, and climate change. How do we typically respond? Most times we ignore said problems altogether. But, sometimes we give some of our time or donate some of our money to groups and organizations that address one or another of our collective ills. Other times we provide political support, such as signing our names to petitions, or protesting, making noise in the streets or online. But some of us, a small number of us, are not content just to drop a pebble into the roiling waters. Some of us are driven to try to make a big difference, in a very few cases a *very* big difference.

Where does this drive come from? What is the source of the lust to leave a legacy that is large and long-lasting and beneficent in its intent? Is it simply altruism? Not necessarily. Beneficence and altruism are not synonymous. Altruism implies helping someone else for their sake – *only* for their sake.[4] But, even when legacies are left for the specific purpose of helping others, we cannot know for certain if even they are motivated exclusively by, or even primarily by, selflessness.

In fact, even the most dedicated of philanthropists can have and sometimes do have selfish interests. These include, for example, two types of so-called good feelings. The first emanates from within. It makes us feel good to do what we want and intend. The second emanates from without. It makes us feel good if what we want and intend elicits the approval of others. Think of the lust to leave a legacy as if it were an urge, an urge that can never be satisfied, but that is quieted, if only temporarily, when progress toward leaving a legacy is realized. This is the essence of lusting to leave a legacy – as opposed to lusting for self-sacrifice. We are not, in other words, writing about martyrs or saints. We are writing about leaders who are self-interested, but whose self-interest can broadly be said to coincide with the interests of others.

Leaders who lust to leave a legacy often do so from a position of considerable strength. Usually they have already achieved a great deal of power, or a great deal of money, or unimagined success. These leaders, then, have the requisite resources – such as large amounts of disposable time and money and ample personal and professional resources – to invest in trying, tirelessly, to satisfy their lust. But, because their own well-being and their lust to leave a legacy are completely compatible, self-sacrifice is not, in any conventional sense of this word, at issue.

The leaders who lust who are our cases in point – first Bill and Melinda Gates, then George Soros – are not materially affected by what they do for others. There is no amount of giving to others that will financially deplete any one of them. Certainly not Bill Gates and George Soros, both of whom reached the pinnacle of their professions early in their lives, long before their lust to leave a legacy came to define who they are and what they do. So, yes, these leaders have already given away vast sums of their own money, and they have already invested vast amounts of their own time in the causes in which they believe. But this is money and time that they *want* to spend just as they are spending it. Spending time and money on a legacy that you are driven to leave is, then, neither a sacrifice nor an act of altruism. It is an act of lust.

How else then, if not altruism or martyrdom, to explain the lust to leave a legacy? There is an explanation that is less associated with having an impact on others and more with transcending our time on this earth. All animals are hardwired to care about what they leave behind at least in one way: reproducing, procreating offspring who will carry enough of our genes to ensure the survival of the species.[5] From an evolutionary perspective, then, reproducing is one way of "cheating death."[6] Another way to, so to speak, cheat death, is through the legacies we leave. Interestingly, Henry David Thoreau never had a child. Nor for that matter did many other legacy-leaving figures such as Socrates, George Washington, Jane Austen, and Vincent van Gogh. Still, they cheated death by leaving so significant a legacy that it lasted, they lasted, long after their deaths.

Finally, there is this explanation for why a certain type of leader might lust to leave a certain type of legacy. "Terror management theory" suggests that some people who somehow accrue enormous wealth seek to alleviate their consciences – their guilt at having so much more of everything that life has to offer than does virtually everyone else – by redistributing their wealth.[7] It is telling that some psychotherapists "have found brisk business in catering to members of the super-rich who feel guilty about having amassed fortunes."[8] However, other members of the super-rich seek a different solution: they donate or, if you prefer, they distribute or redistribute their various, countless, assets in ways that they believe will improve the lives of others. They believe doing this will make others, anonymous others, healthier, safer, and more secure.

Bill and Melinda Gates never lusted for money qua money – money for its own sake. Their vast wealth is in consequence of Bill Gates's lifelong passion for computers. This explains certainly in part why the Gateses have never been conspicuous consumers. (To be clear, nor have they denied themselves. They live in a home estimated to be worth well over $100 million.) Instead they dedicate their lives to bettering the lives of many millions of others, most at a great remove. In some ways similar, in others altogether different, is George Soros. Soros also made a bundle and he also spends vast amounts of his personal and material resources ceaselessly questing to leave a legacy every bit as ambitious – but even more audacious.

Bill and Melinda Gates

In 1994, Bill Gates, the co-founder and CEO of Microsoft, and then the richest person in the world, married Melinda French, a Microsoft product manager. Soon after they married, they began, as a couple, to engage in charitable endeavors. In 2000 they went on to found and, in time, increasingly to devote themselves to, the Bill & Melinda Gates Foundation. Since then their Foundation has become by far the world's largest: it has already made more than $50 billion in grant payments, and it still has an endowment of more than $50 billion.[9] Headquartered in Seattle, it has three overarching interests: global health, global development, and education. The Foundation is particularly committed to improving health worldwide, with a special emphasis on malaria, HIV/AIDS, and tuberculosis. The Foundation also generously invests – it does not "give" or "donate," it "invests" – in initiatives intended to develop "superfoods" in the global fight against malnutrition. In recent years, Melinda Gates has set a related goal: to "lift up" women in society. As she wrote in her 2019 book, *The Moment of Lift: How Empowering Women Changes the World*, "If you want to lift up humanity, empower women. It is the most comprehensive, pervasive, high-leverage investment you can make in human beings."[10]

How great is Bill and Melinda Gates's lust for legacy? Melinda Gates has given a clear answer. "By now the foundation's work has become inseparable from who we are. We do the work because it's our life."[11]

Context

Bill and Melinda Gates are among the most generous philanthropists on the planet. Through the Bill & Melinda Gates Foundation, they donate to their various causes over one billion dollars every year. Of course, having billions of dollars in the first place makes becoming a large-scale philanthropist possible, doable. But many extremely wealthy people practice philanthropy with far less zeal – with far less lust – than do the Gateses. To an extent, their shared passion can be explained by the contexts within which both, separately and together, have been situated their entire lives. These contexts inspired and guided their joint desire to invest enormous sums of money in the causes in which they believe.

For both Bill and Melinda Gates, the families in which they were raised, the Gateses and the Frenches, constituted the original contexts within which giving to others was expected. Both husband and wife have reported being raised to be aware that giving back was not just a good thing to do – it was the *right* thing to do. According to the Foundation, "Both the Gates and French families instilled the values of volunteerism and civic engagement. Our families believed that if life happens to bless you, you should use those gifts as well and as wisely as you can."[12] In February 2018, Melinda Gates used the Gates Foundation's 10th annual letter to respond to a question that both she and her husband frequently are asked – why? Why "really" are they giving all that money away? She answered: "We both come from families that believed in leaving the world better than you found it. ... My parents made sure my siblings and I took the social justice teachings of the Catholic Church to heart. Bill's late mother was known – and his father is still known – for showing up to advocate for a dizzying number of important causes and local organizations." Later in the letter, she gets more specific about their parents' influence: "Our goal is to do what our parents taught us and do our part to make the world better."[13]

Bill Gates credits his strong disposition toward philanthropy primarily to his mother, Mary, who died of breast cancer in 1994. He has said it was she who pushed him to become philanthropic after Microsoft's 1986 initial public offering made him, at the age of 30, a billionaire. After he struck it rich, very rich, his mother urged him to start giving some of his money away. At the time he replied, probably with exasperation in his voice, "I'm just trying to run my company!" But eventually Mary Gates prevailed: she persuaded her son to start a program within his company, within Microsoft, that would raise money for her favorite charity, the United Way. Bill Gates has described an important, indeed memorable letter that his mother wrote to Melinda French the day before her wedding. Her message to the woman about to become her daughter-in-law was simple but pointed: "From those to whom much is given, much is expected." A few months after his mother's death, Bill Gates, with the help of his father, allocated about $100 million to what several years later would become the Bill & Melinda Gates Foundation.[14]

After they became engaged, in 1993, Bill and Melinda Gates traveled together to Africa. For the first time, they experienced firsthand people living in extreme poverty. Bill Gates has described how almost immediately the continent of Africa became a context of consequence, for him and his fiancée. "We went on a safari to see wild animals but ended up getting our first sustained look at extreme poverty. We were shocked." He went on, "I remember peering out a car window at a long line of women walking down the road with big jerricans of water on their heads. 'How far away do these women live?' we wondered. 'Who's watching their children while they're away?' That was the beginning of our education in the problems of the world's poorest people."[15]

Along similar lines, Melinda Gates has recalled that while walking on a beach in Zanzibar, they "started to talk about" how they might use their fortune to help others.[16] Later, after they were married, they continued to travel to places where inevitably they were confronted with people in dire need – including babies and young children visibly dying of curable and in some cases preventable diseases. In retrospect, it's clear that the Gateses were committing themselves to familiarizing themselves with contexts within which they hoped in time to leave a legacy. Their commitment was early in their relationship. It was to all appearances equally shared. It quickly became as informed as impassioned. And it was unusual – their zeal to make a difference, their lust to leave a legacy, distinguished them from their contemporaries, including those who also were exceedingly wealthy. As one reporter wondered, rhetorically, "How many people with access to billions of dollars would sleep in a goat shed in Tanzania or discuss rape-prevention strategies with sex workers in India?"[17]

While the accounts of how Bill and Melinda Gates got to the point they did – the point at which they decided to make philanthropy their life's work – have differed somewhat, their content has been essentially the same. There was no single "Eureka!" moment. Instead there were a series of mutually reinforcing experiences that encouraged their shared commitment to do something meaningful, something that would, specifically, make a major contribution to improving global health and ameliorating world poverty. The stories about how the Gateses became so deeply committed to philanthropy similarly confirm that their continuing travels to places replete with people who had desperate needs further spurred them on. These were two driven individuals who were led, relatively easily and at relatively young ages, to channel their formidable personal, professional, and financial resources into accomplishments so great that they would in time leave a legacy – an imprint not just on single individuals, or even on communities, countries, or continents. They longed to leave their imprint on humanity writ large.

This brings us to another, infinitely larger, context that shaped the Gateses' life's work. Another context that encouraged their lust to leave a legendary legacy. We refer to the rise of global inequality, the shocking, distressing gap between rich and poor, or even the very rich and everyone else, that in recent years has become more frequently and stridently in evidence. More than one quarter of the world's hungry live on the African continent. More than 30 percent of African children suffer from growth disorders. Sub-Saharan Africa is the region with the world's highest infant mortality. More than 25 million Africans are infected with HIV. Africa is, of course, not only a place with many in desperate need. In fact, "notwithstanding widespread poverty and huge social problems, Africa in general is doing better than many imagine."[18]As well, most of us now know full well that striking income inequities are nearly everywhere in evidence, including in countries that are highly developed, such as the United States. Still, it seems that Bill and Melinda Gates were most struck by, most moved by, and most incensed by extreme miseries with which, before they traveled to Africa, they were at least on a personal level unfamiliar.[19]

Some ills, such as poverty and poor health, have always been among us. Moreover, philanthropists have long sought to alleviate both – the impulse among the wealthy to charity is not new. But we now know more, much more, than we once did about people and places remote from our own. Thus, technology, the information revolution, constitutes another context that contributed to fostering Bill and Melinda Gates's enduring passion for making an enduring difference. Bill Gates has said as much. On one occasion he pointed to the power of technology to raise our "global consciousness." As he put it, "It's getting harder and harder for those of us in the rich world to ignore poverty and suffering, even if it's happening half a planet away. Technology is unlocking the innate compassion we have for our fellow human beings. In the end, that combination – the advances of science together with our emerging global conscience – may be the most powerful tool we have for improving the world."[20]

Evidence

The strongest evidence that Bill and Melinda Gates are driven to leave a legacy is that they don't simply give – they work at it. They give exceedingly deliberately and exceptionally precisely. They pay careful and close attention to what they give, to how they give, to when they give, and to whom they give. People who want to donate money can do so all day every day, to the panhandler in the doorway, to the donation box in the supermarket. Such giving is easy. As is writing a few big checks, which is precisely what philanthropists typically do, without so much as breaking a sweat. The Gateses though are different; they have been different from the start. From the start they thought very long and hard about how they would approach philanthropy. Finally, they hit upon what they refer to as *catalytic philanthropy*. A catalytic philanthropist resembles an investor, a traditional investor. Both invest financial resources, and both anticipate high rates of return on their investments.[21]

"We want to give our wealth back to society in a way that has the most impact," Bill has explained, "and so we look for opportunities to invest for the largest returns. That means tackling the world's biggest problems and funding the most likely solutions. That's an even greater challenge than it sounds ... where every dollar you spend is liable to have the greatest impact."[22] Giving away enormous sums of money in a way that maximizes the chances of having "the greatest impact" – that maximizes the chances of leaving a legacy – demands a great deal of time and work. Which is exactly what Melinda Gates did. Each year, as their three children grew older, she gave more time and put in more work. In 2008, Bill Gates followed suit. He made the highly unusual decision to step down from his day-to-day responsibilities at Microsoft in order to join his wife and commit himself, devote himself, full-time, to philanthropy. When he made this life choice, he was in his early fifties, and in good health. Obviously, he was then young enough to continue for many years to do what he had been doing, which, by all reports, he greatly enjoyed. He *liked* submerging himself in the world of changing technologies while running one of Silicon Valley's most legendary companies. Therefore, if evidence of Bill Gates's lust to leave a legacy was needed, it could be argued that his decision at still relatively a young age to give up his day job in order to commit himself full time to philanthropy is evidence enough.

But there is further confirmation of the level of the Gateses' dedication – and of their ambition. For example, their commitment to the eradication of malaria. Not the reduction of malaria – the *eradication* of malaria. A few facts and figures indicate the magnitude of their task: (1) About one million people die of malaria every year. (2) Some 300 to 600 million people are afflicted by malaria each year. (3) Every two minutes a child dies of malaria.[23]

Undaunted by the size and scope of their challenge, at a 2018 conference on malaria held in London, Bill Gates committed his and Melinda's Foundation to spending *at least* another $1 billion through 2023 to fight the disease. To be clear: before the Gateses became interested in malaria, research in the area was badly underfunded. Indeed, when they gave their first big grant to fight the disease, in 1999, the amount of money spent on researching it instantly doubled.[24]

The Gateses' commitment to this disease in particular is not an abstraction – for them it's deeply personal. In 2014 they visited Siem Reap, Cambodia. They never did see the iconic twelfth-century temple ruins at Angkor Wat. Instead, they flew directly to even more remote parts of Cambodia so that they personally could observe small, obscure projects dedicated to eliminating malaria. As Bill Gates remarked, "We may have been the first visitors who passed through Siem Reap and skipped the temples completely."[25] This suggests their joint drive – and their joint pride. Bill and Melinda Gates make it a point to meet people in the areas that malaria is devastating – both patients and public health practitioners. They analyze the research. They vet the scientists to whom they provide support. And they invest in a bevy of technologies ranging from nets with insecticides, rapid diagnosis tests, and genetic engineering intended to create non-malaria-carrying mosquitoes, to new vaccines and "photonic fence" technology – a laser beam device that literally shoots the wings off individual mosquitoes.[26] Clearly the Gateses are in this fight for the long haul. Though in taking on malaria they are taking on a parasite that "has evolved over many millennia to survive," they remain undaunted.[27] Quite the opposite. At every turn they "acknowledge ... their call, and personal commitment."[28]

Nor is malaria the only disease the Gateses opted to take on. In 2012, Bill Gates traveled three thousand miles to speak at a United Nations meeting to issue "a global call to end polio."[29] They also enlisted in the fights against AIDS and tuberculosis, bringing to each of these initiatives their same trademark dedication, ambition, and zeal. Again, their goal is not to remediate but to eradicate. The Bill & Melinda Gates Foundation strives for: "Zero malaria. Zero TB. Zero HIV. Zero malnutrition. Zero preventable deaths. Zero difference between the health of a poor kid and every other kid."[30]

Leaving a legacy is a lot of work. The Foundation receives approximately 6,000 requests each year. "We go down the chart of the greatest inequities and give where we can effect the greatest change," explains Melinda Gates.[31] The Gateses make it a point to invest in general causes and specific projects they conclude have the potential to effect the greatest change. This is not the same as, or, at least not necessarily the same as, responding to the greatest need or, for that matter, giving to the causes about which they care the most. Essentially their philanthropic work is in three steps. First there is assiduous homework and research to prepare them to take step two. Step two is the decision-making process. In which of countless worthy causes will the Gates Foundation invest its time and money? Finally, there is step three, the investment itself, which is usually, by any measure, huge. All this in the service of others. All this in the service of the Gateses' shared intention, shared passion, shared lust to leave a legacy. "From those to whom much is given, much is expected."[32]

But, again, this is not a story about Bill and Melinda Gates sacrificing themselves at the altar of duty. To listen to them is to appreciate their shared enthusiasm for, and excitement about, what they do. "We have fun doing it," Bill has written. "Both of us love digging into the science behind our work."[33] Whether helping to eradicate malaria or polio, or deciding to support the breeding of high-yield "super cows," the process of deciding where to allocate their money often requires them to study, for example, biology, chemistry, and agronomy. But, no matter, they seem to love it all. Bill: "I'll spend hours talking to a crop researcher or an HIV expert, and then I'll go home, dying to tell Melinda what I've learned. . . . It's rare to have a job where you get to have both a big impact and a lot of fun. . . . I can't imagine a better way to spend the bulk of my time."[34]

Of course, despite all their careful research, despite all their painstaking decision-making, some of the Gateses' philanthropic initiatives have failed. And, since they are exceedingly ambitious, sometimes they failed spectacularly. An example is their $575 million public–private, multi-year project to improve American schools, which was launched with a more than $212 million donation. Beginning in the 2009–2010 school year, the Foundation invested in large school districts in, for example, Pennsylvania and Florida, and in a charter school consortium in California. It "tried to pull a bunch of levers to have a big impact on student performance," including new teacher-evaluation systems, individualized professional development for teachers, enhanced teacher recruitment and advancement procedures, and (controversially) bonuses for teachers who performed especially well.[35] The project was heavily criticized, in part for leveraging government money to pursue third-party – that is, Gates Foundation – objectives. But the more fundamental problem was that whatever the school reforms that were tried, they didn't work. By 2014–2015, the Gates Foundation's own rigorous evaluations found that student outcomes in participating schools were no better than they were in schools that served as controls.

What did Bill and Melinda Gates decide to do? In October 2017, they announced their plan to pour another $1.7 billion into K-12 education, this time focusing on helping schools to improve curricula and scale best practices. In other words, instead of giving up, the Gateses doubled down. Rather than walking away, they pivoted, to reaffirm their commitment to improving American education. Moreover, they promised to continue these efforts, until, as Melinda Gates put it, "every student has an effective teacher in every subject, every school year."[36] Not most students – *every* student. In pursuit of their lust to leave a legacy – from malaria eradication to quality education – they learn from missteps, modify their plans, select their next evidence-based strategy, and step back into the ring, apparently undeterred, perhaps even invigorated.[37]

Followers
Bill and Melinda Gates actively seek to find followers ready, willing, and able to adhere to their brand of philanthropy. In fact, as a matter of principle and strategy, the Foundation, despite its colossal endowment and the Gateses' even more colossal wealth, rarely funds a program without a partner. Instead, it seeks other organizations, firms, sometimes even nations to help underwrite their various initiatives. This collaborative approach echoes an African proverb cited by the Gateses and others at the Gates Foundation: "If you want to go fast, go alone. If you want to go far, go with others."[38]

In November 2013, Bill Gates published an article in *Wired* titled, "Here's My Plan to Improve the World – And How You Can Help." He specifically asks his readers to follow the tenets of catalytic philanthropy. Among his "requests" are of readers as individuals. He asks them to "let their representatives know that aid works," and to "learn more about the problems of the poorest and see how you can help." And he also asks his readers who are leaders – especially of technology companies – to get their companies to dedicate "a percentage of their top innovators' time to issues that could help people who've been left out of the global economy or deprived of opportunity here in the US."[39]

The single most stunning example of how persuasive the Gateses have been in mobilizing others, in getting others to follow their lead is, of course, the enticement and ultimate recruitment of Warren Buffett to join them in their philanthropic work. Buffett had long insisted that any sizable charitable donation would be made only after his death. But during the first decade of the twenty-first century, he changed his mind. Why? The first reason was the death of his wife, Susan. For years, during their long if unconventional marriage – while Warren Buffett continued, tirelessly, to work on growing his pile of money – Susan Buffett dedicated her time (and at her death, the larger part of her fortune) to philanthropy. She had long made clear, even publicly, that she thought they should give more of their money away, even as she acknowledged that her husband was not yet prepared to do so.[40] It took his wife's passing to move Warren Buffett, to motivate him finally to change his mind – to give more, finally much, much more of his money away while he was alive.[41]

The second reason Warren Buffett changed his mind about giving now not later was his deep and by then already abiding admiration and affection for both Bill and Melinda Gates. As Buffett explained, "So when I have money to give away, I believe in turning it over to people who . . . are energized, working hard at it, smart, you know, doing it with their own money, the whole thing."[42] In sum, he concluded that he had identified "people who can give it away better than I can."[43] We already saw that Buffett never devoted much if any of his attention to philanthropy. His lust was for money, not legacy. But he responded favorably to the Gateses – Bill had long been a friend and favored bridge partner – especially to their deep dedication to their philanthropic work. Buffett was particularly impressed by the extensive and impressive homework they did – which paralleled his own, albeit in another area of endeavor, finance – all in the interest of making as certain as they could that their money was being invested wisely and well. As Buffett put it, by following the Gateses' lead, his fortune would "have a huge effect on the health and welfare of others."[44]

But Bill and Melinda Gates, now along with Warren Buffett, were not content to stop there. By 2010 all three were intent on getting others to follow their lead – on getting others to commit to giving away at least half their wealth to good causes either during their lifetimes or upon their deaths. To this end, the Gateses and Buffett co-founded the *Giving Pledge*, their formal effort to encourage people of wealth, particularly people of enormous wealth, publicly to promise to be hugely philanthropic. The Giving Pledge has no formal power or authority to compel even those who sign up to do what they say they will do. It relies instead on moral suasion to persuade the super-rich to "dedicate the majority of their wealth to giving back."[45] It enlists followers by persuading them that donating is what they should do, what they *ought* to do.

By 2019, 204 individuals or couples (most of them billionaires) had signed the Giving Pledge. They had committed to donating, in total, in excess of $500 billion. Additionally, is the potential impact of the Giving Pledge to change the norms of philanthropy, especially among the super wealthy or ultra-rich. To prompt them to be more like the Gateses. To get them to give away more of their money – and to get them to do so earlier in their lives, as opposed to in old age or even after they die. All this is testimony to the Gateses' lust to leave a legacy – and to their ability to enlist in their causes cadres of followers who themselves are fantastically well-endowed.

To be sure, the Giving Pledge has its detractors. Not everyone hurries to sign up. The late Robert W. Wilson, for example, a philanthropist who had already given generously, resisted when Bill Gates approached him. Wilson refused because of what he saw as a significant "loophole" (involving bequests to family charities) that rendered the Pledge "practically worthless."[46] Others such as Marc Benioff – the billionaire founder of SalesForce.com – concluded that while the Giving Pledge was a good idea, it was being "poorly executed."[47] A greater concern perhaps has been the lack of clear direction. As one person put it, "One person's worthy cause is another's force for evil."[48] Still, a good number of those who were asked did agree to sign; they signed the Giving Pledge freely, willingly, and in many cases enthusiastically. As Bernard Marcus, co-founder of Home Depot and himself a signatory, summed it up, "All this money is going for charity to help people – what kind of numbskull would find something wrong with that?"[49]

In 2019 the endowment of the Bill & Melinda Gates Foundation was valued at $46.8 billion.[50] But for the Foundation to maximize its impact, it must of course join its financial resources to its human resources. So, the Gateses have, in effect, an army of employees and volunteers, an army of followers who work to realize their mission, to carry out their legacy. The Gates Foundation employs 1,489 people, all or at least most of them "top talent."[51] As one observer remarked, "If you were the richest person in the world out to solve some of the hardest problems on the planet, who would you put on your team?" People who signed on include a "World Bank vice president, a genetic engineer from seed giant Monsanto, the founder of an Internet company in Africa, and the former chief executive of a $100 million cattle-breeding company." All men and women who are "really driven by the mission" and willing to "tackle some tough things with not a lot of road signs on how to do it."[52]

There is still another constituency the Gateses seek to recruit: policy makers. Gates Foundation "staffers testify before state legislatures and Congress. They publish policy briefs that get wide circulation. They're active on social media. They get heard." Moreover, several former Foundation staffers have gone into "influential" and "powerful posts" in government including, for example, former Education Secretary Arne Duncan's first chief of staff, Margot Rogers. In her case, she kept a foot in both worlds. During the Obama administration, she (and several others from the Gates Foundation) were granted "waivers from conflict-of-interest policies to allow them to continue to work closely with the Gates Foundation after joining the Education Department." In 2014, *Politico* observed that the Bill & Melinda Gates Foundation's "priorities [had] swiftly become state and federal priorities." Put differently, the Foundation advances its mission both by drawing on its own enormous resources *and* by drawing on the enormous resources of state and federal governments, some of which have involved "multibillion-dollar shifts in public spending."[53]

A study of the Gates Foundation concluded it has a unique ability among philanthropies "to bring diverse actors together and marshal support for its initiatives." More than its competitors, it has "successfully established ties to both public and private actors," and engaged "a very large [number] of actors to achieve [its] goals."[54] It turns out as well that there are costs to *not* being included in the Gates Foundation network. The outsized impact of the Gates Foundation "has knock-on effects." Organizations and institutions such as universities "that are not recipients of its money or not aligned to its vision can become marginalized."[55] In sum, Bill and Melinda Gates have been able to recruit legions of followers, followers from different places, for various reasons, not least among them their inordinate power, authority, and influence. These emanate from their wealth – but not only from their wealth. Both husband and wife additionally have a demonstrable capacity to exercise effective leadership.

Hindsight
Bill Gates's image as magical mogul and phenomenal philanthropist has been largely unblemished – but not entirely. In 1998, while he was still Microsoft's CEO, his company was sued by the Department of Justice and a coalition of twenty state attorneys general for violating federal antitrust law. (The government ended winning the case.) And in 2019 it was revealed that he met on several occasions with Jeffrey Epstein, the thoroughly disgraced convicted sex offender, who ended, reportedly, killing himself in prison.[56] But, in general, time has been kind. Bill Gates is not only one of the handful of richest men in the world, he is one of the most admired. And now, along with his wife and partner Melinda, he presides over what can best be thought of as an empire – a philanthropic empire that for the indefinite future will dominate the giving landscape.

Finally there is this. With the advent of the coronavirus pandemic, Bill Gates has come to be seen as something of an oracle. In a 2015 TED Talk he said this: "If anything kills over 10 million people in the next few decades, it's most likely to be a highly infectious virus rather than a war. Not missiles, but microbes."

As befits any empire of great magnitude, the Bill & Melinda Gates Foundation has its own preferences and policies. For example, it does not typically dispense funds to small organizations, no matter how great their need for money or support. While there are several compelling reasons for this – for example, smaller organizations tend to have more meager track records – the evidence suggests that the primary reason for this decision is the Gateses' ambition to maximize their impact by thinking big, very big. They are dedicating their lives not merely to doing good, for example, but to eradicating malaria forever. They are dedicating their lives not merely to being philanthropic, but to transforming the world of philanthropy. They are dedicating their lives not merely to being committed philanthropists themselves, but to inspiring others to be committed philanthropists as well. They are dedicating their lives to being transformational leaders – as Bill Gates was a transformational leader at Microsoft. Bill and Melinda Gates believe in catalytic philanthropy. And they are driven to leave a legacy by being catalysts themselves.

Ironically, paradoxically, while the Gateses are committed to giving away most of their fortune, and while they work full time in their multiple attempts to do just that, all the while they are getting richer. By now they have given away more than $45 billion. Yet since 2010, their wealth has nearly doubled, to $97 billion.[57] Perhaps this explains in part why in recent years Melinda Gates has sought to add yet another cause to her philanthropic portfolio. In her apparent quest to leave her own, more personal, legacy – Bill Gates will, after all, forever lay claim to his achievements at Microsoft, and he has become especially interested in problems associated with climate change – she has turned her attention to women. As the daughter of an Apollo program engineer, she remembers being fascinated as a child by the moment of "lift" – the moment when the force generated by the engine of a rocket supersedes the force holding the rocket down. This was the image that she drew on to title her previously mentioned book, *The Moment of Lift: How Empowering Women Changes the World*.

Melinda Gates's recent focus on women can easily be viewed as an extension of her lust to leave a legacy. About half the world's population is female. Still, by nearly every measure, women continue to fare more poorly than men, most notably outside the developed world.[58] No great surprise then that Melinda Gates decided to invest in women and invest big. In 2015 she founded her own investment and incubation company, Pivotal Ventures. In 2018 she announced a $170 million plan to fund global women's equality efforts – in the wake of an earlier $80 million commitment to "end gender inequality" in pay "around the world." But these turned out merely preliminaries. In 2019 she went all in: she announced that she was pledging $1 *billion* to promote gender equality in the United States over the next ten years. By every account it is she, Melinda Gates, who is leading these various gender endeavors both through the Foundation and Pivotal Ventures – not Bill Gates. As she explained it, "I've focused more and more on gender issues, because I've seen repeatedly that the more empowered women and girls are, the stronger their communities are." Later she added, "Equality can't wait, and no one in a position to act should either."[59]

Melinda Gates's efforts on behalf of women are in keeping with the mission of the Bill & Melinda Gates Foundation, and with everything the Gateses together believe in. And also with every-thing the Gateses together try to accomplish, and with everything the Gateses together share – in this case their hallmark, their lust to leave a legacy. When Melinda Gates announced her most recent gift, she proclaimed that it was time finally to "tear down the barriers that keep half the world from leading a full life."[60] That's how they roll, both husband and wife. Doggedly pursuing transfor-mative impact not only at home but also abroad, by making enor-mous investments with deep dedication and conspicuous care. After what by now are many years of complete commitment, neither Bill Gates nor Melinda Gates shows the slightest sign of constraining their vision, diminishing their ambition – or of slow-ing down. Women, yes. But, also, "Zero malaria. Zero TB. Zero HIV. Zero malnutrition. Zero preventable deaths. Zero difference between the health of a poor kid and every other kid."[61]

George Soros

George Soros is a Hungarian-born American hedge fund investor and philanthropist. He is also a phenomenally wealthy one. In 2019 Soros had a net worth of $8.3 billion.[62] This, even though since 1984 he has given away "$32 billion of a personal fortune made in the financial markets."[63] Most of Soros's donations have been funneled through his Open Society Foundations which, as the name implies, reflect Soros's most deeply held belief that, "societies can only flourish when they allow for democratic governance, freedom of expression, and respect for individual rights."[64]

Though Soros was once called "the man who broke the Bank of England" – for a spectacularly successful short sale he made in 1992, betting against the English pound – today he is known pri-marily as a mega-supporter of liberal and progressive political causes. Soros's lust to leave a legacy has been especially far-reaching: his goal has been nothing less than changing certain societies at their core, broadly speaking from authoritarianism to liberalism. It has even been said of him that in the late 1980s and early 1990s he contributed to the collapse of communism in the Soviet Union and, especially, in Eastern Europe.[65]

Soros is a vivid example of someone who lusted effectively lifelong to leave a legacy – open societies the world over. Of course, as is the nature of lust, the more Soros tried to quiet it, pacify it, satisfy it, the more intensive and expansive his lust became.

Context

George Soros's lust to leave a legacy cannot be divorced from the historical context within which he was born and raised – crucially, his experience as a Jewish child in Nazi-occupied Hungary. He was born Gyorgy Schwartz in Budapest on August 12, 1930. To try to avoid Hungary's increasingly ominous anti-Semitism, in 1936 his father changed the family surname, to Soros. Soros had the obvious virtue of sounding Hungarian, as opposed to Jewish. But "Soros" also means something special in another language, with which Soros's father was familiar. In Esperanto it means to "soar." It is not much of a stretch, then, to suppose that Soros's father deliberately gave his two sons a surname that evoked great ambition and achievement. The father was, not incidentally, the more memorable if not also the more dominant parent. When George was a boy of about seven, he wrote a poem that portrayed his father as Zeus, the Greek god who was king of all the other gods.[66]

The Nazi invasion and occupation of Hungary in 1944 and 1945 led to the deportation and murder of over 500,000 Hungarian Jews. Soros and his family managed to survive by securing false identity papers, an experience he later described this way. "Instead of submitting to our fate, we resisted an evil force that was much stronger than we were – yet we prevailed. Not only did we survive, but we managed to help others."[67] On one occasion, when George was ordered to deliver summonses to Jews, his father recognized the documents as essentially deportation notices – to concentration camps. So, he instructed his son to tell the recipients *not* to obey the instructions. Not long after Soros's father arranged for George's older brother, Paul, to move away from the family to a rented room. Soon George was also sent elsewhere, in his case to live with a Hungarian agricultural official, who passed the boy off as his Christian godson. Decades later, Soros would look back and reflect that he emerged from his experience of the Nazi occupation with a "strong defiant streak."[68]

Not long after the Second World War ended, the communists consolidated their power in Hungary. Soros was still an adolescent. Still, he lost no time emigrating, leaving for London in 1947 where he began to study philosophy and economics at the London School of Economics. There he came under the tutelage of the deeply respected and highly influential philosopher of science Karl Popper. It was Popper's body of thought – specifically his liberal ideals and ideas – that constituted the ideological and intellectual foundation on which Soros stood his entire life. Indeed, without some sense of Popper's political philosophy, it is difficult if not impossible to comprehend Soros's lust to leave his singular, very particular, legacy.

Popper's book *The Open Society and Its Enemies* is considered among the most influential of the twentieth century. First published in 1945, it is an unstinting defense of liberalism and an equally unstinting offense against totalitarianism. (Popper was born in Vienna, a Lutheran. But his grandparents were Jewish, so his life, like Soros's, was upended by Hitler.) The lesson that Soros took from Popper is that societies flourish only when they operate freely and openly, and only when they provide adequate protections for individual rights. Open societies encourage rational reflection, and they are, ideally, buttressed by institutions that support democracy, equality, and faith in reason. In contrast, Popper argued, closed societies tend toward conformity and rigidity. They abhor and abjure individuality, creativity, and critical thinking.

While Popper's thesis is highly persuasive to admirers of liberal democracy, it has been critiqued for being (among other things) too narrow and simplistic. Still, his ideas provided the context, the framework, within which George Soros's lust for legacy emerged at an early stage. Though Soros considers himself a thought leader – over time, he developed his own insights about open societies, about which he has written frequently and passionately – he still acknowledges his profound ideological and intellectual debt to Popper. To be sure, Soros's lust to leave a legacy of open societies is also rooted in his own experience, especially during his boyhood in Nazi-occupied Hungary. But by associating himself with Popper, Soros was able years later to transform his philanthropy from the mundane – an ultra-rich person using his or her money in some way to do good – to the grandiose. In contrast to most of his fabulously wealthy peers, Soros has always lusted to leave a legacy that is outsized – and that explicitly is *political*. He seeks to liberate humankind from what he sees as shackles that since time immemorial have, certainly intermittently, held it down, sometimes violently.

Meantime, while Soros became wealthier and then still wealthier, especially in the 1970s and 1980s, his part of the world – the Soviet Union and its satellite states in East Europe, including Albania, Bulgaria, Czechoslovakia, East Germany, Hungary, Poland, Romania,

Bulgaria, and Albania – became more oppressed and depressed. Under the boot of the Soviet Union, the East European communist states were the opposite of open societies. Most were crudely and cruelly closed. Most were increasingly isolated. Most were under the thumb of a Communist Party that tried to enforce near-total ideological control. Most were characterized by enforced conformity and repressive one-party rule. Most were corrupt. Most had in place a "distinct socialist pattern of surveillance" – for example the Soviet KGB and the East German Stasi.[69] Finally, most Soviet dominated communist states were, along with the Soviet Union, subject to central planning under the misguided belief that it was more efficient and effective than free markets. This last point cannot be overemphasized: as much as anything else, it was central planning that led to economic ruin. As a result, the Soviet bloc did not just wither away, it collapsed. And it left in its wake a string of economies in a tailspin, weak civic institutions, lack of the rule of law, and peoples with little or no experience either of democratic governance or of modern approaches to management. A power vacuum was created – which to too great a degree was filled by oligarchs out to pillage whatever they could.

By the time the Soviet Union collapsed, in 1991, George Soros had long been an American citizen – he had moved from England to the United States in 1956 – so it was from an American vantage point that he was witness to what was happening in his native Hungary and, in varying permutations, in every one of its East European neighbors. Given Soros's passion for open societies, and given his now enormous financial resources, he soon saw what he deeply and sincerely believed was an historic opportunity. An historic opportunity to, in effect, write history. On the eve of the Soviet Union's dissolution, when the Union of Soviet Socialist Republics effectively voted itself out of existence, Soros published a book, *Underwriting Democracy*. It "revealed his new strategy: he would dedicate himself to building permanent institutions that would ... model the practices of open societies for the liberated peoples of eastern Europe."[70] In other words, Soros seized the moment. He would invest a considerable portion of his wealth into transforming East European countries from autocracies to democracies – to open societies. In other words, Soros's lust to leave a legacy was so strong a sensation that his was an attempt at nothing less than the reshaping of post-communist Europe.

Evidence

Once George Soros became an exceedingly wealthy man with the means to become, as he himself put it, an "agent of history," this was precisely the goal he aggressively pursued.[71] In 1991, he wrote, "I carried some rather potent messianic fantasies with me from childhood ... when I had made my way in the world, I wanted to indulge my fantasies [of open societies] to the extent that I could afford."[72] As he had become so rich, the extent to which he could afford to "indulge his fantasies" became considerable. So considerable that by 2005 a reporter for *National Public Radio* noted that Soros had been described as "the only private citizen with his own foreign policy."[73]

Soros's lust to leave a legacy manifested itself in several different ways, among others in his attempt to become a thought leader, to influence other people specifically by virtue of his intellectual insights. Once he was asked to "name one thing in the world that he wished he could have," Soros replied, "I want my ideas to be heard."[74] He has said that when he took his first job on Wall Street, in 1956, his goal was to "sock away $100,000 in five years" so that he could quit finance and turn to scholarly pursuits.[75] To propagate his various ideas, Soros has written no fewer than fourteen books. By his own account, he was "greatly disappointed when, upon meeting Bill Clinton for the first time, the president was more interested to glean stock tips than hear about the deteriorating situation in the former Yugoslavia."[76] (Soros was similarly disappointed by President Barack Obama.[77]) But, as it turned out, his legacy would never be what he did in private; it would be what he did in public, in political arenas both at home and abroad.

George Soros is a man of ideas. He is also a man of action, including enormous, audacious wagers on and investments in financial markets. Similar are his wagers on and investments in open societies. In 1989, after the fall of the Berlin Wall, he poured hundreds of millions of dollars into the former Soviet bloc countries to promote civil society and liberal democracy. His lust to leave a legacy of open societies was then, is still, a singularly lofty goal. It is not about erecting a building, funding a program, or even eradicating a disease. He has been seeking to secure liberal values and democratic rule for hundreds of millions of people. He has been talking about transforming political contexts and cultures, and reshaping nations with checkered histories into bastions of Western ideas and ideals. He has been imagining reinventing a region of the world that has had scant if any experience of democratic self-rule. It is in fact on account of that scant experience that Soros has suffered grievous disappointments. But, then, the odds against him were always long – very long.

In his endless quest to secure, to anchor, liberalism in Eastern Europe, Soros created and then supported many different programs and several foundations. His first foundation, established in 1979, was the "Open Society Fund," focused primarily on Eastern Europe. Among his early initiatives was support for various dissident groups including Solidarity in Poland (early 1980s), and Charter 77 (also early 1980s) in the former Czechoslovakia, a loosely knit group protesting the communists' miserable record in human and civil rights.

Later, in the early 1990s, after the collapse of the Soviet Union, Soros went in another direction. He donated over $100 million to support Russian scientists, above all to preclude them from working for countries hostile to the West. He also poured $250 million into a program designed to train Russian teachers. He wanted to promote their critical thinking and to modernize Russian textbooks.[78] Around the same time he instituted his signature initiative: a network of Soros-funded foundations operating around the world under the umbrella, "Open Society Foundations." In general these programs and others similar grew in size and scope, which is to say that in general the pace of Soros's investments in trying to create open societies accelerated.

In the mid-1990s, he poured $5 million into a program that gave free breakfasts to schoolchildren in his native Hungary. Soon after, he poured millions more into an effort to modernize Hungary's healthcare system, for example by purchasing ultrasound machines for hospitals.[79] By 2018, Soros had funded some $400 million worth of projects in Hungary alone.[80] Of course, Hungary was hardly the sole focus of George Soros. A 2017 article in *Foreign Affairs* described his role in the 2003 Rose Revolution, Georgia's pro-Western peaceful change of power.[81] The article also depicted him playing a part in the 2004 Orange Revolution, Ukraine's shift from a corrupt pro-Russia regime to one somewhat less corrupt and somewhat more democratic.

More recently, Soros increased his philanthropy in the United States. He became driven not just to leave a legacy in Europe, but also in the United States, where he has lived most of his life and made most of his fortune. In 2004 Soros gave some

$27 million to try to stop President George W. Bush from being re-elected. A few years later he was an early backer of, that is, donor to, Barack Obama's 2008 presidential campaign. (Later he referred to Obama as his "greatest disappointment."[82]) And in 2016, *Politico* reported that he had quietly emerged "as a leading funder of Democratic politics."[83] In fact, by then Soros had "placed himself in the center of America's culture wars by giving to groups that support abortion, promote the rights of gays and lesbians and ... curb abuses by the police."[84] A full accounting is beyond the scope of this book. But a small selection of Soros's donations suggests the scope of his giving in pursuit of what he deemed an open society, this time in the United States.[85] In 2012 Soros gave:

- $1 million to *America Votes*, "the coordination hub of the progressive community."[86]
- $1 million to *Priorities USA Action*, "a voter-centric progressive advocacy organization and service center for the grassroots progressive movement."[87] (Think super PAC.)
- $1 million to *American Bridge 21st Century*, "the largest research, video tracking, and rapid response organization in Democratic politics" with the mission to "find what Republicans are hiding and make sure voters hear about it."[88]

Why focus on the year 2012? Because it was a year in which there was an election for American president: Democratic Barack Obama versus Republican Mitt Romney. Whoever is president is widely considered the most powerful person on the planet. Given that Soros was hell-bent on leaving a legacy, what better way than generously to help a preferred candidate get elected to the White House? The next presidential election was in 2016: Democratic nominee Hillary Clinton versus Republican nominee Donald Trump. According to a spokesman, George Soros "poured at least $25 million into mobilizing Democratic voters to bolster Clinton and other candidates on the left."[89]

What about the 2020 presidential election? As of mid-2019, Soros had donated $5.1 million to a democratic PAC – the single biggest check any mega-donor had written up to that point. It is more than double the $2.1 million that he gave at the same point during the last presidential election cycle. In short, Soros was "poised to spend heavily" on 2020.[90] In his own words, "President Trump would like to establish a mafia state," and "I consider the

Trump administration a danger to the world." Soros went on to add that he saw the Trump presidency as "a purely temporary phenomenon that will disappear in 2020."[91] Still, obviously, he is somewhat concerned. As he sees it, Trump is endangering every idea, every value, that he, Soros, has fervently espoused and relentlessly promoted. To Soros's credit, to say that he has put his money where his mouth is – especially in Europe and the United States – is to understate it. As of 2018, Soros directly and indirectly, through his foundations, spent more than $14 billion in pursuit of open societies[92] – in pursuit of his lust to leave a legacy.

Finally, perhaps nothing more vividly illustrates George Soros's uphill efforts than his work on behalf of ten to twelve million Roma (or Romani), who live primarily in Central, Eastern, and Southern Europe. The Roma, who used to be called "gypsies," are Europe's poorest "and most reviled people."[93] To provide them with the help he thought they needed, Soros issued a clarion call: for a "Decade of Roma Inclusion" (2005 to 2015). To this end he enlisted both the World Bank and high-level support from twelve countries, including the Czech Republic, Hungary, Bulgaria, Romania, and Serbia. An Open Society Foundations press release announced: "Prime Ministers Endorse 'Decade of Roma Inclusion' called by George Soros." With this single stroke Soros sought to end the Roma's thousand-year-old outsider status. He himself donated generously to their cause, but he also went much further. He undertook a "comprehensive approach" intended to address a range of Roma issues, including "education, employment, housing, and discrimination."[94]

Given that the Roma had long been on the bottom rung of Europe's political, economic, and social hierarchy, trying to make meaningful progress on their behalf was a Sisyphean undertaking.[95] The outcome? Soros's profoundly ambitious and to all appearances entirely well-intentioned project failed miserably. At the end of the ten years there was a dismal evaluation that included this depressing question: should the initiative "be labeled a 'lost decade,' given its spectacular failure in achieving substantial improvements in any four of its objectives"?[96] As was his wont, though his work fell far short, Soros was neither permanently deflated nor defeated. Instead of walking away from the Roma, he doubled down. The Open Society Foundations remain committed to their cause, even announcing a new initiative, *Roma Integration 2020*.[97]

Followers

George Soros has an army working on his legacy – an army of paid professionals whose job it is to make progress toward open societies. In 2019 the Open Society Foundations employed some 1,800 people operating in thirty-five countries.[98] Soros also recruits and engages influential people to serve on his advisory boards. His foundations, then, are the most obvious repository of his followers – mainly though not exclusively paid followers. By no measure have his writings or speeches had similar impact. But, in this as in virtually everything else, Soros remains undeterred. He continues to write and to give speeches. In March 2019, aged 88, he announced his next book, his fifteenth as author or co-author. It will be a "summation of his core beliefs."[99] And in April 2020, he co-wrote an op-ed for the *Los Angeles Times* that urged the federal government to guarantee paychecks for the duration of the coronavirus crisis.

Of course, as we have already seen, Soros has been remarkably vigorous not just in propagating his ideas, but, beginning in the 1980s, in using his vast wealth to get people to follow his lead both in theory and in practice. Specifically, he was looking for followers who could be and would be local change agents, especially in Central and East Europe. To this end, the Open Society Foundations have, among their other initiatives, provided over 12,000 short- and long-term grants to students from the countries that Soros most directly targeted.[100] These programs continue to this day and their intention remains unchanged: to develop a cadre of liberal and progressive leaders committed to opening – and keeping open – the societies within which they live and work.

Some of Soros's followers have become leaders and some have had a significant impact, if only for short periods of time. For example, after Georgia's "Rose Revolution" in 2003, some of Soros's employees and beneficiaries found themselves in positions of power and authority.[101] Moreover, the Rose Revolution was relatively a success; Georgia continues to this day to look to and lean on the West. But, not surprisingly, the path to an open society is not a straight line, to which Georgia's recent history also testifies. Leadership in Georgia – the president, the prime minister, parliamentarians – has been, well, complicated. A society such as Georgia's is impossible to categorize simply as "open" since, despite Soros's best efforts, there persist dramatic instances of abuses of power, including election rigging and voter intimidation.[102]

Romania provides another example of Soros's uneven success, specifically in recruiting followers. In December 1989, Romania's communist dictator, Nicolae Ceausescu, widely feared and despised, for good and ample reason, was overthrown in a violent revolution. The National Salvation Front (NSF) – the group most directly responsible for the revolution – stepped up to form a government to replace the Romanian Communist Party. The NSF was composed primarily not of young revolutionaries, but of former government insiders with whom Soros chose not to work. Instead he associated himself with another Romanian organization, the Group for Social Dialogue, a collection of dissidents, including intellectuals, professors, and journalists. Not only was the group small – it had only about a dozen members – it had played no major part in the revolution. It did, however, consist of the kinds of people with whom Soros thought he could work. Within the week, he had visited the Group for Social Dialogue, ostensibly "to advise" its handful of members. "I think I was the first civilian plane that landed in Bucharest," Soros has since recalled.[103] But, did these few Soros-aligned, liberal, West-leaning intellectuals have a snowball's chance in hell of leading a "social dialogue" with rank-and-file Romanian citizens, of leading Romania toward advancing an open society? It did not.

Soon after, in mid-1990, in the first post-revolution national election, Romanians, by an overwhelming margin, voted into office the party led by ex-communist insiders. They did promise a clean break, and they did make some real changes such as banning the Communist Party, putting the notorious secret police under army control, and preparing for democratic elections. But from the beginning there were accusations that the Romanian revolution for democracy had been hijacked by insiders and former communist leaders. Romania, then, was like Georgia: neither completely successfully became an open society. Neither could claim the outcome that Soros had wanted and intended.

Soros continues to follow a similar, by now familiar path. He continues to operate in Eastern Europe to try to recruit young followers and to socialize them to champion open societies. He offers students fellowships to study abroad, and provides funds for them, as well as for professionals from different fields, to attend international conferences. In other words, Soros still supports programs that expose East Europeans to established systems of democratic governance. His preferred outcome is, obviously, an aspiring leader eager to create change, change that is in keeping with his, Soros's, and with Karl Popper's, ideas and ideals.

Soros's strategy has successfully created a group of followers loyal to the Open Society Foundations as an institution, and to George Soros as an individual. But he has been notably less successful in realizing his vision – in leaving the inordinately ambitious legacy that all along he has dreamed of. Specifically, with some notable exceptions, his followers have been unable, in anything resembling a critical mass, to serve as significant agents of change. Agents of change who can first get, and then continue to hold, the levers of power necessary to do the work that Soros still hopes will get done.

Some of Soros's would-be followers have been little more than cranky and complaining. For example, Mirel Palada, a Romanian, studied with Soros's support at Kalamazoo College in Michigan. After returning home, Palada served in various government posts, including as a spokesperson for the Romanian government. But, for whatever reasons, his experience with Soros left him with a foul taste in his mouth. According to Palada, Soros takes "naïve, young folks, shows them America, pays for their studies, patiently building a network of people" who are supposed to be grateful. But, then, again according to Palada, Soros goes on to use these people for his own political purposes. "Thank God," Palada continued, "I'm not part of Soros's network. [I would not want to feel] indebted and become one of his minions."[104]

Much more important have been a few spectacular cases in which the beneficiaries of Soros's largesse got into positions of power only to reverse course. Not only did they *not* adhere to the principles of open societies, they did the just the opposite. The most ironic, one could even say tragic, example of a one-time follower who turned on a dime is Hungarian Prime Minister Viktor Orbán. Once upon a time Orbán was Soros's admirer. Moreover, early in his life he was a beneficiary of Soros's largesse – only to become later in his life a formidable, some would even say a vicious, opponent. Soros's Open Society Foundations initially provided young Orbán with a scholarship to Oxford. Some years later, Soros supported Fidesz – "the Alliance of Young Democrats" – a Western-oriented Hungarian student organization that Orbán had helped to found. However, not long after, Fidesz devolved into a defiantly illiberal political party and an inordinately ambitious one at that. Orbán meantime went on to have an astonishingly successful political career. He first served as prime minister of Hungary from 1998 to 2002. Later, in 2010, he was re-elected, since then moving swiftly and steadily toward establishing a state evocative of nothing so much as a jingoistic dictatorship. Orbán has regularly and relentlessly attacked Soros personally and he has regularly and relentlessly attacked Soros's Open Society Foundations. Orbán has gone so far as to shamelessly brand George Soros an all-powerful globalist and a money-hungry Jew, who is plotting to overwhelm Hungary with Muslim immigrants to undermine its Christian heritage.[105]

Such enormous, embarrassing failures, on the scale of Orbán, are rare for Soros. But there are lessons here, lessons to be learned about how and when to engage followers and what reasonably to expect them to accomplish. It seems clear, for example, that Soros overestimated the potential power of a relatively small, elite cadre of loyal followers. He struggled from the start to get ordinary people on board, quotidian citizens, if you will, who at some point would have to be on board if his grand ambitions were going to be realized. To be sure, we do not claim to have the perfect playbook for a man such as Soros, a man who has dreamed of doing no less than opening societies – of writing a new chapter especially in the history of Eastern Europe. But it is almost certainly the case that in order to leave the legacy that he wanted and intended, Soros would have had to enlist not only an elite group of followers, but, additionally, large numbers of followers who cut across all levels of society. How this was to be achieved was never really spelled out.

In Eastern Europe there has been a secondary issue as well. By most accounts, Soros has focused heavily on having his open societies look to the West for inspiration, specifically the United States and Western Europe. Long before the advent of Donald Trump, or for that matter, of Boris Johnson, these were held up as models of what open societies should look like. But, at no point did Soros or his Open Society Foundations make it a point to draw on local countries and cultures, such as those of Hungary, or Romania, or Poland. Exactly what would an open society in any one of these places look like? Bill and Melinda Gates learned early on that what works in one part of the world does not necessarily work in another. Different contexts – as in different countries and cultures – demand different approaches. So, if Soros fails in the end to leave the legacy that he has sought for so long to bestow – fails despite his enormous investments and his own deep dedication to democratic ideals and ideas – it will be in part because he never understood that for leaders to succeed they must have at least the tacit support of their putative followers. Not a few of their putative followers, but many if not most.

Hindsight

George Soros at age 90 is as unpopular as he is popular, as infamous as he is famous. For every person who is a strong admirer, there is another who is a fierce detractor. Soros has become a nemesis of far-right nationalists, and, increasingly, of mainstream conservatives, especially in Europe and the United States. In some circles he is vilified as a rapacious capitalist, and as a devilish cosmopolitan, and as a greedy Jew.

Tragically, Hungary, where he was born, has turned out worst of all. Prime Minister Orbán ran his most recent (2018) campaign for re-election as if his opponent were George Soros. Orbán promoted "anti-Semitic imagery of powerful Jewish financiers scheming to control the world," and he had "thousands of posters" plastered all over Budapest that pictured a "grinning Soros with the slogan 'Let's not allow Soros to have the last laugh!'"[106] Additionally, in a personal swipe at Soros, the Hungarian parliament "passed legislation requiring NGOs to declare themselves foreign agents," as well as a "Stop Soros" law that essentially banned individuals and organizations from "providing any assistance to undocumented immigrants."[107] An Open Society Foundations employee summarized the situation: Soros is "a very useful punching bag, because he's both the insider and the outsider, the meddling foreigner and the Hungarian Jew."[108]

Even in the United States, Soros, who among Americans is not widely known, is nevertheless divisive. He is lionized by some "as an influential voice on the global stage whose word is followed closely" by, among others, "wealthy Democratic donors."[109] At the same time, he is vilified by others. One of the more dangerous conspiracy theories paints Soros as a "puppet master of a vast left-wing and globalist elite."[110] Nor is this sort of craziness, this sort of viciousness, limited any longer to the political fringe. In 2010, then Fox News talk show host Glenn Beck described Soros as "responsible for sowing political and economic chaos throughout the world."[111]

Soros's lust to leave a legacy has, however, run up not just against personal vilification, but also against political change. In recent years the world has turned away from the sort of liberal, democratic ideals espoused by the Open Society Foundations and toward rising nationalism and populism. There has been a "boom in voter support for right-wing and populist parties" across Europe.[112] And in the United States there has been increasing evidence not only of tribalism but of outright racism.[113] To be sure, history is cyclical. For example, it is possible that in the United States Republican Donald Trump will be succeeded in the White House by a liberal democrat. It is also possible that in Europe the shift to the right, even to the far right, will be reversed. What is, however, indisputable is that despite his enormous fortune, a misfortune of George Soros's old age is that the open society ideals that he has fervently espoused and lustfully pursued all his life, are showing signs of retreating. Soros bet that an educated, liberal elite can position itself to drive a country's destiny. But, in case after case, it seems that large numbers of ordinary people – particularly those who live outside urban areas – either never accepted the democratic liberalism that Soros so persistently propagated, or, if once they did, now they do not.

Given the mismatch between the man and the moment George Soros could easily have chosen to retreat. But, again, he has not *wanted* to leave a legacy of open societies, he has *lusted* to leave a legacy of open societies. Which explains, of course, why the future will be in keeping with the past. The Open Society Foundations will continue to spend about a billion dollars a year chasing Soros's dream. He once described himself as a "giant digestive tract, taking in money at one end and pushing it out at the other."[114] This seems about right. So long as he is sentient, he will never stop. In 2017 he gave $18 billion to his Open Society Foundations. It was "one of the largest transfers of wealth ever made by a private donor to a single foundation." And it catapulted the Open Society Foundations "into the second-biggest philanthropic organization in the United States." Second only to the Bill & Melinda Gates Foundation.[115]

Coda

Bill and Melinda Gates, and George Soros, have long lusted to leave a legacy. But, interestingly, in some ways, their respective strategies are in striking contrast. The Gateses have always displayed extraordinary sensitivity to context. They pay careful attention to the specifics of the countries and cultures within which they operate. George Soros is different. His vision is a universal one – the philosophical and political ideals and ideas originally associated with the Enlightenment. Which to him have meant that they can and should apply equally and similarly, no matter the specifics of the circumstances.

As we said at the start of this book, we are here to describe, not to prescribe. We describe what is, we do not prescribe what ought to be. Still, we would point out that one of the reasons the Gateses and George Soros are able to operate on such a vast scale is because many if not most governments are to some considerable extent broken, either functionally, for example they are gridlocked, or fiscally, for example they spend far more money than they take in. This explains certainly in part why actors like the Gateses and Soros have the latitude to try to solve problems of enormous magnitude and great complexity. Of course, they also have the resources to which we earlier referred: among them, vast sums of money, high levels of energy, and vaulting ambition. All this allows them, encourages them even, to conduct audacious experiments, whether eradicating a pernicious disease or, as Woodrow Wilson famously put it, "making the world safe for democracy."

Of course, as we have seen, in both cases there were also spectacular failures. Moreover, it would be easy to conclude that whereas Bill and Melinda Gates are on the side of the angels – who can quarrel with eliminating malaria? – George Soros's quest is more controversial. His is in any case far less typical a philanthropic endeavor – hoping to help those who are sick or poor is more obvious a motivation for donating than hoping to transform an autocracy into a democracy. But the overarching point of course is this. Bill and Melinda Gates, and George Soros, have all been driven – and they will continue to be driven, to the end of their days – to leave a legacy. Their lust is the reason for their being. Their lust is the reason for their leadership. Not one of the three lusted originally to lead. Rather their leadership – as philanthropists and activists – has been in consequence of their lust. Though what precisely will be their legacies cannot now be known, what can be known is that each of the three will have left their mark. Tennis great Billie Jean King once said, "No one changes the world who isn't obsessed."[116] Leaders like these – leaders who lust to leave a legacy – *are* obsessed.

EPILOGUE
Lust and Leadership

It turned out we were on to something. Lust matters. It might seem curious, but when we start writing a book such as this one, both of us know generally where we're going and what we want to say, but not specifically, not exactly. In this case we knew generally that despite its being completely ignored in the twenty-first century leadership literature, lust has been of significance in the past and was certain therefore to be of significance in the present. But until we did the research, until we started putting flesh on the bones of our cases, we ourselves did not fully appreciate how much of a driver lust is. Nor did we fully appreciate the symbiosis between lust and leadership. Or that some leaders who lust are exceptional in part, certainly, precisely because of their lust. To reiterate, leaders who lust have a *fire in their belly* that is impossible to douse. Leaders who lust have a *life force* that is impossible to slow not to speak of stop. And leaders who lust have an *appetite so enormous and relentless* it is impossible ever fully to satisfy. Thus is lust a trait, or an attribute, or a characteristic that must be singled out. It is leaders who lust who mostly make history.

So strong is the leadership industry's preference for moderation, so strong is its emphasis on balance as a virtue, including, not incidentally, work–life balance, that looking at leaders who lust is not only aberrant, but also (initially at least it seemed, even to us) slightly unseemly. So be it. For to avoid leaders who lust is to avoid leaders who stand out precisely because they intensely want or desperately need to obtain an object or to secure a circumstance that, temporarily, provides gratification. Moreover, to avoid lust more generally – to avoid ferocious feelings, powerful drives, insatiable appetites, intense desires, and overpowering needs – is to avoid the human condition. Again, in the past, passions such as these were as openly addressed as deeply understood. The classic Sanskrit scripture, *The Bhagavad Gita*, warns that there are three gates to hell: anger, greed, and lust.[1] The Christian Bible, the Gospel of Luke, exhorts us to be on guard "against all kinds of greed; for one's life does not consist in the abundance of possessions."[2] And Buddhists believe that lust precludes enlightenment. "The righteous man casts off evil, and by rooting out lust, bitterness, and illusion do we reach Nirvana."[3]

But, notwithstanding wisdoms and traditions such as these, lust is more complex and ubiquitous an impulse than initially it appears. First, our primary point is about desire itself. Lust is a desire that is near desperate to be satisfied. It is a desire that is relentless, tireless, ceaseless. A desire that virtually immediately after it is satisfied resurfaces, and then again, in continuous loops beyond all reason. Next our secondary point, is that the strong need, the urgent want for temporary gratification is more expansive a conception than the word "lust" usually implies. We have seen that lust can and often does mean an intense desire for sex and, in keeping with the preceding cautions against greed, it can also mean and often does an intense desire for money. But the objects of desire – the responses to the question, lust for what? – are not confined just to these two. Though we limited our study to six different lusts, even this number is double the conventional three: sex, money, and power.

Lust is also more complicated a concept than we usually conceive because the consequences of it are mixed. Contrary to conventional wisdom, lust is not all bad, something that, by definition, is to be abhorred, to be protected against at all costs. As we have seen, not only do desires that are strong and even unrelenting have different objects in mind – including some that rank among our most cherished, such as freedom and independence, liberty and equality, service and sacrifice – as these would suggest lust can produce outcomes that accrue to the benefit not just of a few but of many.

Because we tend to assume that lust pertains mainly to power, money, and sex, we tend similarly to assume that certainly some leaders who lust should hide their hunger. Which is true.

Some leaders who lust end embarrassed and even humiliated, though this depends to an extent on context. As we saw, for many years one of Italy's most prominent leaders was a man whose lust for sex was widely tolerated and, no doubt, among some even admired. In contrast, in other countries and cultures such levels of tolerance for sexual promiscuousness, especially while the leader is in office, are inconceivable.

The prevailing assumption in any case is that passions, extremes, are unattractive and that, therefore, leaders who lust should mask their lust lest it seem excessive in a role that typically calls for temperance. But it turns out that this too is a myth. Though the leadership industry touts the virtues of moderation, in the real world not only does excess often succeed, it is often widely appreciated and even applauded. One could even go so far as to argue that balance and moderation tend more to foster mediocrity, whereas leaders who lust, who are focused laser-like on the object of their desire, tend more to stand out. (Again, think Steve Jobs.) Our point in any case is that in the real world not only do leaders not necessarily conceal their lust, they frequently flout it. (Think "greedy, greedy, greedy" Donald Trump.) They wear their lust on their sleeve loudly and proudly. For good reason. For not only are some leaders eager to display their lust, some followers are equally eager to savor any type of lust that promises to provide them with benefits. These benefits might be direct – such as, in the case of Nelson Mandela, for South African blacks the end of apartheid. Or they might be indirect – such as, in the case of Tom Brady, for his ardent admirers the vicarious pleasures of near perfect performances.

Lust is in any case neither necessarily good nor bad. It can be either, or for that matter somewhere in between. Moreover, while it can reasonably be argued that lust is among the most narcissistic of human impulses, this does not mean, necessarily, that others, followers, do not also stand to benefit. As some of the cases in this book make clear, while lust is self-involved to the point of being narcissistic, sometimes there is, simultaneously, more. For being to an extent narcissistic and being to an extent altruistic are not necessarily mutually exclusive. Bill and Melinda Gates are satisfying their own need to leave a legacy. At the same time, they are satisfying the needs of numberless others to better their health and welfare. In fact, the Gateses are a perfect example of lust and leadership becoming twinned, the one nearly indistinguishable from the other. Their apparently equally shared passion for leaving a legacy of smart and informed, thoughtful and careful, national and international giving has made them leaders in the field of philanthropy. So, not only is it certain that they will leave a legacy, it is equally certain that they will long be remembered as among the greatest philanthropists in American history.

We wrote in the Prologue that each of the six different types of lust both feed into, and are fed by, leadership. We added that this was another way of saying that it was difficult if not ultimately impossible to determine which is the chicken and which the egg. Do leaders want to lead because leading enables them more easily to satisfy, or to try to satisfy, their lust? Or is their lust in consequence of their being leaders? These are not in the end questions to which we were able to provide unambiguous, conclusive answers, at least not answers that apply wherever leaders who lust surface. To track, say, our two examples of people who lusted for power, Roger Ailes and Xi Jinping, is to see that both these men had appetites that grew with eating. The more power they had, the more they wanted. Put directly, the more they grew into, and finally without major impediment held onto, their positions of leadership, the hungrier they became. But, at the same time, both men were hungry early on. Their hunger was not something acquired later in life, after they had settled into their leadership roles. They got to the top because lust drove them to the top in the first place. Lust pushed them, pulled them, prodded and pressured them to excel to the point of being exceptional. Clearly, then, as we suggested at the outset, lust and leadership are mutually reinforcing. They feed into each other and off each other.

Consider the leaders chronicled in this book – how extraordinary a cast of characters! Roger Ailes and Xi Jinping; Warren Buffett and Charles Koch; John F. Kennedy and Silvio Berlusconi; Hillary Clinton and Tom Brady; Nelson Mandela and Larry Kramer; Bill and Melinda Gates and George Soros. They diverged obviously in the objects of their lust. Those in each of the six different groups were hungry for something different, in some cases something very different. They differed as well in the imprint they left – are still leaving. Of course, how history will ultimately judge each of these leaders will depend on what history ultimately decides is good, that is, effective and ethical, and on what history ultimately decides is bad, that is, ineffective and unethical. Still, it is safe to say that Mandela will forever be remembered as akin to a savior, and Berlusconi as akin to a scoundrel. To our point about the importance of context, this did not preclude Italians from electing Berlusconi in 2019, for the first time, baggage and all, advanced age and all, to the European Parliament.

What finally stands out, however, are not the differences among leaders who lust, but their similarities: First, a ferociously intense want or need to obtain an object, or to secure a circumstance that will grant them gratification, if only briefly, temporarily. Second, an urgent, fervent drive, hunger, determination, ambition, or passion that persists to the point of lasting life-long. Third, a resilience that remains no matter how long the odds; no matter the number of setbacks; no matter the personal, professional, or political sacrifices; no matter the quantities and qualities of whatever it is that has already been obtained or achieved. Finally, a focus, a single-minded, single-tracked, laser-like focus that is fixed, that stays in place notwithstanding decades of numberless and various distractions and temptations.

None of this, obviously, is to say that every leader, even every leader who is exceptional, lusts. Nor is it to say that everyone who lusts is a leader. Rather it is to restore to our understanding of leadership that which was understood thousands of years ago: that lust is endemic to the human condition and that lust and leadership can be mutually reinforcing. In fact, though our sample size is small, and though our research is suggestive not conclusive, lust and leadership would appear sometimes to go hand in hand, especially in those cases in which leadership is exceptional. Exceptional in that it is inordinately *effective*; not, or at least not necessarily, in that it is inordinately ethical.

We have made clear that as we define the word, lust cannot be taught. Ergo, it cannot be learned in any conventional sense of this word. Given its genesis is partly biological, partly cultural, and partly experiential, teaching someone how to lust, how to be lustful, is impossible. This does not mean, however, that there is nothing about lust that can and indeed should be learned. Just as it is one thing to teach how to lead and quite another to teach *about* leadership, so it is one thing to teach how to lust and quite another to teach *about* lust. As it happens, there is a lot to be learned about lust. There are, so to speak, several "lust lessons," lessons of consequence to anyone with an interest in leadership that is more than just passing. Some of the following lust lessons are based on findings other than our own; others are based on findings discussed in this book. All of them are extracted from materials already pre-sented. The following list is, then, more summary than expository.

1. *The genesis of lust is complex.* Some of it is primal, inherited originally from our most distant human or even primate ancestors, and passed on to us by parents, grandparents, and great-grandparents whose genes left an imprint. Some of it is cultural, lust being either encouraged or discouraged by various cultures, contexts, and circum-stances. Finally, the genesis of lust is in part experiential, a consequence of the lives we lived, from infancy into adulthood.

2. *Lust can and sometimes does overwhelm common sense – which is, however, not by definition a deficit.* Lust and common sense appear at odds. Why is enough not enough? Why hunger for more when your cup already runs over? Because while common sense is a virtue some of the time, probably even most of the time, it is not necessa-rily a virtue all the time. Sometimes lust overtakes com-mon sense with results that not only are positive, they are downright exciting. One could even argue that the great dreamers in history, the great movers and shakers, are not usually known for their common sense. Rather they are known for having driving passion and vaulting ambition – levels of passion and ambition that not only are not reasonable, that are downright *un*reasonable. Such leaders defy common sense – which is precisely what can and sometimes does make them, in some way, transcendent.

3. *Lust is an inordinately powerful motivator – perhaps the most powerful motivator of all.* Though it has remained so far foreign to the leadership literature specifically, and to the leadership industry generally, we preliminarily con-clude that lust is one of several characteristics that sepa-rates the wheat from the chaff. More specifically, we preliminarily conclude that lust, as much as or maybe even more than anything else, distinguishes merely ordinary leaders from obviously extraordinary leaders. Of course, our sample size is too small to consider this a conclusion; we are content, for now, simply to call it an observation.

4. *Lust is rare.* Earlier we noted that lust is variable. Which of course is true: levels of, say, ambition and passion vary greatly from one individual, from one leader, to another. But it is also true that as we use the word here, lust connotes levels of ambition and passion, of hunger and drive, that are extreme. What this means, in turn, is that lust as we define it is uncommon, infrequent. To be clear: we grant that all leaders or at least most leaders have some level of ambition and maybe even a smidgeon of passion. However, lust, pure, unadulterated lust, is extreme – at the end of the spectrum – which, by definition, means that it is not usual, it is unusual.

5. *Lust cannot, not now at least, be measured.* As indicated, lust, the degree of lust and, arguably, even the presence or absence of lust, is variable. However, we cannot rigorously assess lust; or accurately measure lust; or even precisely compare leaders who lust. We know that sometimes the level of lust is so high, so blatantly in evidence, it's impossible to miss. We similarly know most of the time though not all the time what a leader is lusting for. But there is no lust index. There are no measures of lust other than those that are crude.

6. *Leaders who lust generally are in control, not out of control.* Lustful leaders do not usually behave in ways that are beyond the pale – they are not crazy. Generally, they channel their drive; if they did not, they would increase their chances of being ousted. To be clear, though, being in control is not necessarily a constant. Sometimes leaders who lust – for, say, power – are out of control. Sometimes they are more than power hungry; they are in effect power mad. Either they continue to want more power and then still more power; or they continue to want to cling, indefinitely, to the power they already have. Still, most leaders who lust can and do control themselves. Either they lust in ways that are acceptable to their followers, or they hide their lust, so their followers never know.

7. *Lust is value free.* As we have repeatedly pointed out, and as is evident from some of the stories told in this book, on the one hand leaders who lust can be good – they can be ethical and effective. But, on the other hand, leaders

who lust can be bad – they can be unethical and ineffective. Of course, like other leaders they can also be a mix – either unethical and effective or ethical and ineffective. The point in any case is that though there is modest evidence that lust tends to elicit unethical behavior, there is also evidence that leaders who lust can be additive as opposed only to subtractive. Similarly, lust can derail, and end in the leader's downfall. Equally, lust can propel, and be the driver of a leader who shoots for the moon.

8. *Lust is not a choice*. If it were a choice, it could be taught. But it cannot. In this sense lust is different from grit and drive, which are widely seen not only as virtues to be admired, but as virtues that can be acquired. You too can develop grit; you too can develop drive. Moreover, you too *should* develop grit; you too *should* develop drive. Not so with lust. Because the genesis of lust is complex, it cannot simply be summoned. To be sure, by raising awareness that lust matters and, especially, that leaders who lust can have a significant impact, it is possible and maybe even probable that some leaders, and some would-be leaders will attempt to connect to their inner lust – to surface it, if you will. Still, in the main, leaders either have it, or they don't.

9. *Lust attracts followers*. Contrary to the conventional wisdom that touts moderation as a leadership virtue and excess as a leadership vice, lust is not, at least not necessarily, a detraction. In fact, just as often it is an attraction. Leaders who lust can and often do appeal to followers pulled in by the leader's obvious, sometimes even ostentatious passion, by their fierce ambition, and by their relentless determination. As Freud pointed out almost a century ago, on some fundamental maybe even primitive level, leaders who are strong, who seem driven and maybe even destined to take the lead, appeal to followers forever seeking safety and security, forever seeking a savior. Though our models of leadership now are more complex – think diversity and inclusion, flatter hierarchies and employee engagement, teams and networks – human nature is what it is. For all the changes that have taken place, especially the leveling between

leaders and followers, our need for some sense of order still means that we want someone, we need someone, to be in charge. And, it happens that, sometimes at least, leaders who lust are especially equipped to convey the high degree of confidence that most of us, on some elemental level, continue to seek.

10. *Lust must be seen in context.* Power is perceived differently, and it plays out differently in China than it does in Canada. Money is perceived differently, and it plays out differently in the United States than it does in Norway. Sex is perceived differently, and it plays out differently in Italy than it does in Indonesia. Success is perceived differently, and it plays out differently, in the West than it does in the Middle East, especially as it pertains to women. Legitimacy is perceived differently, and it plays out differently, in England than it does in Poland. And legacy is perceived differently, and it plays out differently, in Japan than it does in Brazil. Of course, context is not just about country. Context is about any holding environment, any situation or circumstance within which leadership and followership take place. Leaders who lust, then, must be understood from the perspective of the time and place within which they are located.

For the sake of this discussion we'll assume that these ten lust lessons have been learned. Now what? What do we do with what has been learned? Lust itself cannot be taught, hence it cannot simply be adopted or acquired. But, as we said, there is much to be known *about* lust – which raises the question of what we can do with what we now know. Is this discussion, is this book only an intellectual exercise? Or does coming to grips with leaders who lust have practical implications? Do the ten lust lessons teach us something of practical consequence?

We want to make explicit what all along has been implicit. If this book, this discussion, is nothing other than a cognitive exercise, it suffices. *It is more than enough for us to stake our claim on the extremely simple but inordinately important proposition that leaders who lust matter.* And that sometimes they matter a great deal – which is precisely why they should be, why they *must* be, part of what constitutes leadership as an area of intellectual inquiry. It happens though that the information and ideas that emerged from our exploration and discussion have implications not only for how we think about leadership, but for how we lead *and* for how we follow. For the sake of simplicity, we divide the information and ideas into two groups. The first is targeted especially but not exclusively at leaders. The second is targeted especially but not exclusively at followers – at everyone and anyone who does not lead every moment of every day.

Leaders

Some leaders who lust are fortunate. Depending on the object of their lust, on their level of self-control, on who are their followers, and on the circumstances within which they are situated, some leaders who lust can use it to good effect. By "use it to good effect" we mean that such leaders can meet one or another need or want of their own, if only temporarily, while *simultaneously* meeting one or another need or want of their followers. Earlier we pointed out – using Bill and Melinda Gates as examples – that lust is not just narcissistic. Lust can also be, at the same time, altruistic, or at least beneficent, an energy harnessed not just for the benefit of the self, but also, somehow, in some way, for the benefit of others. Here then we offer some information and ideas on how leaders who lust can draw on their drive, their hunger, their determination, their ambition, their passion to make a positive difference. Each of the following can be, is intended to be, accomplished by leaders acting on their own. Each is intended to heighten leaders' aware-ness of what lust is, to help them avoid the inevitable pitfalls of lust, and to direct them to muster their lust to good effect.

- Leaders who lust should have a clear understanding of who they are – they should strive to be self-aware.
- Leaders who lust should have a clear understanding of what lust is – and is not.
- Leaders who lust should have a clear understanding of the nature of their lust – of the object of their lust and of how their needs and wants can reasonably and responsibly be accommodated.
- Leaders who lust should have a clear understanding of their followers – their constituents, their stakeholders, those to whom they in some way are responsible.

- Leaders who lust should have a clear understanding of the contexts within which they are situated – both those that are immediate, such as their groups and organizations, and those at a greater remove, such as their countries and cultures. As is probably evident by now, context can encourage lust or discourage it. If, for example, a country or culture is clearly materialistic, it, in effect, encourages, even supports leaders who are greedy. Similarly, if, for example, a country or culture has a long history of authoritarian leadership, it, in effect, encourages leaders eager to accrue power – and then more power.
- Leaders who lust should have a clear understanding of how lust can be harnessed – an asset used to good effect.
- Leaders who lust should have a clear understanding of how lust can be useless – having no destination other than self-gratification, and no end in sight, ever.
- Leaders who lust should have a clear understanding of how lust can be risky – threatening to the well-being of everyone involved.
- Leaders who lust should have a clear understanding of how lust can be dangerous – hurtful or harmful to self and/or to others.
- Leaders who lust should have a clear understanding of how lust is limitless – which can mean that in some situations their lust must be stifled, suppressed, checked, constrained, contained, controlled, channeled, redirected.
- Leaders who lust should have a clear understanding of the importance of monitoring – either they monitor themselves or they enlist trusted others to assist them, others able, as necessary, to speak truth to power.

Followers

Just as some leaders who lust are fortunate, so are some followers. Depending on the character of the leader, and on the circumstances within which they, followers and their leaders, are situated, and on their own needs, wants, and wishes, it is, as we have seen, entirely possible for followers to benefit from having a leader who lusts. But, obviously, the obverse is also true. Depending on the variables just mentioned, some followers with leaders who lust are cursed.

They stand to suffer at the hands of leaders driven mainly by their own appetites, stirred primarily by their own passions, and persistently on the prowl for the objects of their own satisfactions. There are some occasions on which followers are able relatively easily to deal with leaders like these, to displace or to leave leaders whose lust has made them narcissistic and self-aggrandizing in the extreme. But there are many other occasions, many more occasions, on which followers are saddled with leaders like these, but where either removing them, or leaving them behind is difficult if not impossible. What then can be done?

As the literature on, and our experiences with, whistle-blowers amply attests, removing leaders who are bad, including leaders who lust to detrimental effect, is notoriously difficult. This said, here some things that followers need to know when the going gets tough. When they are stuck with leaders who lust – everyone else be damned. Similarly, here some things that followers need to know when the going is good. When they are led by leaders who lust in ways they can legitimately support.

- Like leaders, followers should become lust learners. They should have a clear understanding that some leaders are driven beyond all apparent reason. They should also understand that this drive, this relentless drive for whatever the object of lust, will not diminish over time. Recall that, by our definition, lust can never, other than briefly, be satisfied. It is folly to think otherwise: leaders who lust will never have enough. Given this inevitable relentlessness, followers should try to avoid at all costs leaders who lust in ways that are bad. Sometimes such leaders, such situations, are impossible to avoid. But other times they are not. Other times paying attention to signs that lust is in evidence, paying attention to signs that lust is doing harm, can make a big difference. It can help followers to steer clear of the dangers of coming too close to leaders whose lust should be distrusted.
- In contrast, given that some leaders who lust are good, followers should, whenever and wherever possible, actively seek out leaders whose passions and ambitions match and maybe even mirror their own. Just as it can be awful to be vulnerable to leaders driven in ways their followers despise, so it can be wonderful to be led by

those who, notwithstanding their being driven, share our values and so seek genuinely to motivate us, and to provide our lives with purpose and meaning.

- Followers saddled with leaders who lust in ways that are bad have the option of resisting. Resisting bad leadership, in this case lustful leadership, can take several different forms, essentially along a spectrum from passive to active resistance. The latter is equated with resistance that nearly inevitably is risky. To wit, significant threats directed at whistleblowers – who should be, but often are not, well protected. When in 2019 a whistleblower revealed incriminating information about Donald Trump, the president was enraged, charging that he or she was "close to a spy," and implicitly threatening the still anonymous individual by asking aloud "you know what we used to do in the old days ... with spies and treason?"[4] By this he meant, of course, executing them. How then to get people to guard against the downsides of exposing leaders who lust if doing so puts them at high risk? We cannot here do justice to so complicated an issue, one that nearly always is fraught with personal, professional, and sometimes even political danger. Suffice instead to imagine yourself a powerless employee at Fox News, publicly protesting the all-powerful chief executive officer, Roger Ailes. Similarly, imagine yourself an ordinary Chinese citizen, with no special claim to fame, publicly protesting the all-powerful president, Xi Jinping. In both cases the outcomes likely would have been bad, possibly even very bad. (Of course, as world-famous artist Ai Weiwei could attest, even fame and fortune are no protection against going after leaders who lust for power.)
- At least some followers saddled with leaders who lust in ways that are bad bear responsibility, some not just indirectly, but directly. Any institution or individual who explicitly is charged with oversight falls into this category. For example, we include in this group boards of directors: they are directly responsible for overseeing chief executive officers. And we include in this group members of the United States Congress: they are directly responsible for overseeing the American president. Technically, of course, neither board members nor members of Congress are followers.

But if they fail to take on bad leaders, they are not leading, they are following. This does not of course let the rest of us off the hook. When leaders who lust become bad, if we settle for being bystanders, we are settling for being conformers and colluders.

In the Prologue that bookends this Epilogue we wrote that to do justice to leaders who lust, the definition of "lust" had to be broken into two parts. Part one centered on the idea that to lust is to have a fervor and an urgency, a hunger and a thirst, an ambition and a passion that were ferocious in their intensity and relentlessness. Part two focused on the object of lust – which transformed lust from being an abstraction to having definition. After all, leaders who lust are lusting for something specific – here for power, or money, or sex, or success, or legitimacy, or legacy. We also suggested that when leaders lust, leadership and lust become twinned, the one indivisible from the other. Each, moreover, fuels the other, drives the other, in a relationship that becomes over time symbiotic.

But ultimately there is an irony. For though leadership and lust can be as synergistic as symbiotic, they are of course not the same. Lust is a trait, or an attribute, characteristic of a few leaders but not of all leaders or even of most leaders. Lust is, moreover, in some ways at odds with leadership, directly at odds. For to lead means to proceed, with one or more followers in tow, in a certain direction for the purpose of reaching a certain destination. As in "to lead the way" which implies that whoever is leading the way not only knows the way but knows why – why the group is going where it is going. It is further to suggest that once the destination has been reached, the task has been accomplished. There is closure – closure that is anticipated to bring a sense of satisfaction, resolution, and completion, at least to the leader.

Lust in contrast is never-ending. There is no closure – it is never over. Nor is it ever entirely satisfying. Lust has numberless benchmarks, countless stations but no destination. For every time a goal is reached, an object is acquired, or a circumstance is secured, the goalpost is moved, further into the distance, ultimately beyond reach, indefinitely beyond reach. Lust exemplifies what social psychologists call the "arrival fallacy" – a term for how though we think we'll be happy when we get what we want, we think wrong. Similarly, unlike most leaders who, when they get to where they want to go, are satisfied, content to have accomplished what they set out to accomplish, lustful leaders remain, forever, unsatisfied. Their appetite grows with eating – they always want more.[5] Like the arrival fallacy, then, lust is an illusion. The illusion that reaching a destination and getting satisfaction are one and the same.

Whereas implicit in leadership is a sense of optimism – a sense that when a mission has been accomplished there will be both pleasure and closure – with lust there is no such result. Lust is never ending – which is precisely why leaders who lust last. They last literally – tending to linger as leaders for a long period of time. And they last figuratively – tending to be remembered as leaders for a long period of time.

NOTES

Prologue

1. Bill George, *Authentic Leadership: Rediscovering the Secrets to Creating Lasting Value* (Jossey-Bass, 2003), p. 46.
2. Edmund Morris, *Edison* (Random House, 2019), p. 7.
3. Bernard Bass with Ruth Bass, *The Bass Handbook of Leadership* (Free Press, 2008), p. 107.
4. Angela Duckworth, *Grit: The Power of Passion and Perseverance* (Scribner, 2016), p. 8.
5. We were struck by one reviewer who described a book by Pamela C. Regan and Ellen Bersheid (Sage, 1999) titled *Lust: What We Know about Human Sexual Desire* as follows: "This book is not about lust: that is, wanting to fuck or be fucked so badly that you can't wait to take your clothes off and you'll do almost anything anywhere." Instead the book was assessed as a run-of-the mill discussion of sexual desire. See Jean Duncombe, "Lust: What We Know about Human Sexual Desire." *Sexualities*, 3, 1999, p. 382.
6. Robert Sapolsky, *Behave: The Biology of Humans at Our Best and Worst* (Penguin, 2017), p. 328.
7. Sapolsky, *Behave*, p. 267.
8. Stephanie Cacioppo, Francesco Bianchi-Demicheli, Chris Frum, James Pfaus, and James Lewis, "The Common Neural Bases Between Sexual Desire and Love: A Multilevel Kernel Density MRI Analysis." *Journal of Sexual Medicine*, 9(4), 2012, pp. 1048–1054.
9. www.psychologytoday.com/us/blog/emotional-freedom/201108/lust-vs-love-do-you-know-the-difference
10. Jens Förster, Amina Özelsel, and Kai Epstude, "How Love and Lust Change People's Perception of Relationship Partners." *Journal of Experimental Social Psychology*, 46(2), 2010, pp. 237–246.
11. Minjung Kwon and Younjee Han, "How Love and Lust Influence Self-Control." *Social Behavior and Personality: An International Journal*, 45(2), 2017, pp. 177–189.
12. Jens Forster, Kai Epstude, and Amina Ozelsel, "Why Love Has Wings and Sex Has Not: How Reminders of Love and Sex

Influence Creative and Analytic Thinking." *Personality and Social Psychology Bulletin*, 35(11), 2009, pp. 1479–1491.

13. Terri Seuntjens, Niels van de Ven, Marcel Zeelenberg, and Anna van der Schors, "Greed and Adolescent Financial Behavior." *Journal of Economic Psychology*, 57, 2016, pp. 1–12.

14. Terri G. Seuntjens, Marcel Zeelenberga, Niels van de Ven, and Seger M. Breugelmansa, "Greedy Bastards: Testing the Relationship Between Wanting More and Unethical Behavior." *Personality and Individual Differences*, 138, 2019, pp. 147–156.

15. Duckworth, *Grit*, p. 35.

16. This quote is from the back jacket of Daniel H. Pink, *Drive: The Surprising Truth About What Motivates Us* (Riverhead, 2009).

17. Seuntjens et al., "Greed and Adolescent Financial Behavior."

18. The quotes in this paragraph are from www.nytimes.com/2019/06/24/us/politics/elizabeth-warren-republican-conservative-democrat.html.

Chapter 1: Lust for Power

1. Joris Lammers, Janker I. Stoker, Floor Rink, and Adam D. Galinsky, "To Have Control Over or to Be Free from Others? The Desire for Power Reflects a Need for Autonomy." *Personality and Social Psychology Bulletin*, 42(4), 2016, pp. 498–512. Also see Yona Kifer, Daniel Heller, Wei Q. E. Perunovic, and Adam D. Galinsky, "The Good Life of the Powerful: The Experience of Power and Authenticity Enhances Subjective Well-Being." *Psychological Science*, 24(3), 2012, pp. 280–288.

2. For an extended discussion of America's ambivalence toward leaders, especially if they are powerful and forceful, see Barbara Kellerman, *The Political Presidency: Practice of Leadership* (Oxford University Press, 1984), especially Chapter 1, "Leadership in America," pp. 3 ff.

3. See, for example, David C. McClelland and David G. Winter, *Human Motivation* (Cambridge University Press, 1987). See especially Chapters 17 and 19.

4. Tom Wilson and David Blood, "When Poverty Data Must Toe Kagame's Line." *Financial Times*, August 14, 2019.

5. Jonah Lehrer, "The Power Trip." www.wsj.com/articles/SB10001424052748704407804575425561952689390.

6. The researchers are Joris Lammers and Adam Galinsky. The quotes are in "The Psychology of Power – Absolutely." www .economist.com/science-and-technology/2010/01/21/absolutely.

7. See, for example, Barbara Kellerman, *Bad Leadership: What It Is, How It Happens, Why It Matters* (Harvard Business School Press, 2004) and Jean Lipman-Blumen, *The Allure of Toxic Leaders* (Oxford University Press, 2004).

8. Tim Dickinson, "How Roger Ailes Built the Fox News Fear Factory." *Rolling Stone*, May 25, 2011.

9. Gabriel Sherman, *The Loudest Voice in the Room: How the Brilliant, Bombastic Roger Ailes Built Fox News – and Divided a Country* (Random House, 2017), p. xviii.

10. The quotes in this paragraph are from Dickinson, "How Roger Ailes Built the Fox News Fear Factory."

11. David Brock and Ari Rabin-Havt, *The Fox Effect: How Roger Ailes Turned a Newsroom into a Propaganda Machine* (Anchor, 2012), p. 26.

12. Sherman, *The Loudest Voice in the Room*, p. 19.

13. Ibid., p. 30.

14. Ibid., p. 78.

15. Ibid., p. 142.

16. Dickinson, "How Roger Ailes Built the Fox News Fear Factory."

17. Chris Peters, "No-Spin Zones." *Journalism Studies*, 11(6), 2010, p. 846.

18. Michael Wolff quoted in Brock and Rabin-Havt, *The Fox Effect*, p. 37.

19. This paragraph is based on, and draws quotes from Jeffrey P. Jones, "The 'New' News as No 'News.'" *Media International Australia*, August, 2012.

20. Michael Wolff quoted in Brock and Rabin-Havt, *The Fox Effect*, p. 47.

21. See, for example, filmmaker Alexis Bloom's documentary, *Divide and Conquer: The Story of Roger Ailes*. This strong film testifies to what we write in this chapter. When Bloom was asked what shocked her about Ailes while making the film, she replied, "the depths of his paranoia," quoted in *Newsweek*, December 14, 2018.

22. Ana Swanson and Steven Mufson, "A Big Divide between Fox News Ailes, Sons of Murdoch." *The Washington Post*, July 20, 2016.

23. All figures in this paragraph are from Sherman, *The Loudest Voice*. The quote in this paragraph is from p. 291.

24. Ibid., p. 160.

25. Ibid., p. 269.

26. Jane Mayer, "Trump TV." *The New Yorker*, March 8, 2009, p. 48.

27. Ibid., p. 47.

28. Sherman, *The Loudest Voice*, p. 271. The phrase "shrouded in mystery" in the previous paragraph, is from Sherman.
29. https://en.wikipedia.org/wiki/Gretchen_Carlson.
30. Mayer, "Trump TV," p. 46.
31. Kellerman, *Bad Leadership*, p. 119.
32. In April 2017 the *New York Times* reported that O'Reilly and Fox News had settled five harassment lawsuits against O'Reilly dating back to 2002.
33. This paragraph is based on Dickinson, "How Roger Ailes Built the Fox News Fear Factory."
34. Quoted in ibid.
35. Quoted in Corky Siemaszko, "Breaking News E Mails." *NBC News*, April 3, 2017.
36. Jill Disis and Frank Pallotta, "The Last Year of Roger Ailes' Life was Consumed by Scandal." *CNN*, May 18, 2017.
37. Megyn Kelly, *Settle for More* (HarperCollins, 2016), pp. 301, 302.
38. Jim Rutenberg, Emily Steel, and John Koblin, "At Fox News, Kisses, Innuendo, Propositions and Fears of Reprisal." *New York Times*, July 23, 2016.
39. www.nytimes.com/2018/07/05/us/politics/bill-shine-white-house-communications.html.
40. www.psychologytoday.com/us/blog/slightly-blighty/201711/what-is-the-link-between-sex-and-power-in-sexual-harassment.
41. www.thoughtco.com/men-power-and-sexual-harassment-3534217.
42. In 2005 Ailes was also named Chair of Fox Television Stations.
43. A. J. Katz, writing in *Adweek*, January 29, 2019.
44. Dickinson, "How Roger Ailes Built the Fox News Fear Factory."
45. Sherman, *The Loudest Voice*, pp. 119, 120.
46. Baier and Wallace quotes in Michael M. Grynbaum, "Inside Fox News, 'There are People in Tears.'" *New York Times*, July 21, 2016.
47. Kelly, *Settle for More*, p. 303.
48. Quoted in Demetri Sevastopulo, "Second Thoughts on Engagement." *Financial Times*, January 16, 2019.
49. See Frank Dikötter, *Mao's Great Famine: The History of China's Most Devastating Catastrophe, 1958–1962* (Walker & Co., 2010).
50. Quoted in Yaroslav Trofimov, "Has Xi Stirred a Backlash?" *Wall Street Journal*, August 17–18, 2019.
51. The relevant World Bank statistics are easily accessible and widely available online.

52. Quoted in Minxin Pei, "China in Xi's 'New Era': A Play for Global Leadership." *Journal of Democracy*, 29(2), 2018, p. 36.
53. Bates Gill, "China's Future Under Xi Jinping: Challenges Ahead." *Political Science*, 69(1),2017, pp. 1–15.
54. Zheng Yongnian and Weng Cuifen, "The Development of China's Formal Political Structures," in Robert S. Ross and Jo Inge Bekkevold (eds.), *China in the Era of Xi Jinping: Domestic and Foreign Policy Challenges*, Project Muse (Georgetown University Press, 2016), p. 47.
55. Stein Ringen, *The Perfect Dictatorship: China in the 21st Century*, Project Muse (Hong Kong University Press, 2016), p. 65.
56. Cheng Li, *Chinese Politics in the Xi Jinping Era: Reassessing Collective Leadership* (Brookings Institution Press, 2016), p. 10 and Chapter 1 passim.
57. Quoted in Ringen, *Perfect Dictatorship*, p. 97.
58. https://en.wikipedia.org/wiki/Internet_censorship_in_China.
59. Chase Purdy, "China is Launching a Dystopian Program to Monitor Citizens in Beijing." *Quartz*, November 24, 2018.
60. Quoted in ibid.
61. www.straitstimes.com/opinion/the-confucian-roots-of-xi-jinpings-policies.
62. www.scmp.com/news/china/economy/article/2145938/chinas-economic-growth-story-will-be-cut-short-under-xi-jinping.
63. Hannah Arendt, *Totalitarianism: The Origins of Totalitarianism* (Harcourt, Brace & World, 1951), p. 71.
64. Li, *Chinese Politics*, p. 314.
65. The quotes and facts that pertain to the anti-corruption campaign are in Richard McGregor, "Party Man: Xi Jinping's Quest to Dominate China." *Foreign Affairs*, September/October 2019, p. 24.
66. Gill, "China's Future," p. 2.
67. "All Hail Papa Xi! The Growing Cult Around China's All-Powerful Leader." *The Spectator*, October 21, 2017.
68. The sentence about loyal servants is a paraphrase of Ringen, as is this paragraph, which is based on Ringen, *Perfect Dictatorship*, pp. 90 ff.
69. www.nytimes.com/2019/11/01/world/asia/china-student-informers.html.
70. Evan Osnos, "Hong Kong on the March." *The New Yorker*, September 2, 2019, p. 14.
71. Gideon Rachman, "The Asian Strategic Order is Dying." *Financial Times*, August 6, 2019.

72. www.brookings.edu/articles/how-much-does-xi-matter-new-voices
-on-chinas-foreign-policy/.
73. Pei, "China in Xi's 'New Era,'" p. 43.
74. See, for example, https://finance.yahoo.com/news/nba-needs-
china-revenue-growth-leverage-170102327.html.
75. Ringen, *Perfect Dictatorship*.
76. Rana Foroohar, "President Xi is No Davos Man." *Financial Times*,
January 21, 2019.
77. Elizabeth Economy, "China's New Revolution: The Reign of Xi
Jinping." *Foreign Affairs*, May/June 2018, pp. 60–74.
78. James MacGregor Burns, *Leadership* (Harper & Row, 1978), p. 18.

Chapter 2: Lust for Money

1. www.imdb.com/title/tt0094291/characters/nm0000140.
2. www.chicagotribune.com/news/ct-xpm-1986–12-15–
8604030634-story.html.
3. www.vox.com/2016/1/29/10866388/donald-trump-greedy.
4. Paul F. Knitter and Chandra Muzaffar (eds.), *Subverting Greed:
Religious Perspectives on the Global Economy* (Orbis Books, 2002).
5. www.christianity.com/wiki/christian-terms/what-is-greed-
definition-and-bible-verses-about-greed.html.
6. E. A. Carmean, "A Choice at the Final Moment." *Wall Street Journal*,
September 14–15, 2019.
7. www.theguardian.com/world/2015/jul/10/poor-must-change-new
-colonialism-of-economic-order-says-pope-francis.
8. The quotes in this paragraph are from www.theatlantic.com
/magazine/archive/1915/09/war-and-the-wealth-of-nations
/555902/.
9. www.npr.org/sections/money/2010/09/13/129832608/bankers-
pay-instability-greed-and-selfishness.
10. www.nytimes.com//06/04/opinion/greed-is-bad.html.
11. See Alexander F. Robertson. *Greed: Gut Feelings, Growth, and History*
(Polity Press, 2001); Deby Cassill and Alison Watkins, "Mogul
Games: In Defence of Inequality as an Evolutionary Strategy to
Cope with Multiple Agents of Selection," in Roger Koppl (ed.),
*Evolutionary Psychology and Economic Theory: Advances in Austrian
Economics* (Elsevier, 2005); Gad Saad, *The Evolutionary Basis of
Consumption* (Erlbaum, 2007).

12. See Greg Melleuish, "Greed is Great." *Institute of Public Affairs Review*, 61, 2009, pp. 23–24; Terri G. Seuntjens, Marcel Zeelenberg, Seger M. Breugelmans, and Niels van de Ven, "Defining Greed." *British Journal of Psychology*, 106(3), 2014, pp. 505–525; Michael Rosenberg, *The Power of Greed: Collective Action in International Development* (University of Alberta Press, 2005); Ernst Fehrl and Herbert Gintis, "Human Motivation and Social Cooperation." *Annual Review of Sociology*, 33, 2007, pp. 43–64.

13. Long Wang and J. Keith Murnighan, "On Greed." *Academy of Management Annals*, 5(1), 2012, pp. 279–316.

14. Philip Brickman and Dan T. Campbell, "Hedonic Relativism and Planning the Good Society," in Mortimer H. Appley (ed.), *Adaptation-Level Theory* (Academic Press, 1971).

15. See Ed Diener, M. Suh Eunkook, Richard E. Lucas, and Heidi L. Smith, "Subjective Well-Being: Three Decades of Progress." *Psychological Bulletin*, 125(2), 1999, pp. 276–302; Louise Keely, "Why Isn't Growth Making Us Happier? Utility on the Hedonic Treadmill." *Journal of Economic Behavior & Organization*, 57(3), 2005, pp. 333–355.

16. Sam Polk, *For the Love of Money: A Memoir* (Scribner, 2017).

17. Kurt Gray, Adrian F. Ward, and Michael I. Norton, "Paying It Forward: Generalized Reciprocity and the Limits of Generosity." *Journal of Experimental Psychology*, 143(1), 2012, pp. 247–254.

18. The statistics in this paragraph are from www.fool.com/invest ing/2017/07/23/an-interesting-chart-about-berkshire-hathaway.aspx.

19. www.forbes.com/profile/warren-buffett/#46fac8de4639.

20. www.forbes.com/sites/russprince/2012/03/16/what-is-a-thought-leader/.

21. The quotes in this paragraph are from http://content.time.com /time/business/article/0,8599,1843839,00.html.

22. https://buffett.cnbc.com/about-buffett/.

23. www.cnbc.com/2018/01/26/these-3-people-shaped-warren-buffetts-investing-style.html.

24. The quotes in this paragraph are from www.businessinsider.com /warren-buffett-berkshire-omaha-2012-8.

25. www.berkshirehathaway.com/letters/1988.html.

26. The quotes in this paragraph not otherwise attributed are from www.cnbc.com/2019/05/13/what-warren-buffett-and-kevin-oleary-say-to-do-when-the-market-tanks.html.

27. www.nytimes.com/2008/10/17/opinion/17buffett.html.
28. www.businessinsider.com/warren-buffett-net-worth-berkshire-hathaway-billionaire-coke-mcdonalds-2019–4.
29. www.cnbc.com/2018/01/17/warren-buffett-is-delaying-retirement-heres-how-you-can-too.html.
30. This quote and the quote preceding it are from Alice Schroeder, *The Snowball: Warren Buffett and the Business of Life* (Bantam Books, 2008), p. 187.
31. www.nytimes.com/2006/07/02/business/02buffettkids.html.
32. www.cnbc.com/2018/02/09/heres-what-warren-buffett-likes-to-eat.html.
33. www.cnbc.com/id/49787452.
34. www.architecturaldigest.com/story/warren-buffett-is-willing-to-sell-you-his-laguna-beach-house-for-dollar31-million-less-than-original-asking-price.
35. The quotes in this paragraph are from money.cnn.com/maga zines/fortune/fortune_archive/1986/09/29/68098/index.htm.
36. All quotes in this paragraph are from www.foxbusiness.com/fea tures/warren-buffett-3-practices-that-attract-and-retain-top-talent.
37. www.cnbc.com/2018/05/08/ndamukong-suh-shares-lessons-learned-from-his-mentor-warren-buffett.html; www .barrons.com/articles/berkshire-annual-meeting-fans -51556975705.
38. https://realinvestmentadvice.com/a-walking-contradiction-warren-buffett/.
39. https://finance.yahoo.com/news/guide-berkshire-hathaway-shareholder-meeting-204149963.html.
40. www.bloomberg.com/news/articles/2019-06-03/crypto-pioneer-pays-4-57-million-for-lunch-with-warren-buffett.
41. Tim Wu, *The Attention Merchants: The Epic Scramble to Get Inside Our Heads* (Knopf, 2016).
42. Robert McFadden, "Mogul Whose Fortune Steered American Politics to the Right." *New York Times*, August 24, 2019.
43. www.ft.com/content/59d0f5c4-be9e-11e9-b350-db00d509634e.
44. www.forbes.com/profile/david-koch/#734a319b659b.
45. Daniel Schulman, *Sons of Wichita: How the Koch Brothers Became America's Most Powerful and Private Dynasty* (Grand Central Publishing, 2014), p. 362.
46. This quote and the quote preceding it are from www.kansas.com /news/special-reports/article1100658.html.

47. The quotes in this paragraph are from http://freakonomics.com /podcast/why-hate-koch-brothers-part-1/.

48. The quotes in this paragraph are from www.kansas.com/news/ special-reports/article1100658.html.

49. See Jane Mayer, *Dark Money: The Hidden History of the Billionaires Behind the Rise of the Radical Right* (Doubleday, 2016).

50. McFadden, "Mogul Whose Fortune Steered American Politics to the Right."

51. www.lp.org/platform/.

52. www.pewresearch.org/fact-tank/2014/08/25/in-search-of-libertarians/.

53. www.kansas.com/news/special-reports/article1100658.html.

54. Ibid.

55. The quotes in this paragraph are from www.kansas.com/news/ special-reports/article1100658.html.

56. www.nytimes.com/2019/08/15/books/review/kochland-christopher-leonard.html.

57. www.forbes.com/companies/koch-industries/#6ec9183374ce.

58. www.nytimes.com/2019/08/15/books/review/kochland-christopher-leonard.html.

59. The figures and quotes in this paragraph are from https://time .com/4072398/charles-koch-good-profit/.

60. Christopher Leonard, *Kochland: The Secret History of Koch Industries and Corporate Power in America* (Simon & Schuster, 2019), p. 574.

61. The quotes in this paragraph are from www.npr.org/2019/08/13/ 750449277/kochland-explores-the-money-stream-of-the-famous-brother-duo.

62. The quotes in this paragraph are from Susan Goldberg, "How the Kochs Built Their Business – and Their Power." *The Washington Post*, August 16, 2019.

63. www.politico.com/story/2015/12/koch-brothers-network-gop-david-charles-217124.

64. www.washingtonpost.com/politics/koch-backed-political-network-built-to-shield-donors-raised-400-million-in-2012-elections/2014/01/05/9e7cfd9a-719b-11e3-9389-09ef9944065e_s tory.html.

65. www.cnbc.com/2018/01/27/koch-brothers-network-to-spend-400-million-in-midterm-election-cycle.html.

66. Mayer, *Dark Money*.

67. www.greenpeace.org/usa/global-warming/climate-deniers/koch-industries/koch-industries-pollution/.
68. www.texasobserver.org/kochworld/.
69. www.wsj.com/articles/SB947781616495455358.
70. The quote and figure in this paragraph are from www.newyorker.com/news/news-desk/do-the-kochs-have-their-own-spy-network.
71. Leonard, *Kochland*.
72. www.greenpeace.org/usa/research/koch-industries-secretly-fund/.
73. Mayer, *Dark Money*, p. 11.
74. Justin Farrell, "Corporate Funding and Ideological Polarization about Climate Change." *Proceedings of the National Academy of Sciences*, 113(1), 2016, pp. 92–97.
75. Justin Farrell, "Network Structure and Influence of the Climate Change Counter Movement." *Nature Climate Change*, 6, 2016, pp. 370–374.
76. Nancy MacLean, *Democracy in Chains: The Deep History of the Radical Right's Stealth Plan for America* (Viking, 2017).
77. Ibid., p. 217.
78. www.kansas.com/news/special-reports/article1100658.html.
79. www.huffpost.com/entry/the-empire-strikes-back-e_b_778288.
80. www.nytimes.com/2010/10/20/us/politics/20koch.html.
81. www.huffpost.com/entry/koch-brothers-spending_n_5494963.
82. https://repository.upenn.edu/cgi/viewcontent.cgi?article=1012&context=think_tanks.
83. www.insidehighered.com/news/2018/07/25/koch-foundation-pledges-make-future-grant-terms-public-critics-want-know-more-about.
84. https://publicintegrity.org/federal-politics/why-the-koch-brothers-find-higher-education-worth-their-money/.
85. www.greenpeace.org/usa/global-warming/climate-deniers/koch-pollution-on-campus/.
86. Mayer, *Dark Money*.
87. www.newyorker.com/magazine/2017/10/23/the-danger-of-president-pence.
88. www.pbs.org/newshour/nation/all-of-the-ways-embattled-epa-chief-scott-pruitt-has-changed-energy-policy.
89. www.salon.com/2017/01/11/koch-allies-in-the-white-house_partner.

90. www.forbes.com/sites/danielfisher/2012/12/05/inside-the-koch-empire-how-the-brothers-plan-to-reshape-america.

91. This quote and the quote preceding it are from www.salon.com/2018/11/05/koch-brothers-are-watching-you-and-new-documents-expose-how-much-they-know/.

92. This quote and the quote preceding it are from www.npr.org/sections/itsallpolitics/2015/10/12/447999852/koch-political-network-expanding-grassroots-organizing.

93. www.kansas.com/news/special-reports/article1100658.html.

94. www.ft.com/content/59d0f5c4-be9e-11e9-b350-db00d509634e.

95. www.forbes.com/sites/clareoconnor/2013/05/14/new-app-lets-you-boycott-koch-brothers-monsanto-and-more-by-scanning-your-shopping-cart.

96. www.huffpost.com/entry/koch-brothers_n_6646540.

97. www.newyorker.com/magazine/2016/01/25/new-koch.

98. www.theatlantic.com/politics/archive/2015/03/do-the-koch-brothers-really-care-about-criminal-justice-reform/386615/.

99. www.washingtonexaminer.com/opinion/koch-brothers-tell-republicans-the-free-ride-is-over.

100. www.ft.com/content/59d0f5c4-be9e-11e9-b350-db00d509634e.

101. http://freakonomics.com/podcast/why-hate-koch-brothers-part-1/.

102. www.kansas.com/news/special-reports/article1100658.html.

103. www.nationalreview.com/2004/06/decade-greed-richard-mckenzie/.

Chapter 3: Lust for Sex

1. Tamara Keith, National Public Radio, March 12, 2015. "Hillary Clinton's Privacy Problem."

2. James Beggan and Scott Allison, *Leadership and Sexuality: Power, Principles, and Processes* (Edward Elgar, 2018), p. 6.

3. https://en.wikipedia.org/wiki/Droit_du_seigneur.

4. William Wan, "What Makes Some Men Sexual Harassers? Science Tries to Explain the Creeps of the World." *Washington Post*, December 22, 2017.

5. Quoted in ibid.

6. All the quotes in this paragraph are from Christine Lee, "Moneywatch." *CBS News*, October 27, 2010.

7. The quotes in this paragraph and the paragraph preceding it are from David Greenberg, "Sex and the Married Politician." *The Atlantic Monthly*, October 2011. The "cozy relationship" phrase is Greenberg quoting *New York Times* columnist James Reston.

8. Bobby Baker in Todd Purdum, "Sex in the Senate." *Politico*, November 19, 2013. Baker himself ended up serving eighteen months in prison on tax evasion charges.

9. The quotes in this paragraph are from Kennedy Adonais's Introduction to Steven Watts, *JFK and the Masculine Mystique: Sex and Power on the New Frontier* (St. Martin's Press, 2016), p. 3.

10. Quoted in Sara Stewart, "All the President's Women." *New York Post*, November 10, 2013.

11. Michael John Sullivan, *Presidential Passions* (Shapolsky, 1991), p. 13.

12. Mimi Alford, *Once Upon a Secret* (Random House, 2012), pp. 48ff.

13. Ibid., pp. 74ff.

14. Judith Exner, *My Story* (Grove Press, 1977), pp. 104, 105. The book was "told to" Ovid Demaris.

15. Also see Seymour Hersh, *The Dark Side of Camelot* (HarperCollins, 2014).

16. Kitty Kelley, "The Dark Side of Camelot." *People*, February 29, 1988.

17. See Larry Sabato, "John F. Kennedy's Final Days Reveal a Man Who Craved Excitement." *Forbes*, October 16, 2013.

18. Kelley, "The Dark Side of Camelot."

19. The quote and the sentences on Ellen Rometsch are based on the account by Sabato. For a fuller account of the impact of the relationship between the American president and East German Rometsch, see Larry Flynt and David Eisenbach, *One Nation Under Sex* (Palgrave, 2011), pp. 185ff. The earlier physical description of Rometsch is from Flynt and Eisenbach, p. 185.

20. Alford, *Once Upon a Secret*, p. 42.

21. Sullivan, *Presidential Passions*, p. 65.

22. Godfrey Hodgson, "Obituary: Evelyn Lincoln." *Independent*, May 20, 1995.

23. Adonais in Watts, *Masculine Mystique*, p. 188.

24. K. A. Cuordileone, "'Politics in an Age of Anxiety': Cold War Political Culture and the Crisis in American Masculinity, 1949–1960." *Journal of American History*, 87(2), 2000, p. 521.

25. Ibid., p. 522.

26. Ibid., p. 525.

27. https://en.wikipedia.org/wiki/New_Frontier.

28. Adonais in Watts, *Masculine Mystique*, p. 194.

29. Beppe Severgnini, "Italy's New Marriage of Convenience." *New York Times*, September 2, 2019.
30. www.cnbc.com/2019/05/20/italys-government-is-at-breaking-point -heres-why-its-all-going-wrong.html.
31. All quotes in this paragraph are from Maurizio Viroli, *The Liberty of Servants: Berlusconi's Italy* (Princeton University Press, 2011), pp. xvii ff.
32. Felia Allum, "Silvio Berlusconi and his 'Toxic' Touch." *Representation*, 47(3), 2011, p. 284.
33. https://thesefootballtimes.co/2018/04/18/the-devils-odyssey-how-silvio-berlusconi-turned-ac-milan-into-a-superpower/.
34. Tuomas Kuronen and Aki-Mauri Huhtinen, "Un-willing is Un-leading: Leadership as Beastly Desire." *Leadership and the Humanities*, 4(2), 2016, p. 99.
35. Ibid.
36. www.theguardian.com/commentisfree/2011/nov/13/how-europe-propped-buffoon-silvio-berlusconi.
37. Isabel Crowhurst and Chiara Bertone, "Introduction: The Politics of Sexuality in Contemporary Italy." *Modern Italy*, 17(4), 2012, p. 413.
38. The quotes in this paragraph are from Michael Day, *Being Berlusconi* (Palgrave Macmillan, 2015), p. 134.
39. Peter Popham and Claire Soares, "Friends and Lovers: Berlusconi and his 'Butterflies.'" *The Independent*, July 9, 2008.
40. Silvia Aloisi, "Sex, Cash and Starlets: Berlusconi's 'Rubygate.'" *Reuters*, April 5, 2011.
41. https://en.wikipedia.org/wiki/Silvio_Berlusconi.
42. Day, *Being Berlusconi*, pp. 144, 145.
43. Nick Squires, "Silvio Berlusconi backed by call girl at heart of Bunga Bunga scandal."*The Telegraph*, November 15, 2011.
44. For more on intemperate leaders, see Barbara Kellerman, *Bad Leadership: What It Is, How It Happens, Why It Matters* (Harvard Business School Press, 2004), especially pp. 95ff.
45. Viroli, *Liberty of Servants*, p. xx.
46. Ibid., p. xxi.
47. Allum, "Silvio Berlusconi and his 'Toxic' Touch," p. 291.
48. This paragraph is based on and draws from Rachel Donadio, "Editor Resigns over Berlusconi-Tied Accusations." *New York Times*, September 3, 2009.
49. Francis Rocca, "Berlusconi Sex Scandal Awkward for Vatican." *The Huffington Post*, May 25, 2011.

50. Rachel Donadio and Elisabetta Povoledo, "Italians Protest over Berlusconi Scandals." *New York Times*, February 13, 2011.
51. Elisabetta Povoledo and Rachel Donadio, "Sex Scandals in Italy Fuel Discontent of Women." *New York Times*, February 2, 2011.
52. Silvia Poggioli, *National Public Radio*, January 18, 2018.
53. www.nytimes.com/2019/08/18/arts/music/placido-domingo-opera-harassment.html.
54. Miles Johnson, "Silvio Berlusconi Plots a European Political Comeback." *Financial Times*, January 17, 2019.
55. Francesco Filia quoted in Silvia Amaro, "Berlusconi Has Been in Politics for Nearly Three Decades. This is the Secret to his Popularity." *CNBC*, February 21, 2018.
56. Stephen Gundle, "Berlusconi, Sex, and the Avoidance of Media Scandal," in M. Giuliani and E. Jones (eds.), *Italian Politics: Managing Uncertainty* (Berghahn Books, 2009), p. 72.
57. Reuters report in the *New York Times*, March 15, 2019.
58. www.bbc.com/news/world-europe-47595320.
59. www.goodreads.com/quotes/976229-desire-is-the-kind-of-thing-that-eats-you.

Chapter 4: Lust for Success

1. www.silverkris.com/lebron-james-whatever-success-i-have-had-is-never-enough-i-always-want-more/.
2. Bernard Weiner, "Thoughts and Actions Associated with Achievement Motivation," in David C. McClelland and Robert Steel (eds.), *Human Motivation: A Book of Readings* (General Learning Press, 1973) p. 426. The quote from Weiner is from an article he published in 1969.
3. Abraham Korman, *The Psychology of Motivation* (Prentice-Hall, 1974), p. 181.
4. Monaco Ramirez Basco, *Never Good Enough: Freeing Yourself from the Chains of Perfectionism* (Free Press, 1999), p. 5.
5. Arthur Ciaramicoli, *Performance Addiction: The Dangerous New Syndrome and How to Stop it from Ruining Your Life* (Wiley, 2004).
6. Ibid., p. 1.
7. See, for example, Max Weber, *The Protestant Ethic and the Spirit of Capitalism* (Penguin Classics, 2002; the book was first published in 1904/5); and Samuel Huntington, *American Politics: The Promise of*

Disharmony (Harvard University Press, 1981). See Huntington especially on the American Creed, pp. 33ff.

8. Tyler Okimoto and Victoria Brescoll, "The Price of Power: Power Seeking and Backlash against Female Politicians." *Personality and Social Psychology Bulletin*, 36(7), 2009, pp. 932–933. This finding is supported in nearly all of the literature on women and leadership.

9. https://fortune.com/2019/05/16/fortune-500-female-ceos/.

10. Frank MacAndrew, "Controlling the Conduct of College Women in the 1960s." *Psychology Today*, February 15, 2017.

11. Jeff Gerth and Don Van Natta, Jr., *Her Way: The Hopes and Ambitions of Hillary Clinton* (Little, Brown, 2007), p. 21.

12. Nancy Jurik and Susan Ehrlich Martin, *Doing Justice, Doing Gender: Women in Legal and Criminal Justice Occupations* (Sage, 2007), p. 115.

13. Quoted in Gerth and Van Natta, *Her Way*, p. 53.

14. Nicole Foster Shoaf and Tara Parsons, "18 Million Cracks, but no Cigar: News Media and the Campaigns of Clinton, Palin, and Bachmann." *Social Sciences*, 5(3), 2016, p. 11.

15. https://en.wikipedia.org/wiki/Hillary_Clinton.

16. Michael Kelly, "Saint Hillary." *New York Times Magazine*, May 23, 1993.

17. Carl Bernstein, *A Woman in Charge: The Life of Hillary Rodham Clinton* (Knopf, 2007), p. 207.

18. Hillary Rodham Clinton, *What Happened* (Simon & Schuster, 2017), p. 297.

19. All quotes in this paragraph are from Clinton, *What Happened*, pp. 111, 115, 116.

20. www.nbcnews.com/politics/donald-trump/hillary-clinton-i-m-living-rent-free-inside-donald-trump-n1001026.

21. This term was coined by Garry Wills. He is quoted by Karlyn Kohrs Campbell, "The Discursive Performance of Femininity: Hating Hillary." *Rhetoric and Public Affairs*, 1(1), 1998, p. 1.

22. "Hating Hillary." *The Economist*, October 22, 2016.

23. For a smart discussion of the phenomenon in lay language, see www.pbs.org/newshour/features/hidden-sexism/.

24. Bernstein, *Woman in Charge*, p. 542.

25. James Boys, *Hillary Rising: The Politics, Persona, and Policies of a New American Dynasty* (Biteback, 2016), p. 93.

26. Bernstein, *Woman in Charge*, p. 547.

27. Both quotes in this paragraph are from Hillary Rodham Clinton, *Hard Choices* (Simon & Schuster, 2014), p. 1.

28. Kim Ghattas, *The Secretary: A Journey with Hillary Clinton from Beirut to the Heart of American Power* (Picador, 2014), p. 12.

29. Chimamanda Adichie, "What Hillary Clinton's Fans Love about Her." *The Atlantic*, November 3, 2016.

30. Nina Burleigh, "Meet Hillary Clinton's Inner Circle, the Queenmakers Who Won't Rest Until She's President." *Newsweek*, August 16, 2016.

31. Clinton, *Hard Choices*, p. 6.

32. Gerth and Van Natta, *Her Way*, p. 217.

33. Annie Parnus and Jonathan Allen, *HRC: State Secrets and the Rebirth of Hillary Clinton* (Crown, 2014), p. 64.

34. Clinton devotes a chapter to "Those Damn Emails" in her book, *What Happened*. See pp. 289 ff.

35. All quotes in this paragraph are from Sady Doyle, "America Loves Women like Hillary Clinton – as long as they're not asking for a promotion." *Quartz*, February 25, 2016.

36. Jessica Samakow, "Hillary Clinton Broke Down How Impossible It is For Ambitious Women to be 'Likable.'" *The Huffington Post*, April 2017.

37. Clinton, *What Happened*, p. 126.

38. Katie Rodgers, "I was a Gladiator: Pain, Injury, and Masculinity in the NFL," in Thomas Oates and Zack Furness (eds.), *The NFL: Critical and Cultural Perspectives* (Temple University Press, 2015), p. 143.

39. Ibid., p. 157.

40. Rich Cohen, "How the NFL Reflects American Culture." *The Wall Street Journal*, September 19, 2014.

41. Ibid.

42. Bob Glauber, "A Week in the Life of an NFL Team." *Newsday*, September 4, 2014.

43. This paragraph is based on discussion in James Holstein, Richard Jones, and George Koonce, Jr., *Is There Life After Football? Surviving the NFL* (New York University Press, 2015), p. 46.

44. Aja Romano, "Why Everyone Hates the Patriots." *Vox*, February 3, 2019.

45. Holstein et al., *Is There Life After Football?*, p. 45.

46. Alex Johnson, "For the First Time, NFL Acknowledges Link Between Football and Brain Disorders." *NBC News*, March 14, 2016.

47. Elisabeth Chuck, "Despite Evidence, Skeptics Try to Cast Doubt on CTE-Football Link." *NBC News*, August 30, 2018.

48. The quotes in this paragraph are from Brian Resnick, "What a Lifetime of Playing Football Can Do to the Human Brain." *Vox*, February 3, 2019.

49. www.sportscasting.com/nfl/tom-brady-gisele-bundchen-argument/.

50. Jesse Mez et al., "Clinicopathological Evaluation of Chronic Traumatic Encephalopathy in Players of American Football." *Journal of the American Medical Association*, 318(4), 2017, p. 369.

51. www.imdb.com/name/nm1530018/bio.

52. The quotes in this paragraph are from https://en.wikipedia.org /wiki/Tom_Brady.

53. The quotes in this paragraph are from Michael Holley, *Belichick and Brady: Two Men, the Patriots, and How they Revolutionized Football* (Hachette, 2016), pp. 32ff.

54. The quotes in this paragraph are from Casey Sherman and Dave Wedge, *12: The Inside Story of Tom Brady's Fight for Redemption* (Little, Brown, 2018), pp. 68ff.

55. The quotes in this paragraph and the account generally are based on "Deflategate Timeline: After 544 Days, Tom Brady Gives In." *ESPN*, July 15, 2016. The argument that Brady was treated unfairly is carefully made by David Berger in *HeinOnline*.

56. Sherman and Wedge, *Inside Story*, p. 183.

57. The quotes in this paragraph are from ibid., pp. 110, 113.

58. Ibid., p. 279.

59. Greg Bishop, "Given the Way He Prepares, Tom Brady Won't Be Slowing Down Anytime Soon." *Sports Illustrated*, December 10, 2014.

60. Keven Van Valkenburg, "Tom Brady's Big Reveal." *ESPN*, January 21, 2016.

61. Tom Brady, *The TB12 Method: How to Achieve a Lifetime of Sustained Peak Performance* (Simon & Schuster, 2017).

62. Paul Sommers, "Has Tom Brady Passed His Prime?" *Open Journal of Statistics* (Scientific Research Publishing, 2018).

63. www.usatoday.com/story/sports/nfl/columnist/2019/02/04/super-bowl-2019-tom-brady-patriots/2765897002/.

64. Holstein et al., *Is There Life After Football?*, p. 77.

65. This quote is from Adam Kilgore, "Hi, I'm Tom Brady." *Washington Post*, January 12, 2019. This paragraph and the one preceding are based on this article.

66. The quotes in this paragraph are from Tyler Sullivan, "Stephon Gilmore Says What Makes Tom Brady a Great Teammate." *247 Sports*, February 13, 2019.

67. "We asked 9 Patriot Players to Give Their Best Tom Brady Stories and They Did Not Disappoint." *USA Today Sports*, January 29, 2019.
68. Mike Reiss, *ESPN*, January 4, 2019.
69. Mike Reiss, "Tom Brady Says Everyone Thinks Pats Suck and Can't Win Games." *ESPN*, January 14, 2019.
70. Ben Mathis-Lilley, "A Patriots Fan on What It's Like When you Win all the Time and Everyone Hates You (Updated)." *ESPN*, February 4, 2019.
71. All quotes in this paragraph are from Deron Snyder, *Washington Times*, January 28, 2019.
72. Zack Cox, "Bill Belichick's 'Thriving' Relationship with Tom Brady Fueled by Football Curiosity." *New England Sports Network*, March 29, 2019.
73. Gary Myers, *Brady vs Manning: The Untold Story of the Rivalry that Transformed the NFL* (Penguin, Crown Archetype, 2015), p. 197.
74. Jason Gay, "Gisele Bündchen is a Force of Nature." *WSJ Magazine*, March 27, 2018.
75. Cindy Boren, "You've Got to Let Him Do What he Loves." *The Washington Post*, December 13, 2018.
76. www.boston.com/sports/new-england-patriots/2019/04/19/tom-brady-parents-anniversary.
77. Van Valkenburg, "Tom Brady's Big Reveal."
78. Tyler Dunne, "Does Tom Brady Still Have It?" *Bleacher Report*, December 12, 2018.
79. Both players are quoted in Henry Bushnell, "How is Tom Brady Still Going? Early Patriots Reflect on Tom Brady's Longevity." *Hindsight*, January 9, 2019.
80. Michael Hurley, "15 Biggest Takeaways from Tom Brady's Oprah Winfrey Interview on TV and in Podcast." *CBS Boston*, June 18, 2018.

Chapter 5: Lust for Legitimacy

1. Aldon D. Morris and Suzanne Staggenborg, "Leadership in Social Movements," in David A. Snow, Sarah A. Soule, and Hanspeter Kriesi (eds.), *The Blackwell Companion to Social Movements* (Blackwell Publishing, 2004), pp. 171–196.
2. Ibid.
3. Ibid.
4. Joseph R. Gusfield, "Functional Areas of Leadership in Social Movements." *The Sociological Quarterly*, 7(2), 1966, pp. 137–156.

5. David E. Rast III, Michael A. Hogg, and Georgina Randsley de Moura, "Leadership and Social Transformation: The Role of Marginalized Individuals and Groups." *Journal of Societal Issues*, 74 (1), 2018, pp. 8–19 ; Ashleigh Shelby Rosette and Robert W. Livingston, "Failure is Not an Option for Black Women: Effects of Organizational Performance on Leaders with Single Versus Dual-Subordinate Identities." *Journal of Experimental Social Psychology*, 48(5), 2012, pp. 1162–1167.

6. Kurt Lang and Gladys Engel Lang, *Collective Dynamics* (Crowell, 1961).

7. Morris and Staggenborg, "Leadership in Social Movements."

8. Robert D. Benford and David A. Snow, "Framing Processes and Social Movements: An Overview and Assessment." *Annual Review of Sociology*, 26, 2000, pp. 611–639.

9. See Herbert C. Kelman, "Interests, Relationships, Identities: Three Central Issues for Individuals and Groups in Negotiating their Social Environment." *Annual Review of Psychology*, 57, 2006, pp. 1–26; Herbert Kelman and V. Lee Hamilton, *Crimes of Obedience: Toward a Social Psychology of Authority and Responsibility* (Yale University Press, 1989).

10. www.archives.gov/files/press/exhibits/dream-speech.pdf.

11. See David A. Snow and Robert D. Benford, "Master Frames and Cycles of Protest," in Aldon D. Morris and Carol McClurg Mueller (eds.), *Frontiers in Social Movement Theory* (Yale University Press, 1992), pp. 133–155 and David A. Snow, E. Burke Rochford, Jr., Steven K. Worden, and Robert D. Benford, "Frame Alignment Processes, Micromobilization, and Movement Participation." *American Sociological Review*, 51, 1986, pp. 464–481.

12. We put the phrase "just society" in quotes because while the term is widely used, alongside "social justice warrior," it has no one agreed-upon definition. Indeed, there are many different and at times competing views of what constitutes a "just society."

13. www.dailymail.co.uk/news/article-6508403/Alexandria-Ocasio-Cortez-taking-time-self-care-beginning-new-role.html.

14. www.dw.com/en/nelson-mandelas-mixed-legacy/a-44691481.

15. Nelson Mandela's statement at the opening of the defense case in the Rivonia Trial
(Pretoria Supreme Court, South Africa, April 20, 1964).

16. www.un.org/en/events/mandeladay/court_statement_1964.shtml.

17. http://news.bbc.co.uk/onthisday/hi/dates/stories/march/21/newsid_2653000/2653405.stm.

18. www.theguardian.com/world/2017/may/04/sharpeville-massacre-judicial-inquiry-south-africa-1960.
19. www.bbc.com/news/world-africa-23618727.
20. Ibid.
21. www.huffpost.com/entry/nelson-mandela-taught-us_b_4411010.
22. www.nelsonmandela.org/news/entry/i-am-prepared-to-die.
23. www.un.org/en/events/mandeladay/court_statement_1964.shtml.
24. www.mandela.gov.za/mandela_speeches/before/850210_udf.htm.
25. This quote and the quote preceding it are from Nelson Mandela, *Long Walk to Freedom* (Back Bay Books, 1995), p. 523.
26. www.latimes.com/archives/la-xpm-1990–02-11-mn-1049-story.html.
27. www.nytimes.com/1996/04/14/magazine/south-africa-july-7–1985-a-rare-talk-with-mandela.html.
28. www.red.org/reditorial/2018/7/18/8-ways-nelson-mandela-changed-the-world.
29. www.theguardian.com/world/2013/dec/06/nelson-mandela-aids-south-africa.
30. www.red.org/reditorial/2018/7/18/8-ways-nelson-mandela-changed-the-world.
31. www.history.com/this-day-in-history/mandela-writes-from-prison.
32. Mandela, *Long Walk to Freedom*, p. 584.
33. https://truthout.org/articles/media-and-the-end-of-apartheid-in-south-africa/.
34. www.theguardian.com/world/2013/dec/06/nelson-mandela-life-quotes.
35. https://truthout.org/articles/media-and-the-end-of-apartheid-in-south-africa/.
36. www.nytimes.com/1990/04/17/world/mandela-urges-support-for-sanctions.html.
37. www.latimes.com/archives/la-xpm-1990–02-11-mn-1049-story.html.
38. www.inc.com/peter-economy/17-wise-nelson-mandela-quotes-that-will-inspire-your-success.html.
39. www.cnn.com/2013/12/05/world/africa/nelson-mandela-retirement-years/index.html.
40. Ibid.
41. Ibid.
42. https://usun.usmission.gov/remarks-at-the-nelson-mandela-peace-summit/?_ga=2.236587076.412309926.1568738765–1668630922.1568738765.

43. www.npr.org/sections/goatsandsoda/2018/04/02/598864666/the-country-with-the-worlds-worst-inequality-is.
44. https://foreignpolicy.com/2013/12/06/think-again-nelson-mandela/.
45. The figures and quotes in this paragraph not otherwise attributed are from https://foreignpolicy.com/2013/12/06/think-again-nelson-mandela/.
46. www.bloomberg.com/news/articles/2019–04-17/south-africa-s-decline-worst-of-nations-not-at-war-model-shows.
47. www.latimes.com/la-oe-kramer20mar20-story.html.
48. https://news.harvard.edu/gazette/story/2003/10/activist-larry-kramer-is-not-nice/.
49. This quote and the quote preceding it are from www.latimes.com/archives/la-xpm-1990–06-20-vw-179-story.html.
50. https://people.com/archive/larry-kramer-vol-34-no-1/.
51. http://nymag.com/nymag/features/62887/index5.html.
52. www.nytimes.com/1995/01/12/garden/at-home-with-larry-kramer-when-a-roaring-lion-learns-to-purr.html.
53. www.nytimes.com/2017/05/19/nyregion/larry-kramer-and-the-birth-of-aids-activism.html.
54. Ibid.
55. https://newrepublic.com/article/117691/aids-hit-united-states-harder-other-developed-countries-why.
56. Beth Baker, "Larry Kramer." *Common Cause Magazine*, 22(1), 1999.
57. www.latimes.com/archives/la-xpm-1990–06-20-vw-179-story.html.
58. www.indymedia.org.uk/en/2003/05/66488.html.
59. www.poz.com/article/Larry-Kramer-HIV-20772–4898.
60. Larry Kramer, *Reports from the Holocaust: The Story of an AIDS Activist* (St. Martin's Press, 1994), p. xxvi.
61. The quotes in this sentence and the sentence preceding it are from www.nytimes.com/1990/01/03/nyregion/rude-rash-effective-act-up-shifts-aids-policy.html.
62. www.chronicle.com/article/Yale-Makes-Peace-With-Larry/27932.
63. www.nytimes.com/1997/07/09/nyregion/writing-own-script-yale-refuses-kramer-s-millions-for-gay-studies.html.
64. www.insidehighered.com/news/2009/04/28/larry-kramer-questions-gay-studies.
65. http://nymag.com/news/features/62887/index2.html.
66. https://news.harvard.edu/gazette/story/2003/10/activist-larry-kramer-is-not-nice/.
67. www.latimes.com/archives/la-xpm-1990–06-20-vw-179-story.html.

68. www.nytimes.com/2014/04/27/opinion/sunday/bruni-the-angel-in-larry-kramer.html

69. www.theatlantic.com/entertainment/archive/2013/02/the-plague-years-in-film-and-memory/273449/.

70. www.washingtonpost.com/wp-dyn/content/article/2005/05/08/AR2005050800988.html.

71. www.npr.org/sections/health-shots/2019/02/09/689924838/how-to-demand-a-medical-breakthrough-lessons-from-the-aids-fight.

72. www.ncbi.nlm.nih.gov/pmc/articles/PMC3780739/.

73. www.nytimes.com/2018/01/16/obituaries/mathilde-krim-mobilizing-force-in-an-aids-crusade-dies-at-91.html.

74. www.nytimes.com/2018/01/16/obituaries/mathilde-krim-mobilizing-force-in-an-aids-crusade-dies-at-91.html.

75. Ibid.

76. www.nytimes.com/1990/01/30/nyregion/painful-political-lesson-for-aids-crusader.html.

77. www.latimes.com/archives/la-xpm-1990–06-20-vw-179-story.html.

78. www.hivplusmag.com/people/2013/07/24/activist-and-playwright-larry-kramer-surprises-parade-magazine-interview.

79. www.washingtonpost.com/archive/lifestyle/2005/05/09/the-pessimist/fd291b11-3322-412d-aecd-0bc591f1486c/.

80. www.nytimes.com/2017/05/19/nyregion/larry-kramer-and-the-birth-of-aids-activism.html.

81. The quotes in this paragraph are from www.nytimes.com/2017/05/19/nyregion/larry-kramer-and-the-birth-of-aids-activism.html.

82. This quote and the quote preceding it are from www.latimes.com/archives/la-xpm-1990–06-20-vw-179-story.html.

83. www.poz.com/article/Kramer-vs-Kramer-11501–8020.

84. www.poz.com/article/finding-larry-kramer.

85. www.theatlantic.com/entertainment/archive/2014/05/the-normal-heart/371482/.

86. This quote and the quote preceding it are from www.poz.com/article/finding-larry-kramer.

87. www.nytimes.com/2018/07/11/opinion/gay-rights-larry-kramer.html.

88. Ibid.

89. www.hollywoodreporter.com/news/larry-kramer-talks-gay-marriage-805685.

90. www.usatoday.com/story/news/nation/2019/06/24/lgbtq-acceptance-millennials-decline-glaad-survey/1503758001/.

91. www.nytimes.com/2018/07/11/opinion/gay-rights-larry-kramer.html.
92. www.tikkun.org/nelson-mandela-a-jewish-perspective.

Chapter 6: Lust for Legacy

1. For a discussion of the influence of Thoreau on Mahatma Gandhi, see Anthony Parel, *Pax Gandhiana: The Political Philosophy of Mahatma Gandhi* (Oxford University Press, 2016). The quotes in this paragraph are from Robert D. Richardson, "Walden's Ripple Effect: Henry David Thoreau's Meditation Remains the Ultimate Self-Help Book." *Smithsonian Magazine* (August 2004).
2. www.sfchronicle.com/business/article/Big-bucks-in-biotech-but-what-about-Jonas-Salk-6148858.php.
3. www.who.int/features/factfiles/polio/en/.
4. https://bigthink.com/scotty-hendricks/does-altruism-exist-science-and-philosophy-weigh-in.
5. Richard Dawkins. *The Selfish Gene* (Oxford University Press, 1976).
6. https://blogs.scientificamerican.com/guest-blog/is-the-meaning-of-your-life-to-make-babies/.
7. Jeff Greenberg, Tom Pyszczynski, and Sheldon Solomon, "The Causes and Consequences of a Need for Self-Esteem: A Terror Management Theory," in R. F. Baumeister (ed.), *Public Self and Private Self* (Springer-Verlag, 1986).
8. www.marketwatch.com/story/therapy-for-the-1-why-its-not-easy-being-rich-2015–10-20.
9. www.gatesfoundation.org/Who-We-Are/General-Information /Foundation-Factsheet; John Jurgensen, "In Bill Gates's Mind, A Life of Processing." *Wall Street Journal*, September 11, 2019.
10. Melinda Gates. *The Moment of Lift: How Empowering Women Changes the World* (Flatiron Books, 2019), p. 27.
11. www.cnbc.com/2018/02/13/why-bill-and-melinda-gates-give-away-billions.html.
12. www.gatesfoundation.org/Who-We-Are/General-Information /History.
13. This quote and the quote preceding it are from www .gatesnotes.com/2018-Annual-Letter.
14. The figures and quotes in this paragraph are from www .businessinsider.com/bill-gates-mother-inspired-philanthropy -2015–5.

15. The quotes in this paragraph are from www.wired.com/2013/11/bill-gates-wired-essay/.
16. This quote is from www.aarp.org/politics-society/advocacy/info-2017/melinda-gates-trip-to-africa-that-changed-everything.html.
17. www.wsj.com/articles/the-moment-of-lift-review-one-target-for-smart-giving-11555873259.
18. David Pilling, "Africa poised to play a major role in the world." *Financial Times*, August 28, 2019.
19. The statistics in this paragraph are from www.sos-usa.org.
20. www.wired.com/2013/11/bill-gates-wired-essay/.
21. www.gatesnotes.com/About-Bill-Gates/The-Power-of-Catalytic-Philanthropy.
22. www.wired.com/2013/11/bill-gates-wired-essay/.
23. These statistics are from www.unicef.org/health/files/health_afri camalaria.pdf.
24. www.gatesnotes.com/Health/Mapping-the-End-of-Malaria.
25. www.gatesnotes.com/Health/What-It-Takes-to-Kill-Malaria-Mosquito-Week.
26. www.devex.com/news/gates-vs-malaria-how-bill-gates-aims-to-win-the-fight-of-his-life-91996.
27. www.devex.com/news/gates-vs-malaria-how-bill-gates-aims-to-win-the-fight-of-his-life-91996.
28. www.seattlepi.com/local/article/WHO-chief-joins-Gateses-call-to-eradicate-malaria-1252850.php.
29. www.gatesnotes.com/Health/A-Global-Call-to-End-Polio.
30. https://fortune.com/2017/02/14/data-sheet-gates-foundation/.
31. This quote and the statistic before it are from http://northwest primetime.com/news/2017/apr/28/melinda-gates/.
32. www.inc.com/business-insider/how-bill-gates-mother-pushed-him-to-be-a-philanthropist.html.
33. www.gatesnotes.com/2018-Annual-Letter.
34. www.inc.com/scott-mautz/bill-melinda-gates-just-taught-a-leader ship-lesson-by-answering-10-toughest-questions-they-get.html.
35. www.pbs.org/newshour/education/why-didnt-this-program-aimed-at-boosting-teacher-effectiveness-help-students.
36. www.gatesfoundation.org/Media-Center/Press-Releases/2009/11/Foundation-Commits-$335-Million-to-Promote-Effective-Teaching-and-Raise-Student-Achievement.
37. The figures and quote in this paragraph are from www .edweek.org/ew/articles/2018/06/21/an-expensive-experiment-gates-teacher-effectiveness-program-show.html.

38. www.philanthropy.com/article/A-View-Inside-the-Gates/175661.
39. The quotes in this paragraph are from www.wired.com/2013/11/bill-gates-wired-essay/.
40. https://finance.yahoo.com/news/mental-him-warren-buffetts-wife-203500031.html.
41. http://community.seattletimes.nwsource.com/archive/?date=20060626&slug=gatesfoundation26.
42. https://buffett.cnbc.com/video/2007/05/05/morning-session–2007-berkshire-hathaway-annual-meeting.html.
43. www.nytimes.com/2006/06/26/business/26cnd-buffett.html.
44. https://givingpledge.org/Pledger.aspx?id=177.
45. https://givingpledge.org.
46. https://nypost.com/2014/01/01/bill-gates-told-that-his-charity-pledge-is-worthless.
47. www.nytimes.com/2010/11/11/giving/11PLEDGE.html.
48. www.salon.com/2012/09/21/billionaire_charity_isnt_always_praiseworthy.
49. www.nytimes.com/2010/11/11/giving/11PLEDGE.html.
50. www.gatesfoundation.org/who-we-are/general-information/foundation-factsheet.
51. www.seattletimes.com/business/want-to-work-for-the-gates-foundation/.
52. The quotes in this paragraph are from www.seattletimes.com/business/want-to-work-for-the-gates-foundation/.
53. The examples and quotes in this paragraph are from www.politico.com/story/2014/02/bill-gates-microsoft-policy-washington-103136.
54. www.duo.uio.no/handle/10852/17671.
55. www.theguardian.com/commentisfree/2009/aug/05/gates-foundation-health-policy.
56. www.nytimes.com/2019/10/12/business/jeffrey-epstein-bill-gates.html.
57. www.vox.com/future-perfect/2018/12/11/18129580/gates-donations-charity-billionaire-philanthropy.
58. https://data.worldbank.org/indicator/SP.POP.TOTL.FE.ZS.
59. The statistics and quotes in this paragraph not otherwise attributed are from www.cnbc.com/2018/03/05/melinda-gates-is-spending-170-million-to-promote-womens-equality.html. Melinda Gates's later statement was part of her explanation of the $1 billion grant she made in 2019 from www.forbes.com

/sites/elanagross/2019/10/02/melinda-gates-pledges-1-billion-to-gender-equality/#302de37346b8.

60. www.cnbc.com/2018/03/05/melinda-gates-is-spending-170-million-to-promote-womens-equality.html.

61. https://fortune.com/2017/02/14/data-sheet-gates-foundation/.

62. www.forbes.com/profile/george-soros/#5565f2422024.

63. www.opensocietyfoundations.org/newsroom/open-society-foundations-and-george-soros.

64. www.opensocietyfoundations.org/newsroom/open-society-foundations-and-george-soros.

65. www.theguardian.com/news/2018/jul/06/the-george-soros-philosophy-and-its-fatal-flaw.

66. Michael T. Kaufman, *Soros: The Life and Times of a Messianic Billionaire* (Vintage, 2002), p. 4.

67. www.nybooks.com/articles/2011/06/23/my-philanthropy.

68. www.nytimes.com/2018/07/17/magazine/george-soros-democrat-open-society.html.

69. Amir Weiner and Aigi Rahi-Tamm, "Getting to Know You: Soviet Surveillance and Its Uses, 1939–1957."*Kritika*, 13(1), 2012, pp. 5–45.

70. This quote and the quote preceding it are from www.theguardian.com/news/2018/jul/06/the-george-soros-philosophy-and-its-fatal-flaw.

71. www.nytimes.com/2018/07/17/magazine/george-soros-democrat-open-society.html.

72. George Soros, *Underwriting Democracy: Encouraging Free Enterprise and Democratic Reform Among the Soviets and in Eastern Europe* (Free Press, 1991), p. 3.

73. www.npr.org/templates/story/story.php?storyId=4635465.

74. www.newyorker.com/magazine/2004/10/18/the-money-man.

75. www.nytimes.com/2018/07/17/magazine/george-soros-democrat-open-society.html.

76. www.tabletmag.com/jewish-news-and-politics/274870/the-truth-about-george-soros.

77. www.nytimes.com/2018/07/17/magazine/george-soros-democrat-open-society.html.

78. This figure and the figure preceding it are from www.latimes.com/archives/la-xpm-1994–03-17-mn-35234-story.html.

79. This figure and the figure preceding it are from https://hungarianfreepress.com/2018/04/20/open-society-foundations-to-leave-hungary/.

80. www.nytimes.com/2018/07/17/magazine/george-soros-democrat-open-society.html.

81. www.foreignaffairs.com/articles/central-europe/2018–04-06/how-illiberal-leaders-attack-civil-society.

82. www.washingtontimes.com/news/2018/jul/18/george-soros-obama-was-my-greatest-disappointment/.

83. This quote and the statistic preceding it are from www.politico.com/story/2016/07/george-soros-democratic-convention-226267.

84. www.forbes.com/sites/laurengensler/2018/10/23/how-george-soros-became-one-of-americas-biggest-philanthropists-and-a-right-wing-target/#6449696539ba.

85. We refer here to donations made personally by George Soros as well as to those made by the Open Society Foundations. The Open Society Foundations describes Soros's foundation role this way: "Under George Soros's leadership . . ." (www.opensocietyfoundations.org/george-soros). Other US organizations which have reported receiving donations from George Soros and/or the Open Society Foundations include, but are not restricted to: the American Civil Liberties Union, Black Lives Matter, Center for American Progress, Center for Public Integrity, Media Matters for America, Millennium Promise, MoveOn.org, Planned Parenthood, and Win Justice.

86. www.huffpost.com/entry/george-soros-political-donations_n_1498610.

87. https://priorities.org/.

88. https://americanbridgepac.org.

89. www.chicagotribune.com/nation-world/ct-george-soros-interview-20180609-story.html.

90. www.politico.com/story/2019/07/31/soros-launches-super-pac-2020–1442748.

91. www.realclearpolitics.com/video/2018/01/27/soros_trump_will_disappear_in_2020_or_even_sooner.html.

92. www.forbes.com/sites/laurengensler/2018/10/23/how-george-soros-became-one-of-americas-biggest-philanthropists-and-a-right-wing-target/#28e17fb639ba.

93. www.independent.co.uk/news/world/europe/roma-shown-to-be-europes-poorest-and-most-reviled-people-7609052.html.

94. This quote and the quote preceding it are from www.opensocietyfoundations.org/newsroom/prime-ministers-endorse-decade-roma-inclusion-called-george-soros.

95. www.economist.com/graphic-detail/2016/11/30/poverty-among-europes-roma-community.
96. thepolitic.org/charity-from-above-george-soros-and-the-anatomy-of-roma-rights-activism/.
97. www.opensocietyfoundations.org/voices/why-roma-integration-rare-opportunity-western-balkans-and-turkey.
98. www.nytimes.com/2018/07/17/magazine/george-soros-democrat-open-society.html.
99. www.apnews.com/ca73f8ef6d8d466dbeddc4dee95c8e3a.
100. www.opensocietyfoundations.org/publications/scholarforum-alumni-update.
101. Two examples are Alexander Lomaia and Monica Macovei.
102. See www.reuters.com/article/us-georgia-saakashvili-verdict/georgian-ex-president-sentenced-in-absentia-for abuse-of-power-idUSKBN1JO2RJ ; www.ecfr.eu/article/commentary_wildest_dream_a_costly_election_for_georgias_ruling_party; and www.apnews.com/39ade7392c614324b01259b7d69b4b2e.
103. https://medium.com/@JD_Grandstaff/george-soross-antidemocratic-influence-on-romanian-politics-34cedad51774.
104. All quotes in this paragraph not otherwise attributed are from https://medium.com/@JD_Grandstaff/george-soross-antidemocratic-influence-on-romanian-politics-34cedad51774.
105. www.theatlantic.com/ideas/archive/2018/12/viktor-orban-and-anti-semitic-figyelo-cover/578158/.
106. www.politico.eu/article/viktor-orban-anti-semitism-problem-hungary-jews/.
107. www.vox.com/policy-and-politics/2018/6/22/17493070/hungary-stop-soros-orban.
108. www.theguardian.com/world/2017/jun/22/hungary-viktor-orban-george-soros.
109. Gabriel Debendetti, "The Most Influential Democratic Donors," *New York Magazine*, August 19–September 1, 2019, p. 18.
110. www.salon.com/2019/06/04/scapegoating-george-soros-how-media-savvy-far-right-activists-spread-lies_partner/.
111. www.theatlantic.com/politics/archive/2010/11/was-glenn-beck-s-george-soros-takedown-anti-semitic/343439/.
112. www.bbc.com/news/world-europe-36130006.
113. See, for example, www.theatlantic.com/politics/archive/2017/11/the-tragedy-of-president-trumps-tribalism/544739/; www.newyorker.com/news/daily-comment/a-new-report-offers-insights-into-tribalism-in-the-age-of-trump; and www

.baltimoresun.com/opinion/columnists/dan-rodricks/bs-roughly-
speaking-rodricks-trump-political-tribalism-impeachment
-20190603-htmlstory.html.
114. www.jacobinmag.com/2015/03/george-soros-
philanthrocapitalism-millennium-villages/.
115. www.nytimes.com/2017/10/17/business/george-soros-open-
society-foundations.html.
116. www.govinfo.gov/content/pkg/CREC-2004–04-27/html/
CREC-2004–04-27-pt1-PgE655-3.htm.

Epilogue

1. Gavin Flood and Charles Martin, *The Bhagavad Gita: A New Translation* (W. W. Norton, 2013).
2. Amy-Jill Levine, *The Gospel of Luke* (Cambridge University Press, 2018), p. 34.
3. Day Amy Willis, "17 Quotes, Poems, Sayings and Messages to Mark Nirvana." *Metro*, February 15, 2018.
4. www.nbcnews.com/politics/white-house/trump-says-our-country-stake-whistleblower-account-made-public-n1059011.
5. www.nytimes.com/2019/05/28/smarter-living/you-accomplished-something-great-so-now-what.html.

INDEX